Also by Ralph Wiley

———

WHY BLACK PEOPLE TEND TO SHOUT

WHAT BLACK PEOPLE SHOULD DO NOW

DISPATCHES FROM NEAR THE VANGUARD

Ralph Wiley

ONE WORLD

BALLANTINE BOOKS • NEW YORK

A One World Book
Published by Ballantine Books

Copyright © 1993 by HIP, Inc.

All rights reserved under International and Pan-American Copyright Conventions. Published in the United States by Ballantine Books, a division of Random House, Inc., New York, and simultaneously in Canada by Random House of Canada Limited, Toronto.

Portions of the book originally appeared in *Emerge*, *Los Angeles Times Book Review*, *One*, *Premiere*, *Sports Illustrated*, *Washington Post*, and *Washington Post Book World*.

Grateful acknowledgment is made to the following for permission to reprint previously published material:

JAMES BALDWIN ESTATE: Excerpts from James Baldwin's preface to *To Be Young Gifted and Black: An Informal Biography of Lorraine Hansberry* which originally appeared as "Sweet Lorraine" in *Esquire* Magazine in 1969. Used by arrangement with the James Baldwin Estate.

EYEBALL MUSIC: Excerpt from the lyrics of "Voodoo Woman" by Koko Taylor. Copyright © 1975 by Eyeball Music.

FARRAR, STRAUS & GIROUX, INC.: Excerpts from *Approaches to Writing* by Paul Horgan. Copyright © 1968, 1973 by Paul Horgan. Reprinted by permission of Farrar, Straus & Giroux, Inc.

PATTI LABELLE, SAMI MCKINNEY, MICHAEL G. THOMAS, WHOLE NINE YARDS: Excerpt from the lyrics of "Love Never Dies." © 1991 by Whole Nine Yards/Avid One Music/Mactom Music/Zuri Music/Project CLM Music. International Copyright Secured. All Rights Reserved. Written by Sami McKinney/Clarence McDonald/Michael G. Thomas/Patti LaBelle.

PATHFINDER PRESS: Excerpts from *Malcolm X Speaks* by Betty Shabazz. Copyright © 1965 and 1989 by Betty Shabazz and Pathfinder Press. Reprinted by permission.

HARPERCOLLINS PUBLISHERS INC., JONATHAN CAPE LTD., AND JOHN HAWKINS & ASSOCIATES, INC.: Excerpt from *Black Boy* by Richard Wright. Copyright © 1937, 1942, 1944, 1945 by Richard Wright. Reprinted by permission of HarperCollins Publishers Inc., Mrs. Ellen Wright, Jonathan Cape, and John Hawkins & Associates, Inc.

RONDOR MUSIC INTERNATIONAL INC.: Excerpt from "I Can't Stand the Rain" lyrics and music by Donald Bryant and Ann Peebles and Bernard Miller. © 1973 Irving Music, Inc. (BMI) All Rights Reserved. International Copyright Secured.

THE WASHINGTON POST: Excerpt from "At Brown, A Hard Lesson in Free Speech" by Jonathan Yardley. © 1991 The Washington Post. Reprinted with permission.

Library of Congress Catalog Card Number: 94-94287

ISBN 0-345-38044-4

Cover design by Kristine V. Mills

Cover photograph by Michael Britto (adapted from hardcover edition)

Manufactured in the United States of America

First Ballantine Books Trade Paperback Edition: November 1994

10 9 8 7 6 5 4 3 2 1

For Dorothy, Helen, Elizabeth, Marcell, and Donzaleigh

Acknowledgments

My endless gratitude goes to the sparkling array of people whose patience, resources, and thought processes helped put this book into your hands: Colen Wiley, DTB, Holly Cypress, Marla V. Jones, Demetra Johnson, Barbara Vance, Edgar McGee, Janice Coleman, Dasha Smith, Linda Blanks, Philip Spitzer, Mary Armstrong Spitzer, Tyrone Perry, Terria Ladner, Eliza Bergman Krause, Raghib Ismail, Jacquie Jones, Brother Tarif, Brother Jamal, and Brother el-Razzaq; Wendy Carlton; and especially to all the smart sisters at One World/ Ballantine, Beverly Robinson, Tamu Aljuwani, Kristine Mills, and Brenda Brown; and most especially to my editor, Cheryl D. Woodruff, for helping me to say what I wanted to say, in the end. And to everyone mentioned within the text who tried to hold still for this self-portrait by an ungainly artist, I'm most grateful—even though it may not seem that way at times.

Ralph Wiley
Washington, D.C., 1993

Contents

Contents

About Perceptions

About Travel

About Life

WHAT
BLACK PEOPLE
SHOULD DO
NOW

What Black People Should Do Now: An Introduction

Order, please come to order, people. (You might as well stop pulling on my sleeve, Brother Carruthers. I know order brings power, and power corrupts, and corruption results in chaos, so why bother in the first place; but I ask for order so we can convene this latest general session. So let go the arm and fight off that old urge to hold me back. Thank you.)

The first item up for consideration is a sizable and entangling one—the question of what Black people should do now, especially since the government has decided to pay some attention to us. We all know that having the government pay its attention to us is one of the surest ways to ruin on the public record. An overreliance on others is a mistake.

Worse, scholars have taken to writing articles and books about us lately. Well, not about us, exactly, but about what they expect we'll do, as Blaaacks, given our lack of temperance, social graces, and redeeming values. So the first problem we must solve is which acceptable Black people will decide our course and relay our intent to the world. We must have our spokespeople. It is protocol. Are we agreed?

What?

Wait, now—before you tear the place up, let us succumb to reason for a while. Let us *think*.

Let us take into account the many volunteers for the job of spokesperson. Granted, many of these volunteer spokespeople are as slippery as live baby eels swimming in a bathtub full of drawn butter. But we are not trying to grab hold of them, are we? We're asking them what we must do now, so we shan't hold their slippery ways against them.

Frankly, many of their answers have given us small satisfaction in the past, even though we see their pictures in the newspapers and their powdered faces on television. Even when they lead some of us on the occasional outing, mostly what we hear is the faint sound of their own axes grinding. So we are usually left to admire the cars they drive and the private schools their children attend, and the way they always seem to voice proper opinions. But, I must ask you this, what has it gotten us lately except a few bunions, a bad sense of direction, and an envy complex?

What good did spokespeople do Yusuf Hawkins, who was only trying to buy a secondhand car when he was killed? Or Anita Hill, who was minding her own business when she was privately and then publicly humiliated? Or Leanita McClain, who was trying to write editorials for the *Chicago Tribune* when she decided she had to kill herself? Or Rodney G. King, who was just trying to give up, just give up completely, when he was beaten in systematic fashion by members of the Los Angeles chapter of the Fraternal Order of Police? What

4

good did the leaders do a young boy in Mobile named Michael Donald, emblematic of so many other young men, who was swung from a tree, lynched, right here in America in the latter twentieth century, merely for walking with a girl his own age who happened not to be Black? Why did no leader advise former basketball star Wilt Chamberlain, who later bragged, however erroneously, that he'd lain with twenty thousand women? Why did no spokesman tell him that this was not a feather in his cap, nor a hallmark of his manhood, but was instead directly related to the stiffened, bloated body of Michael Donald in Mobile, or to the younger former basketball star Earvin "Magic" Johnson, who knew, as Wilt was allowing his shortcomings to be so well publicized, that he, like so many others, was suddenly HIV-positive?

Yet our leaders seem satisfied with their own advice, so we should be content with it. Brother Carruthers, among others, says that "it will get better by-and-by. We must be careful not to let our imaginations run away with us."

Are we agreed? No?

Brother Whitlock over in the corner says there's a strong rumor going around now that different ones of us need to do different things, and that we don't need to be telling all that we're doing now, because people will blab and ruin it. He says what Black people must do now is stop listening to people who say they know what Black people must do now.

Although I admire Brother Whitlock's spunk, he is getting to be known here and there as a flaming radical. He used to be nice and predictable. If he weren't getting along in years, I'd say he could be dangerous. He says the people who are telling him what he must do now aren't helping him "raise his edifice." We want to know where the ugly rumor of Black people beginning to stand up two feet at a time got started. And certainly we want to know when an old turnip farmer like Whitlock began using words like "edifice" instead of "barn," when we all know barn is what he meant. Is this all the fault of Whitlock? Or could his wife, the evangelist, be involved? Or could it be his brother Simon—you know Simon, who left his wife for a man with a goatee? Why can't we become one unified voice? We're all on the same track, all headed for hell or heaven in the same handbasket! What happens to one will happen to all! Agreed? Speak up!

I think I shall give no more currency to the wishes of this gathering—or should I call you the peanut gallery? Would that make you happy? No, I didn't think so. Why is it you agree with nothing I put forth? Please refrain from attempting to answer my questions from now on, unless you are going to answer them in just the way I'd like. That's one of the privileges of hogging the microphone at general sessions in this society. You can change the direction of the conversation at your whim. We ought to get the microphone moving more often. That is, after I'm done with it.

Most of us are sick of singing "Ain't Gon' Let Nobody Turn Us Around" in that sweet, mournful, slurring way we have, swaying back and forth, and then singing "We Shall Overcome" for good measure. We surely do want somebody to turn us around, because we don't like the direction we're headed in, do we? And we certainly would rather "overcome" in fact, in practice, rather than just singing about it.

So let us try a different lyric. Let us sing "Ain't Gonna Let Nobody Run a Better Business Than Me" and "We Shall Not Buy from Racists." Those are the songs we should sing today. Let us change the harmony and surprise everyone, including our spokespeople. In fact, let us put the most ineffective of our leaders into another business altogether! Let them become lawyers and charge usurious fees up front.

Black people must *drive the hard bargain*.

Why haven't I heard a single "Amen" or a few hissed "Yesses" coming from the middle rows to back me up? Have you nothing to offer me but derisive laughter in response? I'm beginning to question whether any of you know what it is to be Black and lectured, although surely you must by now.

Now, getting back to Brother Whitlock, yes, just as we suspected, he admits having spoken to Brother Mulhew and Sister Pendleton. They're on the record. Mulhew says there's hardly any true racism against Black people anymore, that it's mostly in our overly vivid imaginations. He says even the most racist hatemongers have reformed, and we Black people only hold ourselves back now. He makes it hard to argue with him in the end because he always adds that part about us holding ourselves back, and we all know we do that, but this doesn't take any starch out of the racism, oh no; it makes it seem like so much more hardened concrete poised over all our heads, held only by strings on the fingers of the big shots. But Brother Mulhew can talk up an electrical storm and not let you get a word in edgewise, all without your knowing what he just said. He can talk you dumb. Look what he did to Whitlock, who had a cross burned on his lawn and said it didn't bother him as long as they didn't burn his "edifice." He lives not far from here. Not far from you. We told him, "Whitlock, your barn's going up in flames next, and we doubt if Mulhew will be there to help put it out!"

Now, Sister Pendleton remains unmarried and, more to my point, unasked, even to this day, if you don't count that White man who married her for her money, and got it. Let us point that out to you for better or worse, for it is a fact. Please, if you're going to throw things at me, at least let the fruit be ripe. You might as well let me speak my mind. Sister Pendleton would like us to believe the only relevant question is what should Black women alone do now, since she and her following have decided Black men are too heavy and ill-mannered to carry to small New England colleges and cable television studios and other very respectable places. My advice to you is not to be alone in a room with Sister Pendleton, as she may accuse you of nudging her, or thinking of it, or approving it, or worse. She will find some way to have you strung up or, at best, brought down beneath the heel of her boot, begging forgiveness, all in the name of progress. And a boot is a boot from the view beneath it. Who wears the boot matters not if it is pressed down on your neck.

Granted, Sister Pendleton also writes books and makes the occasional good point, but let us not confuse the issue today. The women who feel they cannot be women without being contentious toward *all* men are much too far ahead of their time to do us any good now. Women prove nothing by receiving judgments at the expense of Black men while White men do the same as they've always done. If Mike Tyson cannot force himself on you, but William Kennedy Smith or a platoon of soccer players can, where's the progress, really?

Sister Richardson is as skeptical as Sister Pendleton, but she stops short of cynicism, nor does she often allow herself to be used to facilitate the new world order of the day, which is plain-as-day death to Black men. Oh yes, that memo was leaked. So if women had a few more general sessions like this one, decided a few more things among themselves, as Black people perhaps we'd have less serious matters on our agenda. We must go on together, whether we like it or believe it best or not. We can't afford the luxury of not liking each other. But it is foisted upon us so fetchingly that I admit it can be hard if not impossible to resist.

Many of you advise waiting as a strategy. Freedom and justice are not buses that make the same rounds on the half-hour and stop and open their doors and have plenty of empty seats. You can't wait for freedom and justice unless you are still waiting for yourself to realize freedom comes first from within. You say this sounds suspiciously like some of our old spokespeople's oratory? Well if you're going to get ugly, I'll suspend philosophical ramblings for the remainder of my brief time at the microphone. You three can sit back down and stop shaking your fists at me. Some folks will always want to hear good preaching. What? None of those folks are here today? I see my time is growing short.

So far we've come up with only one resolution, and that was article A, which states that Black people, specifically Black men, should now stop shooting each other with bullets. This resolution is all we've been able to get passed, and that was by the slimmest of margins. Let's hope we stick to this. We all know a Black man's life is not worth 25 cents, according to Hoyle, or whichever White man is making up the rules these days. But we must refrain from blowing holes in quarters, because quarters wisely kept add up to dollars. I know it may be hard work because if you feel like shooting something, a Black man sure seems to be the cheapest way to go—cheaper even than going to the pistol range and shooting at cardboard targets. But let us leave this shooting of Black people to the police and to the heroes in bad films, the Klan and Aryan nations and to National Guardsmen. They are the experts at shooting us. Let us provide them with agile, moving, nonexistent targets, rather than doing their work for them.

And speaking of expertise, let us try to develop more with some of these quarters, while we still have a few of them on us. Let us expand our expertise in all areas, but let us not be so quick to abandon those areas where we have a foothold already because we are so creative, in the arts and entertainment and politics and sports. Let us not give up on those quite yet merely because people say they are what we do naturally. Let us understand these fields better, so we can manage them, instead of the other way around.

One item put up by Brother Peck concerns reparations. This is a damned solid idea, reparations, as long as they're not publicized as being given to us. If reparations are said to be "given" to us by government program, then you can bet it will not turn out right, that government program will be somehow misspelled on all the documentation and come out government *pogrom*, and the people will become confused, and when people are confused they go with what they know, which is killing Black people. And if we are dead, it probably will take all the utility out of any ensuing reparations.

I've heard the motions about proposed reparations, that they need not be cash, although I don't know what's wrong with cash. Some of our people say cash paid to Black people would make some White people bitter and resentful. Well? Where would be the change in that? In some cases it would be an improvement. What have White people been getting paid with all these years? Gingerbread cookies? I think not.

Drive the hard bargain, I say.

Other submotions on the subject of reparations concern free college tuition to any Black American with a lineage to slavery. Fine for the people who want to go to college, but what of agrarians like Whitlock, or mechanics like Brother Ali, or carpenters, or trapeze artists? Another submotion concerns a ten-year suspension of income taxes; another good idea, except I doubt it will happen under the circumstances. We have to be in position to negotiate, or at least palaver, and leverage is hard to come by. You must *think* to get it. You must *drive the hard bargain*. This brings us to the last item. We have decided that new ideas are to be allowed—for a trial-basis probationary period, of course. I propose what Black people should do is buy Whitlock's turnips, Mulhew's insurance, and Pendleton's and my books, all for a pittance.

Yes, Sister Richardson, you're telling it straight as you usually do; you'll get my vote even though you are the one who is loudly pointing out that I wrote this book and that it's to my advantage to tell Black readers to buy and read it. My position is this: We should stop apologizing for doing business with each other. I never heard a White man apologize for making money. If he did, it was an apology for not making more of it sooner, eh? As long as you are giving something back, I see nothing wrong with making it. If you don't make it, where can you find something to give back?

I know everybody resents paying us. Black people are supposed to volunteer (slavery was volunteerism of a sort, according to Brother Mulhew) and do all the hard work for leftovers and coupons, if not for free, but we need to take a hard look at past policy. While it reflected a wonderful magnanimity on our part as human beings, it said little in the way of our business acumen and gets no reparations. Most businesses I know won't accept magnanimity unless it's in the form of a check that will not bounce. We need to run our own businesses more, and we need to run them the way DuBois ran Niagara, the way Healy ran Georgetown, the way Johnson ran *Jet*, the way Gaston ran part of Birmingham, the way Gordy ran Motown, the way Reggie Lewis ran Beatrice. We must learn to run our businesses even better than that.

We consume goods faster than they can be slapped with a brand name, without a single check of policy. Buy foolish and die foolish. The time to do something about it is before it happens. Black people who do business with anybody who doesn't respect them, and keep on returning that business, deserve what they get, which will be nothing in the end, let me tell you, nothing but some possible holes in their heads.

Maybe there's an honest dollar in an honest day's work, as long as you are working with someone honest in the first place. I know, another rumor—but perhaps we should test its veracity, hold our collective breath, throw caution to the wind, and do some business together—men, women, old, young, straight, gay, left, right, light, dark, country, city, class or no class. Find some ways to do business with each other, no matter how wrong it seems at face value. Ice is ice. It is cold no matter who sells it—just as long as you make absolutely sure you're getting real ice in the first place. Now, before I yield the floor to Sister Richardson, I offer my final word on what black people must do now:

Turn the page, ladies and gentlemen. Turn the page.

ABOUT MEDIA

Why Black People
Don't Buy Books

I know what I know, and I know what I know is never enough. This is my credo. Actually, I have many credos that I pull out as they become convenient. Another one is "How, and more important why, did you become involved and lost in the bizarre and confusing world of book publishing?"

I call myself a writer (I know what I know). This means I have to understand at least some of the nuances of book publishing (I know what I know is never enough).

I first heard that "Black people don't buy books" from my friends and operatives who translate the book publishing business for me. Most of the book publishers, to give them credit, were too polite to say this to my face. In fact, they were too polite to say anything to my face. I have never talked to them, would not know them if I saw them except for those looks of self-satisfaction on their faces. I've only talked to editors, and the majority of them were engaging and garrulous people who were often encouraging and quite helpful. They pointed out things I might have seen myself had I not been looking so hard. They were unwavering in their compliments. But in the end, they insisted they were quislings (I had suspected as much) and at the mercy of their mercenary bosses. These would be the book publishers I have not seen, although they are rumored to be White people who live in ivory towers who have their own way of seeing things; not the happiest set of circumstances if you are a Black writer.

There are no people named Henry Holt or Alfred Knopf around anymore, but they have left proxies in their stead. And the proxies don't believe Black people buy books. Supposedly they discovered this by reading balance sheets and the body language of their competitors to find out if Black people do buy books, since most of them could only ask their Black maids if this was really true. They could call up Bill Cosby to ask him, and get left on hold. Cosby's books sell quite well, even though as a writer Bill Cosby is a great comedian—which, luckily for him, still works out.

The editors' pronouncements left me in confusion. First of all, just about all the Black people I know and have kept up with over the years buy books by the pound. Of course, it depends on what you're selling. Black people did not rush out to buy *Scarlett*, for example. And why should we? But Black people went right out and bought *Roots* by Alex Haley, and *The Color Purple* by Alice Walker, and *Waiting to Exhale* by Terry McMillan. But if there are no interesting Black people in your book at all, well, then the book had better be entertaining in some other way if you want Black people to buy it. It had better be funny, powerfully convincing, or a wonderful story, or at least look good on the coffee table.

Waiting to Exhale sold more than 750 skijillion copies in 1992, theoretically opening doors for other Black authors whose growing numbers include all political persuasions. This does not change the perception that Black people don't buy books, just because Black people, more specifically Black women, now go on the best-seller list occasionally. We are subtly told this means Black women *write* books (which might get read by White people on occasion). We are given that, reluctantly, by the book publishers. We are even given that we might *read* books every so often. But Black people still are certainly not seen as *buying* books. Only White people *buy* books. More publicity is given to Black people *stealing* books than buying them. Think about it.

For me the issue pertains to mental health. Was saying Black people don't buy books another way of saying, "Your book is the drizzling shits, and nobody could read it even if they made the mistake of buying it"? No matter how bravely we mutter, writers are always afraid somebody with half a brain will say that to them and be self-satisfied and, worse, correct. So I searched and searched (actually I engaged a man named Philip to search for me) until I found a publisher inventive enough to take in my curious work. My would-be book was then published, but the theory was left unchallenged; I was told, in essence, "Black people still don't buy books, *nyah-nyah-nyahnyahnyah*, but we'll publish your book anyway, young bizarre Black fellow, because some White people may need coasters and cutting boards."

Then the mysterious process of turning what you have written into a book begins. Once-garrulous editors turn sober. They come calling with red and blue pencils to change what they can before the manuscript can be copy-edited, printed, and finally bound. The printing involves the setting of type of varying degrees of felicity to particular grades of paper, then reading printed galleys over and over for errors. The paper is bound between hard covers usually made of cloth; the cloth cover is then covered again with a glossy paper diaper called a book jacket. For this jacket, the editors call up people and hypnotize them into writing nice things about the author that will help sell the book to people too busy to read it. Then a few quiet prayers are muttered, candles are burned, pentagrams are drawn, blood is smeared, and surreptitious meetings are held where White people shake their heads and do not laugh. Then the book distributors are notified that a new book is coming out. Their orders depend on how enthusiastic the book publishers are—how many copies of your book they've printed, and how desperately they smile when they are talking about it.

By the time the entire process is completed, the book you have written is three years old—seven years if you are a Black writer, because it takes four years instead of one to talk some White book publisher into undertaking all this delicate surgery on your behalf in spite of what his maid says. By the time you see your book you hardly remember it. People have to remind you what your own book was about.

Of course most of this is slightly exaggerated, all except the part about people in publishing saying, "You know, of course, that Black people don't buy books." Actually the editors in book publishing are far more skilled and humane than their contemporaries in both newspaper and magazine publishing—which is like saying lethal injection is more skilled and humane than the electric chair or a stout club.

After I had the fortune (I don't know whether to call it good or not, since I've yet to see this fortune) to have a book published, I decided to use to my own advantage this perception among White people that "Black people don't buy books." I went to sign books at bookstores. I'd wait for some unsuspecting Black person to come near my table and make the slightest eye contact with me, and then I would blurt: "White people tell me Black people don't buy books."

Almost immediately the Black person would frown, become cross, and mutter, "Well now. Which one said that?"

"Oh, any number of them," I would reply, as if confident of my sources. "A whole moblike group of them, for the most part located on or near Madison Avenue in New York City."

"Well, that's just ridiculous and a half," the Black person would usually say. "I buy books when they're on sale, and so do my sister Loretta and my brother Chuckie Lee. And I'm going to buy yours—if it's on sale. What's it about?"

"Oh," I'd answer absently, "situations like this."

"How much does it cost?"

"Does price matter when you're proving a point?" I would ask, trying to bring character points into the fray.

"Price matters even if you don't have a point," the unblinking Black person would answer. *"Is it on sale?"*

This is where I would usually mutter the price, at the same time attempting to keep my eyes from darting around.

"Wow," the Black person might say. "That's a lotta money. I could go to the matinee three times for that."

"True," I'd say. "But you can't take the matinee home. You can use a book twice. Read it, then give it away for Christmas. If you take the cover off before you read it and don't break the spine as you turn pages, it's like new."

"Hey, good idea. Is it on sale?"

And sooner or later, after about thirty minutes of solid huckstering, I would sell a book. But sometimes when I would say, "White people say Black people don't buy books," the Black person would say, "In your case they're right. Apparently all White folks ain't as stupid as you say."

But sooner or later I'd have to leave the bookstore, and business would go back to usual. If it wasn't a bookstore specializing in books by and about Black people, the Black people who came in would be forced to ask, "Where is your section on African-American authors? I'm looking for a new release by Whatshername." They have to ask because no such books are visible, unless, of course, they are by Bill Cosby. The bookstore manager, depending on his or her mood, might point it out. "Af-Am? Other than the Cosberino? Back there, to the left, past that narrow aisle, under that wobbly ladder Irene is standing on. The bottom two rows."

"Irene says the book I want isn't back there."

"Well? What do you want me to do about it?"

"Could you order it for me?"

"Just one?"

"Well, that's all I care to read at one time."

"Oh, all right, I suppose. Check back next December. You're probably going to give it away as a present, huh?"

"Forget it. Guess you've got *Mein Kampf*, eh?"

"No, but we can have it here in 24 hours."

"Never mind."

Black people don't buy books. Let's call this a given among White people—the way some of them think Black people use Brazil nuts for toes, or run down property for the hell of it. I wonder why this stereotype has come to be uttered so smugly? Certainly it is unprecedented. Why, as recently as 127 years ago, White people gave Black people just released from bondage cash premiums to buy books, enticing them to become avid readers. "Reading is the key!" all White people said. "If you don't read, it will be difficult to better yourselves! Read and understand! Read and gain perspective! Read and find control and penetrate the job market! If you show potential after reading, we'll hire you! We'll publish your books and put them up in front of the bookstores! So read! Read and feel sad, happy, reflective! Forget that 'cast down your bucket' stuff. Read! And if you're too lazy to do it, at least make your children read!"

Again I exaggerate. I've read there were a few Quakers and some other honest, fair White people who might have said this to a few Black people who needed it. But I know this: If

I had been born one hundred years earlier, a bare sliver of time's difference, I could have been shot or hanged for reading a book, let alone for writing one and trying to get it published. I wonder if knowing this helps me avoid blocks and keeps me studying the locks and bars on the publishers' gates. I know that what I don't know is always too much.

It's Greek to Me

"You think me a fanatic tonight, for you read history not with your eyes but with your prejudices."

Wendell Phillips

Who are the opponents in the battle for History? In the blue corner, delicate nostrils flaring, stand defenders of Western thought, the Eurocentrists. We'll call them the "Frics" (the smart money is said to be on them). In the red corner, ready to have at it, smiling through bowed, fleshy lips and all that melanin, are the defenders of the African diaspora, the Afrocentrists. We'll call them the "Fracs."

Fine for them. But the real question is, *who are we?* Here we sit, as confused as deaf bats by all the strategic posturing and shrill bleating and cool pronouncements. We care nothing for their "your people" this and "our people" that. Their "don't listen to him, listen to me." We would like to know the real story of the past because we'd like to get to the future. We might be called the multiculturalists.

We know we would like to believe in ourselves. We'd like

to know if the diaphanous presence of Black people in what is accepted as civilization's recorded history is accurate. We have our suspicions about it—it seems stunted, blunted, and then its sections halved. So most of us don't want history as it has been taught for years (unless we're the most egotistical of White males, for that is His Story—Eurocentrism; specifically, Anglocentrism). But we don't want unreasonable accommodations on the part of the new wave (for that's a mystery, My Story—Afrocentrism). We wouldn't know what to do with any accommodations on our part, in fact, so inured are we to the taking of the hard road uphill. Still, we demand the *real* story.

I can think of at least one better recorded spokesman for Western culture as distilled in America than the late Professor Allan Bloom or the historian Arthur Schlesinger, Jr., whom I'll ask to speak shortly. For now, however, let us concentrate on the former. Professor Bloom was a mind employed by the University of Chicago as a teacher, a molder of other minds. In 1987 he wrote a book entitled *The Closing of the American Mind*, which was a general lamentation, albeit an effectively written one, over the fact many universities were no longer making the classroom the exclusive province and hunting ground of Great White Philosophers that Professor Bloom had learned to admire and emulate. People were trying to say that maybe black or brown or yellow or red people, possibly even a rare woman or two, might have had something to say in the past that was worth noting and remembering. This was too much for Bloom to handle—all this questioning, challenging, and curiosity. Certainly it was out of place in a college classroom. He liked things as they'd been reflected most often in the past; things reflected in an image like his. He had always taken his own security and peace of mind for granted until he discovered it was not guaranteed anymore by genetic caveat. Security and peace of mind had been his truth. He was made uncomfortable by any new way of seeing history. He was uncomfortable with change. Why?

It would mean having to learn much more than he'd learned up to that point. It seemed intimidating and made him mutter about a lowering of standards because the canon was expanded to include more—as if bigger would not be better in this case, as if each White writer and philosopher studied at universities were William Shakespeare. As if Bloom himself might be related to Shakespeare. Of course, that is the inference. It can go a long way in helping one's confidence as a writer. What humans believe they are, they become. We are powerful. Bloom constructed his book powerfully, no doubt. It consists of more than three hundred effective pages, wave after wave of the work, effect, and legacy of European scholars, and maybe a few Asian ones too, if you count Russia as Asia, which Bloom did not. His book could have been entitled *The Closing of the European Mind in America.* Now let us go back to those recent days of yesteryear in America when White men were the only ones being studied, and Blacks were lucky to study at all, let alone be studied, unless it was as a rhesus monkey is studied. Given this unfortunate recent history, Bloom's position seemed strange to me right on the face of it, because where was he in history? In Chicago, and on the South Side of Chicago at that. This is an area shaped and molded by those very people Bloom chose to determine not to exist on the same plane of thinking as the Great White Fathers of Western civilization.

Chicago is a mighty city, named by the indigenous Native American population and later "discovered" by a Black explorer named Jean Baptiste Pont DuSable. Chicago and its affluent suburbs were made what they are today by a vast combination of white immigrants from Eastern Europe, black immigrants from the southern United States, brown immigrants from south of the American border, and yellow immigrants from the Far East. One of the reasons Chicago is a great city in the first place is because of its many Black citizens. Minister Malcolm X (Bloom would have me believe by exclusion that he was not an orator or philosopher, I'd imagine) explained it in this manner: "If everyone in this room gave me their salaries for a week, I'd be well off. If everyone in this room gave me their salaries for a year, I'd be rich. This happened to black people for over three hundred years!" No wonder Chicago is a mighty city.

Yet, in spite of being located at a university smack in the middle of all the fruits, sour and sweet, of all these collective lives and labors, Bloom insisted that the culled ramblings of White men who never saw America, never knew it existed, were the only ones worth studying at the local universities of most renown. When you get down to it, that makes him no better than those who say, "You can go back to where you came from, now that we are all settled and prosperous and everything," which ignores the central fact. We are from here. Black people came from America—at least many of the ones in Chicago did. Black Americans were made in the U.S.A., and they made the U.S.A. in their image as well. Do people believe there will never be an accounting for the way America was constructed, merely because they think it beside the point? Writing in Chicago, how could one, given the discovery, creation, and root sustenance of the city itself, not include the works of Gwendolyn Brooks or Lorraine Hansberry or Richard Wright in a study of any contemporary or otherwise relevant literary canon? We're talking about a wing of a canon *right there in Chicago*. How to miss all three without trying?

This is because Black people are not seen by most White people as being within the same value system—a convenient blindness that allows them to think what they like and make it come true. Most White people cannot see Black people in the same way that they see themselves. That way they can never be outdone. Worse, they don't realize that this is a result of how they were educated in schools and universities, and what they were fed by the equally exclusionary media.

Bloom used Saul Bellow, another Chicago writer, though supposedly a far more famous and accomplished one than, say, Richard Wright, as the author of his foreword. Bloom had no problem placing Saul Bellow up there in his great constellation of the worthy, and Saul had no problem agreeing with him. No matter to me that Saul won the Nobel Prize. Who gave it out? More White men. Black people might never be seen for themselves in such a world. Deeds, hard work, and accomplishment would happen unheard, unseen.

Imagine some time in the distant future, where Bellow's work has been, well, not forgotten, but appropriated into some miasma called, let's just say, Afrocentrism. And in this future time, suppose what Bellow had written was subtly changed. Some of the references moved, for example, or entire texts altered or in some cases transmogrified; indeed, his whole authorship limited to one or two of his works and the rest appropriated and placed under someone else's name. Let's say his work became not Saul Bellow's but a man named Willie Horton's, for the sake of argument, and not trying to start anything. You don't lack such imagination if you are Black. Are the ramifications of the scenario clear?

At first I thought, "What does he fear?" I think fear has to be in the equation. If Black people were not feared, then why deny them access to the books, which was done in this country for more than three hundred years? This behavior leads to a Professor Leonard Jeffries, the radical Afrocentrist who had to spend his life understanding that reason had nothing to do with the way he and his history had been treated. He went a little overboard, but if you ask me, people like Bloom asked for it. I learned more in a book by another late professor from the University of Chicago. The book was entitled

A River Runs Through It, and it was given to me by a friend named Nick. The author was Norman Maclean. And although by then I was not predisposed to books authored by elderly University of Chicago professors, I found it to be a simpler, better book than *The Closing of the American Mind*, a classic that did not ask to be anointed as such. Some of my faith in human nature and education in the city of Chicago was salvaged, at least for the time being.

Later on, in 1991, Arthur Schlesinger wrote a book entitled *The Disuniting of America: The Reflections of a Multicultural Society*, which, among other things, stated that so-called "politically correct" curricula led to "the reduction of history into ethnic cheerleading." He rode the Afrocentrists hard and put them away wet, claiming that in their unenlightened rush to heighten the low self-esteem of young Black Americans, the Fracs were replacing the world's "true" history with an ideology of racial separatism and/or superiority, and with foolish myths about the role ancient African civilizations played in the world's history. He uses the word *tragic* a great deal in discussing the grasping of history by the likes of Na'im Akbar, Asa Hilliard, Ivan Van Sertima, and John Henrik Clarke, some of the more intractable Afrocentric academicians who give presentations as cooly efficient as Schlesinger's. He doesn't quite dismiss ancient Egyptian civilization but can hardly see how it relates to history. He makes it plain that we don't know what "race" the Egyptians were, or even if "race" was a valid concept to these Mediterranean people. He also says people in America have to accept the "New Man" theory. That is downright funny, because Black people were not the ones rejecting DeTocqueville's "New Man" theory of America. We were the ones who truly *became* it. One drop of blood made a White American a Black person. It was not us who denied reality. Schlesinger's rationale was born of guilt because he succinctly described what Eurocentrists have done since King James: having appropriated the whole cloth of history, they now sit back smiling and wondering why anyone would try to change it. Tragic? I'll tell you what is tragic. The Middle Passage was tragic. The disfigured features on the faces of those ancient relics are tragic. The story of the Sphinx's disfiguring is tragic. Ten thousand lynchings are tragic. Murder is tragic. Not untold is the story of the usurper who scorched the earth, then called it "tragic."

Schlesinger is an accomplished man, a flag-bearer of liberalism. He was one of the people who showed up on September 26, 1992, at the University of the District of Columbia to honor Joseph Rauh, a White lawyer and staunch defender of human rights for fifty years. This makes it even more troublesome that Schlesinger would have written such a book, or that Whittle Communications, the company behind Channel One, perhaps a new way to educate upper middle-class American children, saw that the book was published.

I'd now like to suggest two better spokespeople for the American Outpost of Western Civilization as we know it today. The first one is an African-American writer from Philadelphia named Lorene Cary. In this case a Philadelphia writer is nearly the same as the proverbial Philadelphia lawyer: someone to heed. In 1991, Cary wrote a book called *Black Ice* that is to *The Disuniting of America* what *A River Runs Through It* is to *The Closing of the American Mind*. That is to say, her book is better, an American classic. And as for my other spokesman, I'll let him speak for himself.

We were glad to have seen the land which was the mother of civilization—which taught Greece her letters, and through Greece Rome, and through Rome the world; the land which could have humanized and civilized the hapless children of Israel, but allowed them to depart out of her borders little better than savages. We were glad to have seen that land which had an enlightened religion with future eternal rewards and punishment in it, while even Israel's religion contained no promise of a hereafter. We were glad to have seen that land which had glass three thousand years before England had it, and could paint upon it as none of us can paint now; that land which knew three thousand years ago, well-nigh all of medicine and surgery which science has *discovered* lately; which had all those curious surgical instruments which science has *invented* recently; which had in high excellence a thousand luxuries and necessities of an advanced civilization which we have gradually contrived and accumulated in modern times and claimed as things that were new under the sun; that had paper untold centuries before we dreamt of it, waterfalls before our women thought of them; that had a perfect system of common schools so long before we boasted of our achievements in that direction that it seems forever and forever ago; that so embalmed the dead that flesh was made almost immortal—which we cannot do; that built temples which mock at destroying time and smile grimly upon our lauded little prodigies of architecture; that old land that knew all which we know now, perchance, and more; that walked in the broad highway of civilization in the grey dawn of creation, ages and ages before we were born; that left the impress of exalted, cultivated Mind upon the eternal front of the Sphinx to confound all scoffers who, when all her other proofs had passed away, might seek to persuade the world that imperial Egypt, in the days of her high renown, had groped in darkness.

Mark Twain

This was Mark Twain? Yes. I'd say he is the king of American letters. And when you get right down to it, maybe he was even more productive and intuitive than either Arthur Schlesinger or Allan Bloom, maybe even a better writer than Saul Bellow. Possibly. To find out for sure, we'd have to ask other White men. Judgments are beyond us, as "blaaacks." There's sure to be a panel of White men convening somewhere right now for the sole purpose of handing out more awards.

Now, before 1865, America was nowhere near the cultural

leader and award-winner of the world. Not even close. But America certainly considers itself the cultural leader of the world now. This upward movement started, coincidentally, about the time of Twain—*and the time slavery was abolished*. Was *Huckleberry Finn* the Great American Novel? White men have awarded it so. What to do with it now? Take it back? Or, perhaps more efficiently, teach it improperly?

Who is Huck? Adolescent White male who means well, is called "master," and whose opening premise to us is *I don't want to be civilized*. And who is Jim? Mature Black male who means well, is called "nigger slave," and wants *freedom*. The story is of their trip, by all necessity together, down the Mississippi River on a raft. The raft is America, and the river is history. Some of us don't see it that way. Recently some Black people whose children were in the school system of Plano, Texas, protested the use of the novel in the school curriculum, because of the number of times that term of endearment, *nigger*, is used. As though these Black people have never heard that word or used it themselves, as though the word must never be confronted in Great American Culture.

It doesn't matter that none of us have liked some of the things that have happened in the ensuing years. American culture grew from this. And one of the best the culture has produced in letters is Mark Twain. If Plato's *Republic* is your idea of giving insight into the formation of the Great American Culture, then write your own essay, turn it in to a tenured college professor, and come away with your A, your 4.0 GPA, your feeling of comfort and acceptance. If that is your world, your private grove, then so be it for you. We live in the world. Give me Twain and keep me out of school.

The passage excerpted above is from *The Innocents Abroad*, written in 1868 and 1869, after Twain had visited Europe, East Asia, the "Holy Land," and Egypt itself. He was disappointed in most of the Old World wonders (it was not his America, the New World), and he did send them up over there, his targets including natives of three continents and his traveling companions. As we know, under Twain's pen nothing was so sacred it could not be sent up royally, and turned on its head, and laughed at. But at times he could be serious. He really was one of the original multiculturalists. So even in classrooms that have recently been seen as the exclusive habitat of the White male, some Eurocentric myths that were taught or held in error have been shattered. I have also heard what has become the old saw of the Eurocentrist: "Well, okay, maybe you have a tiny point here. But so what? Whom could it help now? And haven't we done a good job civilizing you?"

The truth always helps people, gives them the idea they can find it again. An acquaintance of mine, American Black man by definition, light tan by true color, went to Williams College as an undergraduate. There he was made to feel very uncomfortable in one of his classes by a professor smiling slyly at him, the only Black man in the class, while talking about genetics, about who was naturally inclined to do what, amid tittering and sniggering from my acquaintance's fellow students who just happened to be White American boys and girls who were learning what kind of men and women to one day become. I don't know if my acquaintance ever got over this humiliation. He remembered it well enough to relate it in detail fifteen years later. Oh, but that he had arrows in his quiver then to fire back at the smug assassin of character. They should've been at his disposal. I always wondered if his confidence had been eroded just enough to hold him back after that—not enough to keep him from doing well, but enough to stop him from becoming truly great.

One must stretch beyond self for greatness. You must think you have the stuff of greatness in order to even attempt to become great. You must feel culturally and historically linked to excellence in order to excel. You must feel deeply culturally obligated to perform in order to feel free to reach your finest performance. In order to feel historically, culturally obligated to contribute to society, you must be made strong by your contributions already made.

Actually, it is the Eurocentrists who are panicking that the untrue among their myths are being exploded. It seems they're unwilling to stand on their own two feet with little help from the past, but they insist that we do it.

There was a famous scholar—British, of course—named Bernard Knox, who, here in the America of 1992, went around the country giving a lecture entitled "The Oldest Dead White European Males." His aim was to point out the follies of multiculturalism by celebrating the accomplishments of the mighty Greeks. Knox said that all civilization stemmed from the Greeks—and they were white men, so there.

I thought this was funny, to see this man grasping just as hard as the Afrocentrists; funny, for the Greeks are considered White men only when it suits the whimsies of Eurocentrists. The ancient Greeks are considered White men until a White(r) professor's White(r) wife wants to take a vacation alone in Greece. Then the Greeks become "those uncivilized bastards." Nobody's trying to stop the legacy or the effect of the Greeks. We all should be made to study them. The point is, we should neither start nor stop with them. Were they the first men to stand on their own two feet? Were they the first men to think for themselves? They all were struck by inspiration at once?

Homer's *Iliad* and *Odyssey* are the Rosetta Stone of Greek culture. Plato and Socrates are credited with inventing philosophy as formed by questioning. Ptolemy is given credit for astronomy (here is where Eurocentrists say, "Which Ptolemy, from what dynasty of Egypt?" What difference does it make now, I say, as they've said to me. When the word *Ptolemaic* is uttered, nothing astronomical leaps to mind; I know I am less for that; I know this ignorance dulls the taste of blood or wine, takes the red from a rose, inhibits my senses; I wonder how I can live without it).

But how could Ptolemy have "discovered" astronomy, when the Pyramids had already been standing for more than two thousand years and were built in accordance with the rotation of the Earth and the stars' configuration in the universe? Somebody knew something about astronomy then. And in pre-Columbian Europe, the consensus was that the Earth was flat? Even counting on one's fingers, it doesn't add up.

As for the *Iliad* and the *Odyssey* themselves—who was Agamemnon, the king whose fury over the loss of Helen began the Trojan War? Where was Troy? Who was Helen? What did she look like? Like Yvette Mimieux? Like Grace Jones? Like Lena Horne? Like Merle Oberon? Do you know who and of what people are? Whatever she was, it wasn't Scandinavian, or Teutonic, or of the British royal family. Scholars admit that for many years the great epics of the *Iliad* and *Odyssey* had many editors, many "Homers," because each copy of Homer's work had to be inscribed individually by scholars—there were no printing presses then—so they could be passed along and the Greek children could read them and learn passages by heart. Many variations were thus left. And on what were these first copies of the *Iliad* and *Odyssey* written? On papyrus, from the Egyptian plant, made long before Homer. Who was Homer? Omar? The Moor? Then do we discuss Spain and the culture of North Africa out of Spain that began the end of the Dark Ages. . . . But I am getting into precisely that which I hope to avoid when I wish to be informed about today, about who we are now, together.

When people deny the complexities of the past, it drives the likes of a Jeffries, college professor in the State University of New York system, into the corner. In the end Jeffries was no better—or worse—than Schlesinger, though less dangerous to me. It is the realization of these hidden complexities that drove Martin Bernal to write *Black Athena*; Molefi Kefe Asante to pen a beautiful polemic, *Afrocentricity*; Henry Louis Gates to write *Loose Canons*; all protesting the unsettling shadows over history in their differing ways.

I try to understand them all. How dare historians sit there and try to deny what they themselves long ago admitted, just so their consciences will never emerge from the big sleep? How dare a Eurocentrist say, "What does it matter?" It must matter a great deal for this information to have been twisted and destroyed for centuries as it was. Knox and the rest of the calm Eurocentrists must think it matters a great deal to hold onto it so very, very tightly.

As a beginning, Afrocentricity is good to strip away those layers of doubt and self-hate in Black people, the way old paint is scraped away for a new coat to adhere properly. But sooner or later we folks in America must admit to ourselves we are not pure African at all—we are out of Africa. Just as the origins of humanity are out of Africa. We here are the children of the New World, children of a different kind. This difference is now being explored by the likes of Kwame Anthony Appiah, whose very name is the fruit of multiculturalism. The New World (and the Old World as well) was grounded and built on multiculturalism. America was, without a doubt, so we are not trying to fool anybody. We have been fooled. But no more. Appiah's contribution to the discourse is a book called *In My Father's House: Africa in the Philosophy of Culture*. When speaking of the mixture of European and African in many of us, he makes a very powerful statement: "We might instead seek to turn to our advantage the interdependence history has thrust upon us."

The reason the Afrocentrist is so strident is because of centuries of crass rejection suffered from Eurocentrists. Multiculturalism changes things right away, for you need no one's authority or permission or debate to make it real and legitimate; you may immediately use it, embrace it, and under-

stand it, and not go back to being told who you are by someone who doesn't know you or want to know you, no matter
what the color of their skin, the letters after their name, or
the secret location of their heart of hearts.

I was fortunate enough to travel to Egypt recently and was
at once claimed as a citizen, a lost friend, or at least an expatriate who would be briefly tolerated.

People who had been in Cairo all their lives came up to me
and asked in their fluent Arabic for the time of day or the
nature of my business or if the day was pleasant enough for
me. I looked at them evenly and told them I was sorry, but I
didn't speak Arabic. They would gently punch me in the
shoulder or look at me with disbelief. Why of course I knew
Arabic. It was plain. They had just seen me, dressed differently, appearing less Americanized, just a fortnight ago, running a vendor's tent in the bazaar of Khan El Khalily, looking
to hook tourists into buying scarves.

I made attempts to tell them they must have been mistaken.
I was a tourist myself. American. I was not from there. "Sure,"
they said with those doubting eyes, or the Arabic equivalent,
smiling and clicking their palates with their tongues. "Sounds
like a good trick you're playing, friend, Good luck with it."
If it doesn't pan out, their eyes said, they would see me again
in another fortnight, perhaps peddling camel rides at Giza.

A short time later I went to the Egyptian Museum for a
tour. One had to pay to enter with a camera. There were
valuables inside, so valuable that one must pay even to photograph them. There is no point in my being specific. You
would have to see them to believe it. There were large rooms
for each of the many periods of Egyptian history, such as it
was re-created, with ancient appointments made of finely
crafted faience, lapis lazuli, ebony, ivory, gilded wood, pink
granite, quartzite, incense, linen, gold, and alabaster adorning

the statuary, the Bed of Osiris, the Treasures of Tutankhamen. There were stacks of sarcophagi, each with a story inscribed on its flanks, copious writing meticulously done,
obviously the life story of the person within. I admired the
sure richness of workmanship in each piece, until it occurred
to me that there must have been an entire class of artists in
this society, and that it must have been a huge class of people,
and that therefore certain necessities of survival must have
been made simple. Who were they? Here was all this art,
room upon room of it, wave upon wave, reflecting a pro-
found power of concentration. And this was just what remained after thousands of years of neglect and freebooting.

Of all these artisans behind this work, I knew not a name.
Not one. I knew the name Michelangelo. *Who were they?*

The figure of Isis was carved from black granite so perfectly
you could almost see the firmness of the flesh, the grip of
muscle over the curve of the hip and thigh, beneath the stone-
made gossamer wrapping. This was art of a very high order,
and I could never know the name of the artist the way I know
the name Michelangelo. But this was art, though the artisans
themselves and the vast majority of what they accomplished
are lost in the mists of time. What they created remains in
"newer" works of art. Who among us can say it won't be the
same for us five thousand years from now? Who among the
Western artists can say this? To forget the place of the bridge
is to forget how to cross over.

I cannot impress upon you what it has been like to go to
museums on and off for thirty-five years here in the New
World of my living, learning to be impressed by all the art
there, and learning to accept those depictions as being what
art is, grand but unlike you at all; and when like you, like
you in a way you might not wish to be but must accept as
the only way you can be represented in art. I can't tell you
what it feels like to go to a museum where the images resemble you, or people you've known, or could have known. I

cannot express to you the peace and reassurance of these waves of feeling. But if you are White, I don't have to express it. You simply accept it. It never occurs that others require the feeling of accomplishment, of foundation, of priceless-ness, of knowing their history, of being essential to the panoply of civilization.

I assure you: Word is getting around.

Multiculturalists require a common truth of history. If college professors and other school teachers don't like this, well, that's why they call it hooky. We will find out for ourselves, share the knowledge, hope the raft doesn't sink before we gather at the mouth of the river to account for our brief time here.

Why Black People Don't Often Go to Baseball Games

Progress can be a tricky business, especially when one does not know exactly what it is one is progressing toward. Is that the light at the end of the tunnel up ahead—or is it the headlamp of the Amtrak Metroliner? Writing about progress can be even trickier. By the time you say you've made progress, it's no longer progress, it's history, and subject to people changing its meaning.

My mission here is to discuss the American game of baseball. Baseball is one of the best games ever dreamed up. In fact, some White men are loath to admit that there are any other games worth playing at all (outside of golf, which was, among other things, the official sport of the Nazi Party). You and I know better. But recently I've been noticing that many periodicals have printed stories observing the lack of Black participation in dreamy games of baseball in inner-city lots, and noting dwindling numbers of Blacks in organized baseball's dream-laden minor leagues, and checking Black people's declining presence as fans at major league ball parks across America's field of dreams. I cannot tell if the stories are whimsical or if they are to be taken seriously, like the horoscopes and editorial pages. These baseball stories are regularly written, along with those about baseball being right next to heaven, or those about an upcoming pheenom, real or dreamed up, usually the latter. You really can't believe half the things you read about baseball; not many people are authorities on it, as it is a game of skill.

Personally, I'm more concerned with the lack of jobs, libraries, and fresh produce in the inner cities and the mysterious proliferation of cheap handguns there. Baseball is like breathing. It seems to take care of itself, more or less. As for turning out for big league games, apparently many Black people are too busy buying lettuce and paying up the utility bill to come to the games in droves, especially when you can watch the games that are on television for free. I'm sure major league baseball will rectify this in the future and declare that the World Series must be paid for, even just to watch it on television. No doubt baseball team owners will say this will not be to raise revenue, but only so that the participation of young Black men in baseball can rise again.

It's funny how young Black men seem to be the catalytic agent for so much behavior. They even shape the protocol of White baseball executives. And let a young Black woman not be able to find a husband, or a young White man not be able to find a job, or a young Polynesian not be able to resist taking steroids to look good at the beach, and they will tell you it is not their fault, but the residual effect of a young Black man somewhere. I had no idea young Black men were so influential in everyday American life.

Some people look at organized baseball's minor leagues,

see fewer Black players there, and say, "Hmm. Black people must be losing their interest in baseball." A man I knew once wrote a similar story in the late '70s for a small newspaper in Northern California called the *Peninsula Times-Tribune*. He wrote that the Black baseball player was the California condor of athletes, because there weren't many Black baseball players in the minor leagues then, either. Later, he asked me what I thought of this piece of sterling prognostication. We were in Candlestick Park in San Francisco, so I pointed at Dave Winfield and Ozzie Smith and said, "Don't ask me, ask them."

Personally, I enjoyed the baseball season in 1989, when the Baltimore Orioles had just about all White players, a Black manager, Frank Robinson, and just about all Black coaches. They played good ball and nearly won the pennant, which they might have been able to do had they had a few more Black ballplayers or a good catcher of any hue.

I also enjoyed 1990, when Eric Davis made a few plays to help win the World Series for the Cincinnati Reds. In the National League playoffs against the Pittsburgh Pirates, Davis was playing left field instead of his customary center field. This was because he had injured a knee by running into any number of walls, trying to catch baseballs, because doing the impossible is often the play to make in the big leagues, and unavoidably for the greater glory of the Reds.

In a close playoff game at Pittsburgh's Three Rivers Stadium, a Pirate batter named Bobby Bonilla (he happened to be Black) cracked a whistling drive that sped on a line over the Cincinnati center fielder's head. The Cincinnati center fielder was named Billy Hatcher (he is Black, too, but that wouldn't help him catch this missile). He gamely raced back, leaped mightily, vainly, and crashed inelegantly into the center-field wall. He'd had no hope of making this play. The screaming 400-foot line drive made a sound like a gunshot as it banged into and then caromed high off the 12-foot boards.

Hatcher slumped beneath them, beaten. It seemed Bonilla might have an inside-the-park home run, and the Pirates might find themselves in the World Series.

But that meant not taking Eric Davis into account. When the ball left the bat, he had raced over into center field from his station in left, and he played that ball on a big hop off the center-field wall. That in itself was an amazing play, a ballplayer's play, which would hold Bonilla to a well-deserved triple. But Davis knew that was not the only play to make, so he wheeled back toward the infield and with no time to gain his bearings, no time to hesitate, fired a blind, shoulder-high, impossible fastball strike toward third base. His true throw sped toward the infield on a line and took one flat hop over the big right shoulder of the sliding Bobby Bonilla. Chris Sabo, the Cincinnati third baseman (who is White, as a change of pace), caught this great throw and applied a sweeping tag to a sliding and now incredulous Bonilla. Sabo called Davis's throw "a bullet from nowhere."

Eric Davis spent parts of six seasons in the minor leagues, beginning just about the time that my colleague at the small newspaper wrote that sterling lie. Davis seemed thin as a reed, but his thin limbs were heavily waxed at key points— forearms, wrists, waist, shoulder—by hard and quick muscle. He appeared to be thin from far away, but he certainly seemed bigger than life when you were close up on him. When he went up to hit, he held his hands low and close to his right hip and twisted them slowly around the handle of the bat, as if he were cracking the combination of a safe, or perhaps summoning some private genie from its wooden trap. In the batter's box, Davis held his feet in something of an exaggeration of the first position in ballet. Despite his form, or perhaps because of it, he could still turn on any known fastball delivered by a human arm—if it was thrown straight—with the possible exception of Nolan Ryan's or Dwight Gooden's or Roger Clemens's or the arms of their historic brethren like

Johnson, Paige, Wood, Smokey Joe Williams, Feller, etc.— and then only their best stuff, when they were young.

Unfortunately for the Oakland Athletics, none of these pitchers played for the A's in 1990. In that World Series against the A's, in his first at-bat of the first game, Davis got his arms out and socked a three-run home run to dead center field off Dave Stewart, the A's Black pitching ace, setting off a mad demonstration of affection from the Cincinnati Reds' fans, who lost their heads, and from his teammates, who seemed to suddenly gain theirs. Maybe the mighty Oakland A's of Rickey Henderson (Black) and Jose Canseco (Latin) and manager Tony LaRussa (Overrated) could be beaten after all. The CBS-TV network, in the first year of a contract to televise these baseball games live, did not get the shot of Davis's home run going out on that breathtaking parabola. The CBS cameramen weren't quick enough. As for the Cincinnati fans, they cheered because they sure saw it. They would be back to booing Davis as hard as rain by the next year. One reason Black people may avoid attending big league games is because of the dreamy behavior of fans going to heaven. At a ball game, "Hey Davis, you fuckin' stink like horseshit!" qualifies as crisp theater.

Cincinnati swept Oakland in four games. In the final game Davis split a kidney making a full-out diving catch on the green grass of the Coliseum field in Oakland. He somehow caught the ball, but then he dropped his arm in pain before being able to hold it up for the umpire to see, which is the way they verify a catch in the big leagues. The big leagues are not about dreams, about might-have-beens, but about reality. Eventually, after a long delay in which Davis and the Reds waited for his pain to subside (it never did), he finished playing for that half-inning and jogged haltingly to the dugout. There, he doubled over, waiting for the pain to recede. It worsened and kept him doubled. He was taken to Merritt Hospital, where doctors told him he was bleeding like a stuck pig inside. They asked if he'd been trying to kill himself or something. No thought of that, just trying to make the play and win the World Series as a result.

These Reds, once they had won the World Series later that day, celebrated, marveling at their four-game sweep of the mighty A's. Without a second thought they happily piled onto their jet plane and left Oakland with Davis in the hospital. It wasn't like he was Joe DiMaggio. Joe DiMaggio was gone; there was even a dreamy song written about it.

Who by comparison was Eric Davis? Just a ballplayer. They were both just ballplayers, the difference being that the Reds didn't even want to pay for Davis's trip back to Cincinnati from Oakland, once he was well enough to travel, with tubes and wires still plugged into him. All this after Eric Davis had aided the Cincinnati Reds in their quest to win the major league World Series of baseball, which is the reason they are in business. You can imagine what it must be like, then, for a more ordinary Black baseball player in the minor leagues, if this is what happens in the bigs.

Approximately two years later, in November of 1992, it came out that the Cincinnati Reds team owner, Marge Schott, was in the regrettable habit of ranting in richly bigoted terms that would be exemplary, if a bigot could be seen as an example to anyone. She had unaffectionately called Davis (who had since moved on to the L.A. Dodgers—wisely so, it appears in hindsight) and a former Cincinnati teammate, Dave Parker (who was retired but had been perhaps the best native-born Cincinnati athlete in history, after the boxer Ezzard Charles), her "million-dollar niggers." Schott also called some business associates and competitors "those Jew bastards" and "money-grubbing Jews."

Oddly enough, Marge had more money than about all of the people she dissed. I think her harangue was partially designed to aid her own survival in the world of other baseball captains of industry—owners who, other than Marge, were

White men. Schott also kept a Nazi swastika armband at home, implying it was a party favor, symbolic of nothing more than a good time. She'd said Hitler was "good at first, but then went too far."

Schott also charmed participants in a conference call among owners of the major league baseball teams by saying, according to a listener, that she "would rather have a trained monkey working for [her] than a nigger." This call had been set up by Sharon Jones, who was at the time a midlevel executive with the Oakland A's. She was the listener in question. Jones, who is an African-American, heard what Marge Schott said clearly, as did the rest of the team owners who were on the line at the time, and by their silence they approved it.

I have sat and spoken with the Charles O. Finleys and the Donald Trumps while they surveyed various ball fields and their walking depreciable assets. What Marge Schott said was in line with the way they thought when I saw them, rather when they saw me, and they didn't have to say anything, although they usually did. And their every gesture, action, smirk, and uncomfortable off-color aside made their distastes abundantly clear.

I have seen Sharon Jones. There isn't a trained monkey in the world you could confuse with her, unless of course you were the White owner of a major league baseball team. Whether or not she was a good baseball executive was beside the point. She was not a monkey. I think Marge has more of a resemblance to a chimp than Sharon. All you'd have to do is see the three of them together to notice this. Such a meeting is not likely now.

Within two weeks of this information being made public, there was an outpouring of support for Schott in the Cincinnati area. Cincinnati is also called "the Rhineland" because of its proportion of descendants of German immigrants. This fact may not be relevant, but now seems a good time to mention it. The Reds are even called "the Rhinelanders" by some old heads among baseball writers. The Rhineland gave Schott a vocal mandate for her crass, self-delusional bigotry, even though she had not done anything worthy of note—other than marrying a rich man who died. What she had done might be debatable, but Schott had never caught a baseball or hit a home run that helped the Reds win the World Series.

The 1993 Cincinnati home opener sold out in record time in the fall of '92, after Schott was found out. The good baseball patrons of "der Rhineland" couldn't wait to support her with a standing ovation. Local newspapers and radio stations conducted polls showing she enjoyed upwards of a 70 percent approval rating for her ringing honesty. The National Council of Negro Women, headed by Dorothy Height, as much as said that what Schott uttered didn't bother it, and that we should forgive her, collectively. Finally, the captains of baseball slapped her ample wrist, gave her a $25,000 fine, the baseball equivalent of a jaywalk ticket, and then "suspended" her for the 1993 season although she could come to the games and sit in the owner's box and run her club from there. What they should have made her do was hire some Black people in her front office in key positions. But it was hardly even suggested that she do that. In a way, it's too bad the author Shelby Steele didn't become a ballplayer instead of a college professor. He might have seen the racism he insists is often imaginary in a more incisive light.

If what happened to Eric Davis is what can happen to a Black ballplayer in the big leagues, one imagines what the minors are like. No wonder those who aren't good enough for the majors become plumbers or professors instead of career minor leaguers. No wonder there aren't many Black people in the front offices.

I'll tell you what I'd like to see—more Black people like Frank Robinson serving as general managers and coaches and doing those sorts of things in and about baseball. It's not like Black people have to prove they can *play* baseball. Jackie

Robinson played. Henry Aaron played. Willie Mays played. And Eric Davis played. After that, what's the point?

As for what may happen to Black attendance in the near future, let's just say that in, oh, ten years or so, twenty people will look up from a single pay-per-view video screen after the last out of the 2002 World Series. The Black owner of the screen will say, "Well, that was $200 well spent," while collecting $35 from each couple, regardless of color, creed, or continental origin. Another Black person will add, while handing over his money, "Yeah, but in retrospect Susan and I would just as soon have bought a head of lettuce."

MEMORIAL STADIUM, BALTIMORE, MARYLAND

THE BOYS AND I

I took my boy and his friend to see the Yankees, even though I'm a National League man all the way. I was born in 1952, and Jackie Robinson had come up with the Brooklyn Dodgers of the National League five years before that. Branch Rickey, the owner of the Dodgers, paid not a cent for his contract to the Negro League team that employed him, the Kansas City Monarchs. In fact, no major league teams paid for the contracts of Negro League stars they signed. Cumberland Posey's Homestead Grays routinely drew 30,000 people to D.C.'s Griffith Stadium in the '30s and early '40s, when the white Washington Senators were barely drawing 3,000, according to records and John Holway, author of *Blackball Stars*. "It was like coming into a men's store and stealing everything off his shelves," said Cum Posey. Thus, Negro League teams, instead of being absorbed, instead of being institutionally included by integration, were stripped of their talent, and allowed to die. Isn't integration wonderful?

As a result, for me, when I was a boy, major league ball was all the National League.

St. Louis was the closest big-league town to where I grew up, and Bob Gibson became my favorite pitcher because he was mean and threw hard and didn't waste time out there and won more often than he lost. My favorite ball team played in Milwaukee, then in Atlanta, and they were called the Braves. They were my favorite team because of one ballplayer, whom I'll name later. Most of the Black players who were in the major leagues were in the National League in the '50s and '60s, which is why the National League won nearly all the All-Star games over the nearly carnation-white American League in those years. The difference was that the National League was drawing from a bigger pool—the total pool of all available ballplayers, the pool that included me and would one day include my boys. But then I grew up and my relationship to baseball changed—as far as what I could do with it went. The American League had long since wised up. I took my boys to see the Yankees at Baltimore's now-abandoned Memorial Stadium one spring evening in 1987. Spring is when all boys hope to be major league hitters and all-around tough outs. My boys are no different from anybody else's, I decided. My boys need a little fun and deserve an education. They need to feel the thrilling shock of hitting a ball well race up their arms, and they need to realize the work it takes to hit. This was part of a complete and unrestricted enjoyment of childhood—to go and see the bat swung right.

Damon is my son Cole's friend. He was nine back then and liked to pore over dead bug anatomies. He may grow up to own the Yankees. Cole was six and was going off his own way. He believes he can do anything he sees done once. But he is shy, so sometimes I dream for him. If my son saw it done, and I could convince him to do the work behind it, maybe he could grow up to hit like Rickey Henderson. People might call him a hot dog, but I think I could live with that.

At the time, Rickey Henderson was employed by the New York Yankees. Also with the Yankees at that time were Dave Winfield, Jack Clark, Don Mattingly, Claudell Washington, Gary Ward, Mike Pagliarulo, Jose Cruz, Don Slaught, and Willie Randolph, all of whom, at one point or another, were good big-league hitters with some good pop in their bats. They could drive the ball—there was not a Judy among them. Mostly, I took the boys to see Rick and Jack.

MARINERS' CAMP, TEMPE, ARIZONA

ME AND RICK

Rick's the best ballplayer I ever seen up close, ever day, Black or White, and that's my problem, first, tryin' to pick one out, and then, pickin' Rick. Rick ain't never been Mr. Popularity. Ain't never gone for it. Me and him was rooks, him on the A's, me up to look, just a lookieheresee and coffee. I'll never forget the first chat we had in Tempe, back in '77, '78, or '79, or whenever it was we was rooks.

We was warmin' up for a sprang trainin' game against Seattle. Me and Rick done come in early, and we was already warmed up good, but we seen allathem sportswriters lookin' like we didn't know what we was or what we was supposed to be doin', and they did. I'd have to say the very worse thing about bein' a big-league ballplayer, outside of damn good pitchin', is sportswriters. Billy, who was managin' the club, called sportswriters "the evil necessities of the game," whatever that meant. I'll get back to Billy directly.

We set on the bench, Me and Rick, spittin' at blue and green iridescent horseflies and squintin', me sort of loungin' around (it ain't hard to look and see), Rick just a ball of coiled-up pythons. The pressure was on him, really, because it was either the Show or back to the minors, where it goes without sayin' don't none of us wanna be. We was waitin' for Billy to post the line-up card. Me, I didn't have nothin' to worry about. I knew I wasn't in there.

Rick got a soft way of talkin'—hell, he got a soft way of being loud—and he couldn't what they call consecrate a verb for his life. But he got a real easy laugh, and he will laugh at himself, or he would back then, anyway, and people who consecrate verbs for a livin' cain't see what Rick seen as he laughed real easy and watched the Seattle pitcher warm up in the dry sprang desert air. Air carry sound good down there, and a catcher's mitt was being walloped by the Seattle pitcher's serious stuff. Somebody's hand was gonna need Epsom later. There was pressure on this rookie pitcher too. Makin' the big leagues ain't no tiny small thing to do.

There was other sounds to be heared, too: There was the hollow knock of fungo bats as two coaches hit grounders from the on-deck circles to infielders; there was those little whams and blams of battin' practice throws hittin' the mat in back of the cage after they was swung on and missed or took because they was not good pitches to hit (a bad battin' practice pitcher can cost you your shot, you know); and there was them crackles and chatters of the fellows who get the luxury of still bein' boys in sprang.

"Think I'll hit one 450 feet first time up."

That was Rick talkin' to me. So I'm sittin' all naive and not knowin' it. I think, "Yeah, sure, rook." I'm sittin' there watchin' this pitcher. Look like he from the Dominica, judgin' by his curl, and he's gotta be throwin' ninety-five easy, I'm thinkin', and his ball got a tail. And the Kid says he's gonna take him deep first time out the box. I'm thinkin' I'm an authority, not a kid myself, and that Rick, pleasant though he might be, got a lot to learn about ball.

So the first time up—Rick ain't never been nothin' but a

leadoff batter—Rick hits the first ball out of this Dominica pitcher's hand, I mean hits the stankin' dogshit out of it, hard, one a beeline, into sagebrush back behind the service road that run past them bleachers out beyond left field—450 feet if it went one. Then Rick said, "heh-heh," and tap-tapped them snakes of his around the bases.

It got real quiet in Tempe. Pretty soon I closed my mouth, but Rick made my jaw drop again many times just by doing amazin' ball stuff. Around 55 times since then, Rick done led off an oh-fishal major league ball game with a home run. Nobody ever done that before. So it wudn't no accident, what he done back then, that's what I'm sayin'. At the time the Oakland A's manager was Billy Martin—yep, the same Billy from before—and the great thing about Billy Martin was that he just let Rick play ball. Now me, Billy never had no use for. Billy knowed talent when he seen it.

I seen Rick score from second base on a sacrifice fly—not once but two, three, four times. I seen him score from second on a ground ball to the shortstop. If the shortstop threw to first to get the out while Rick was goin' to third, Rick just kep on comin'. Seen him go from first to third on a ground-ball out to the infield. Seen all that regular—not once in a lifetime. Rick stole somethin' like 1,000 bases so far. Nobody in big-league ball ever done it before. Rick changed his number to 24—Willie Mays's number. Good.

It was funny, though. Everybody talked more about the way Rick talked than how he done amazin' ball stuff. They talked about the way he didn't consecrate verbs, or talked in circles after games when they kept after him and after him and said, "Talk, Rick, we need you to talk for us." They couldn't write about the way Rick played. They needed him to explain it to 'em, I guess, and it just wasn't Rick's fort, talkin' and playin'. Now, me, that's another story. They shoulda asked me, only I wasn't there, but I can sure talk a good game. When Rick stole no. 939 in 1991, he tore third base out the ground and held it over his head in Oakland. They stopped the game then and asked Rick to say a few words. Shoulda asked him to steal a few more bases, and everybody woulda been satisfied with him. Rick thanked Billy Martin and another manager named Tom Trebelhorn for helpin' him to realize his potential (although he left me out, for some reason.) Then he said, "I'm the greatest." White folk give him a hard time about that until this day. Well, if he wasn't the greatest, who was? You asked him to talk, right?

People said he wasn't motivated and didn't always play hard. He sure set a lot of records and closed many a throat and dropped a lot of jaws and won a lot of ball games for the A's and the New York Yankees for a soft ballplayer.

In 1981, the Oakland A's did not have a good major league baseball team. But they won their division anyway—because of Rick. Then he stole somethin' like 130 bases one season, which was a record for one season, a record by far. The old record was held by Lou Brock at 118. That year when Rick broke that record, in *Sports Illustrated* a story come out sayin' that the stolen base wasn't all that important no more in ball. I laughed. Rick took all the shine off of it for 'em, I guess. I laughed hard, tell the truth. The story was wrote up by man name Bill James, baseball stastistician, I guess pretty much like the stastisticians we remember at the high school football, baseball, and basketball games. 'Member that kid? Growed up and become Bill James. Bill James explained, with numbers, verbs, and whatnot, that what Rick had accomplished wasn't all that much, really, and that a stolen base wasn't all that important in a ball game.

I found this hard to follow because most baseball managers is glad to give up an out for a base in a close game—not to mention get a base for free. It brings them into a situation where a base hit—not an extra-base hit, any base hit—will score a run. And runs is what wins games.

The best games ain't high-scorin' because it's the pitcher's game, baseball, and a hitter who is on them hard only three times out of ten is considered Hall of Fame stuff. I don't know from no Hall of Fames—but I know Rick. Rick helped win the American League Championship Series and the World Series for the A's in 1989. Hit .400, stole bases, hit home runs, raced down line drives. Hit. Ran. Made plays. Looked good doin' it, like I remember. That's my problem.

CANDLESTICK PARK, SAN FRANCISCO

JACK AND MEMORY

I'm a little partial to Jack Clark only because he has one of the sweetest swings I ever saw, and any man who can swing the bat like that can make you forget whatever else might be right or wrong with him. We also traveled.

When we first talked back in the '70s when he was a rookie with the San Francisco Giants, I told him, "Jack, you know, I think you can hit 400 home runs in the major leagues."

He didn't answer me right away. Jack wasn't the greatest talker in the world, and by no stretch was he the brightest guy in the world, or even in the clubhouse. But he could swing the bat. He is of Italian and Irish blood. Now I can't say as it helps either way, but he could hit. Not one of these ping hitters. A long-ball hitter. And he was fluid when he hit. He was fluid when he walked up to hit. He was just fluid, with an ease in his motions many people label "Black style." This is simply the style of a person who is very comfortable with what he is about to do, has done this singular activity so many times, has honed it down so sharp, that it's almost like going to sleep. That was Jack.

At times, when he was younger, batting third with the San Francisco Giants, it seemed he could go weeks being intentionally walked, or not being given good pitches to hit by the pitchers who were taught in meetings, "Don't let Clark beat you." When he was younger this would frustrate him and he'd complain to us baseball writers, who were famous for digging out these legitimate frustrations of susceptible ballplayers and then displaying our tin ears for such whining, as we called it, unless we were complaining ourselves about our own shops and our trials within them.

But even the most comic among us, if they had common sense and one good eye, knew Jack could hit. Once he hit three home runs and two doubles in one doubleheader in Atlanta against the Braves. Didn't help. The Giants lost both games. We knew he could hit. Later, as Jack was inevitably traded and moved on to other teams and listened to more advice from older hitters, he became more patient. He told me one day, "There's always gonna be pitches to hit," and I knew Jack was going to be bad news for somebody until he retired.

His most famous moment came in 1985, I believe, after he had moved on to play for the Cardinals in that cavernous ball park in St. Louis called Busch Stadium, where home-run hitters often go to die. The place was not set up for them. The power alleys were 383 feet away, and the wall curves only a little toward the hitters down the lines, and the air in summer off the Mississippi River is as thick as consommé. Nobody hits 30 home runs in a season while playing half of his games in Busch Stadium, unless his name is Dick Allen or Jack Clark. But Jack was a home-run hitter, a long-ball man. He could turn a ball park into a living room if you were unfortunate enough to give him something he could drive.

The home run is a singularly classic American sporting accomplishment. I don't believe it is more difficult to do than, say, run 70 yards for a touchdown against big-league competition in football, not at all. In fact, it is often much easier because sometimes pitchers do make bad pitches. But to hit a good major league pitch for a home run—that's a matchless athletic accomplishment. There is nothing else quite like it, from the awesome sound of the bat on the ball to the majestic sight of the ball going out. And to hit home runs the way Jack did, where there was no doubt as soon as the bat struck the ball and turned it into a flowing blur of light—that was a unique experience to watch and hear. In the words of a former baseball manager, Dick Williams, "He [Jack] takes all the air out of the park when he swings."

The Cardinals were in a playoff against the Dodgers in that year of 1985 to decide who would go to the Series, and in the final game, at Dodger Stadium in Los Angeles, Jack came up with runners at second and third and two outs and the Cardinals down a run or two. The Dodger manager, Tommy Lasorda, decided to have his pitcher, Tom Neidenfuer, pitch to Jack instead of walking him to the open first base and pitching to a less dangerous hitter, which at that time would have been any other hitter in the National League, much less the man hitting behind Clark, an excellent center fielder named Andy Van Slyke who was known for his glove but not for his home-run-hitting prowess.

It is axiomatic, an immutable baseball law: A home run hitter tends to hit more home runs if a home run hitter is hitting behind him. Jack held in his surprise that Lasorda, the best manager in baseball, would flaunt this law in Jack's face and pitch to him rather than walk him and pitch to Andy Van Slyke. Shortly, with that fluid swing, Jack drove a white-blur nail into God's sky, blasted a line-drive homer over the wall in left, deep into the bleachers and many hearts. Dodger Stadium became a morgue. Tommy Lasorda knew he'd have to do some tall explaining to all those tin-eared baseball writers for once. The left fielder, Pedro Guerrero, didn't even turn to watch it go. He knew. He fired his glove to the outfield grass in disgust. There are a lot of people in baseball who don't care for Jack Clark to this day—people who laughed at him when he filed for bankruptcy, a million-dollar ballplayer, during the summer of '92. But we all know Jack could hit. And in the end, that's something.

THE BOYS AND I

I turned to the boys as we walked in the red crushed dirt and gravel, crunching past the dugout an hour before the game between the Yankees and the Orioles. "Boys, you might as well know this now. The Orioles are like an itch you can't scratch. They usually play good ball."

The Yankees were taking batting practice, and when Rick got out the batting cage we were there like three catchers blocking the plate. Rick started to frown, because I am not the only father in the world who wants his son or his daughter to meet the likes of Rickey Henderson, and that ever-constant attention can become annoying, and Rick never was one who liked to have people in his way, but there was a click in Rick's head when he saw me, I almost saw it. He remembered the old days, when he was a rook, and he smiled a bit and stopped and extended his hand for the boys to shake.

"Boys," I said, "this is Mr. Henderson. Rick, these are the boys, Cole and Damon." Damon stared open-mouthed at Rick after shaking his hand. My son stared at his own feet after shaking Rick's hand. Rick laughed that easy cartoon laugh.

"Well, at least look at him," I said to Cole. Along about the fifth inning, after Rick had stolen two of the three bases he'd get that night, my son turned and said, "How will we know if we ever see a better player than Mr. Henderson?"

"Oh, you'll know. I'll never see a better player, but you might, and you'll know it when you do."

"Oh," he said, not satisfied with this vague answer. Maybe

he'll grow up to be a writer instead. People will still call him a hot dog, but I know I can live with that.

"What's a pennant?" Damon asked.

"The league championship, which the Yankees won't win in spite of all these good hitters because they're missing a good shortstop and pitching. Pitching wins pennants."

"What's a Judy?" my son asked.

"What Mr. Clark and Mr. Winfield are not," I said. The boys had shaken Jack's hand, too, and Winfield's, and Dave had demonstrated how he waxes and bones the handles of his bats to keep them stronger and less likely to break when he takes his hard cuts. "A Judy's a weak hitter. A ping hitter."

"Because it's a girl's name?" Damon asked skeptically.

"No, because of a couple of old puppets called Punch and Judy. It's really the Punch part that tells the story. People shortened it to Judy. A Punch-and-Judy hitter, who thinks a single-and-a-half a game is doing some hitting."

The Yankees obliged us. Rick set a good standard for me by stealing three bases and scoring two runs. Once, while on second, he let a base hit by Randolph go by in front of him before going to third. It seemed the center fielder, a good one, Fred Lynn, would have a play at the plate, at least on an ordinary ballplayer. Rick scored standing up. "Mr. Henderson just stole home plate!" my son hollered.

"No, son, it just looked like it."

Jack ripped one 404 feet to center field, but Fred Lynn had been playing him in the next county, and he flagged it down for the Orioles. Winfield had two hits. And my son missed his first major league home run. A friend of mine, a Black man with gray hair, sat with us in the stands and kept talking to the boys about baseball instead of letting them watch it slowly unfold. He was in the middle of asking if they had baseballs at home. Cole was watching Claudell Washington hit. But my friend was adamant about getting his attention, and my son has been taught to be polite, so when he turned to answer my friend, Claudell caught hold of one and sent it deep into the right-field bleachers.

"Right field! It's a home run!"

But my son had no quick sense of bearings on the field. He was new to it. He looked left, center, and by the time he looked right, the fans had covered the ball and were sitting back down and Claudell was simply trotting around the bases.

"You missed it," I said, sadly. "Claudell went deep."

"Yeah, and he got all of it, too," said my friend. Your friends make you wonder sometimes, don't they?

Two pitchers named Tommy John and Cecilio Guante shut out the Orioles, 4–0. So the boys got to see a little bit of everything at a major league game. On the parkway, they expressed sadness for the Orioles, then fell asleep in the car underneath their brand-new Yankee ball caps and slept soundly all the way home. They had dreams of their own.

I HAD A HAMMER

BY HENRY AARON AND LONNIE WHEELER

Henry Louis Aaron, the first name in the *Baseball Encyclopedia*, is also known as the game's most prolific hitter. His numbers, accomplished while with the Milwaukee and Atlanta Braves and the Milwaukee Brewers from 1954 through 1976, loom like a range of the Himalayas, boggling the senses of even the most jaded fans once they see them up close. Aaron hit more home runs than Babe Ruth, drove in more runs than Lou Gehrig, scored more runs than Willie Mays, and had over 12 more miles in total bases than the all-time runner-up in that category, Stan Musial. As a nineteen-year-old at spring training, Aaron hit a ball so hard Ted Williams came running out of a Sarasota clubhouse because he'd *heard* it and wanted to know who could make a ball sound like that. "They don't make 'em like that anymore" understates Aaron's skill. They didn't make 'em like that back then, either.

Whether or not Aaron had a good book in him was open to debate, however, mostly due to the perception that the Hammer never had much to say. He was a quiet man who might offer up the occasional drop-dead one-liner, but in the same way your eight-year-old might. As a personality, he was right up there with Pat Sajak. That didn't matter when he was at the plate, but did it have an effect on his as-told-to autobiography, *I Had a Hammer*, written with Lonnie Wheeler?

Both Aaron and Wheeler took great pains to make sure it did not. They combined for a corker of a book reflecting both man and player. Like Hank Aaron himself, *I Had a Hammer* is a triumph not of substance over style, but of substance and style. Wheeler's style is so fluid you do not notice it, which of course is the best style of all, as Henry Aaron the ballplayer proved many times over. As-told-to autobiographies are as tricky to write as they are to identify in a sentence. Wheeler was well armed for the job, having grown up in middle America, away from the legends of Mays and Mickey Mantle in New York. In middle America, in the 1950s, the dependable knock of Aaron's bat made him an icon, something of a tomahawking noble savage not unlike the Native American "brave" his team was supposed to represent.

Wheeler freely admits he was one of the cheering tribe, then moves aside and shows his wisdom and skill by pulling from Aaron a thoughtful awareness that many people who cheered him were not aware the slugger possessed. It is Aaron who shows us how good a player his teammate Eddie Mathews was. With outfielder Aaron hitting third and third baseman Mathews hitting fourth, they combined for 1,267 home runs—easily the most by two teammates in baseball history. Mathews was also the man who said there wasn't a fastball without a tail or some kind of movement on it that he could not hit. No man could throw it fast enough to throw it by him. He would just adjust the gauge on his hitting trigger, quicken his swing, time the fastball. He was a true National Leaguer. It is also Aaron who admits he could never resolve whether Warren Spahn was unaware of his own prejudice.

Wheeler juxtaposes opinions from Aaron's family, teammates, and friends in periodic italics. This technique starts out powerfully in the early sections of the 333-page work, then loses its edge in the middle. I had an unsettling fear it would end up stumbling like an old ballplayer hanging on, but Wheeler stays with it, and it becomes a good spice to Aaron's pronouncements.

On Willie Mays: "My guideline. I've never seen a better all-around player than Willie Mays, but I will say this: Willie was not as good a hitter as I was. No way."

On Stan Musial: He "hopped the fence [at Cincinnati's Crosley Field] and came running out onto the field when I beat out my three-thousandth hit."

On the home runs of Babe Ruth, who was nearly his polar opposite in every way but hitting baseballs out of ballparks; "He made outfielders look up at the sky." On his own home runs: "I made shortstops bend their knees."

On coming to the big leagues in '54: "I never doubted my ability, but when you hear all your life you're inferior, it makes you wonder if the other guys have something you've never seen before. If they do, I'm still looking for it."

On going home to Mobile, Alabama, as World Series hero in 1957: "It was one thing for a Black World Series hero to speak at their club, but it was another thing to have his Black daddy sitting with the good White men in the audience. . . . A few days later, seven crosses were burned around the city."

This is the unbreakable thread Wheeler and Aaron have spun of Bad Henry Aaron, a young African-American boy from Mobile who hit cross-handed until a scout changed his grip, then hit a home run on his next at-bat. He didn't even know how to put on a uniform at one time. His naiveté soon went away, but public reaction to his race never did. His life was threatened many times, not always via letter, during the heat of the chase to break Babe Ruth's old home run record of 714. By the way, Aaron leaves no doubt that the home run he hit in 1957 to win the pennant for the Milwaukee Braves is infinitely preferable to home run No. 715 as an event in his recollection. That recollection is sound and strong, full of evocative detail and genuine reflection. If it is unnerving for the reader that the effect of being Black never seems to go away in Aaron's life, then he makes you know what it was like for him. In the introduction, Wheeler asks, "How could a man hit 755 home runs and have nothing more to offer?" What a ballplayer! His book is comparable.

The Friends of the Library in Memphis, Tennessee, asked me down to say hello and sign books. The Friends are a good group of people. They said Henry Aaron would also be in Memphis, at the main library on McLean, signing books. I went down.

Hank Aaron is a compact man, though not as compact as Rickey Henderson. When Aaron was a great young ballplayer with the Milwaukee Braves, he was built more like Eric Davis than like Henderson. Or, they both were more like Aaron. You can see where Aaron was once at peace with his frame. He still moves easily, casually led around by his stomach now—a bit portly, thickened up, with little silver hairs curling among the black ones along his hairline. His wrists are still as thick as a baker's rolling pins, though, as thick as they were when he hit the home run that clinched the 1957 pennant for the Braves. And they needed to be. The main library on McLean in Memphis was choked with people, and they were not there to see me. These hundreds of people, the overwhelming majority of them White, were there to see the Home Run King of Baseball in the flesh and have him sign their copies of his book. He smiled at them, his gums pink, his teeth white, his eyes nicely offset in his broad, mahogany face.

"Did you take care of me?" asked the Home Run King, whispering into my ear, still smiling.

"Sure, Supe."

Before he'd arrived, I'd read a little to the assemblage from a review I'd written on Aaron's book and from another story about athletes and what people think about them. The crowd was made up mostly of middle-aged people, but there were many youngsters there, young would-be ballplayers brought by their parents because they wanted them to see the man who they knew had swung the bat right. And in some way, his mahogany color did not matter to these people who came, because they knew Aaron could hit a baseball like nobody's business. He was that man the boy in them had always wanted to be. So in some ways it must be a great game, baseball, because it can make many people colorblind, albeit for very brief stretches of time. Again, it is a game of skill.

I called Aaron "Supe" because I knew toward the end of his career most of his younger teammates on the Atlanta Braves team called him Supe, short for Superstar, Superman. Aaron's family, when he was young boy, called him Man. He'd always seemed to have lived beyond his years, some-how.

"One thing I can't figure, Man," I said to him as the crowd waited expectantly for him to speak. "I can't figure how the 56-game hitting streak of Joe DiMaggio, which conceivably can be done by a rookie in less than half a season, became the greatest baseball record, over the home run record, the 755. Seems like it's you and Babe Ruth."

Henry tilted his head to one side and shifted in his seat as if to say, "I know what you mean, but it doesn't matter because there is nothing to be done about it. I did what I could do." At least that was how I read his simple gestures and lack of expression about the subject. He was tired. Aaron was working for the Braves in an executive position, and he'd been making some White people in baseball concerned because he refused to shut up about how few of these great Black ballplayers ended up as executives, when the most mediocre White ballplayers ended up as executives. He had complained to the commissioner of ball many times.

He rose to speak. His beloved Braves would play in the World Series that fall against the Minnesota Twins. They would go seven games before losing, 1–0, in extra innings, in the final game, after a bad outfielder and good hitter, a Black ballplayer named Lonnie Smith, proved how lousy a baserunner a Black ballplayer can be. He was tricked by a Minnesota middle infielder (a rookie, White, just to show you they can still play) named Chuck Knoblauch, who turned a double play in front of Smith with a phantom ball. Smith was running from first on a pitch as teammate Terry Pendleton hit it for a double to right center field. But Smith never picked up the flight of the ball, stopped running at second base, and never scored. They don't call old Lonnie "Skates" for nothing. Willie Mays or Rickey Henderson or Eric Davis or Henry Aaron would have scored and been in the dugout making a phone call for dinner reservations by the time the ball Pendleton hit had been relayed back to the infield. But Mays doesn't play anymore. Rickey's old for a ballplayer now, and Eric's headlong rushes have cost him his health.

The Braves lost. But they won all three World Series games played in Atlanta, so 1991 was good. The next year, they defeated Pittsburgh and its brilliant manager, Jim Leyland, in the playoffs. Then they faced the Toronto Blue Jays in the World Series. The Jays won in six games. Dave Winfield, the same one and only California condor from Candlestick, doubled in two runs in the top of the 11th inning, and the Jays held on to win, 4–3. It would have been over in five games, but Lonnie Smith hit a grand slam home run in Toronto to win a game. The teams played well. Toronto was managed by Cito Gaston, and he did a good job. A good year all around.

Henry Aaron had twenty-two such years. The home run is the classic American sporting achievement. If you hit thirty-five home runs a year for twenty-one years straight in the major leagues, you will still find yourself behind Aaron in home runs. That's why people will even come to a library to see him.

"Baseball is a great game," said the preternatural Man. That's what I remember of what he said to all those upturned faces. He hemmed a bit—he wasn't a great talker, but he was better than Rick. Then he tried to tell about some troubles he'd seen, but his heart wasn't in telling these people about all that, not just then. He decided to let them dream. He told the stoic youngsters and their starry-eyed parents not to worry if they couldn't hit 755 home runs in the big leagues during their lifetimes. He never would have believed it possible himself. Never. "Baseball is a great game," said Man, and then he smiled and signed an awful lot of books.

How Skeeter
Became the Boss

"We offer love."
Cathy Hughes, WOL, 1450 AM

Cathy Hughes is a warrior
born. This might not be the first description that comes to
mind among those who listen to her each weekday morning
on the radio in Washington, D.C., or to those who don't and
who say they wouldn't listen if she were the last talk-show
host on earth. But because of some and in spite of many,
Cathy Hughes works her wonders as the controversial lightning rod of "The Morning Show" on WOL, 1450 AM, right
out of northeast Washington. The studio is down on H Street,
Jack, across a bridge and a chasm of opportunity from Cable
News Network headquarters in D.C.

Cathy cast her lot in the ground-floor front window of the
sizzling sauce, in full view of the worst poverty and degra-
dation any major city can offer. She was offered one of the

worst places to do business, then did good business by giving people an invaluable product: information. You're also going to get an opinion along with it, but that's the price of doing business with her. If it's Black, relates to Black, and in town, Cathy Hughes is usually on it. Hard.

She sidled up to the microphone in a spring-loaded chair on roller casters one morning in the summer of 1992 as I listened closely to record her daily agenda on this, a typical day. The format isn't supposed to work, talk on a so-called "soul" station. The people who assume this don't know Cathy. She laughed to kick things off, laughter that is her calling card. Cathy laughs like laughing is all right. She laughs like Tarzan wished he could've hollered. She read a news item: Reginald Lewis, CEO of TLC-Beatrice, had given a $3 million gift to Harvard Law School, which he attended, for an international law center to be named for him. Cathy reflected, and added this, like a talking conscience: "Just what Harvard needed, $3 million from a Black man!"

This is Cathy Hughes. Why clutter up a good line with additional facts? Lewis had also given a $1 million gift to Howard University, and gifts totaling another $1 million to thirty-five other institutions, including Virginia State, his alma mater, and Gallaudet University in Washington. But that was not what came across the Associated Press wire, and that was the point Cathy was making—not about Lewis, whom she admired (and who would be dead within six months, a victim of brain cancer and a cerebral hemorrhage).

Cathy just does not like to bite her tongue. Next she discussed possible use of psychological depressant drugs like Ritalin on young Black schoolchildren. This was being proposed by an official group of White men, who were soon to meet on the campus of the University of Maryland, with the apparent blessing of the National Institutes of Health. "Whose health, they don't say," Cathy allowed. Then she gave precious air time for some senior-citizen phone-in callers to announce funerals, meetings, and the like. Then she helped a man launch a twice-weekly newspaper, and then took calls from parents of school-age Black children who were mad about the Ritalin that the official group of White men were trying to convince the National Institutes of Health would be a good thing to pass out. Finally she savaged the sitting mayor, Sharon Pratt Dixon Kelly, and her predecessor, Marion Barry, in a such a way that I could only nod my head in bemusement and chuckle, "She's right, and when she isn't right she's still interesting!"

All this happened in fifteen minutes. Cathy may be no threat to New York's Howard Stern, but he's no threat to her, either—not in my mind. She is across the chasm from CNN owner Ted Turner, but she can wave to him. They are in the same business. Not only does Cathy Hughes perform at station WOL, she *owns* station WOL, and three other stations as well.

"Eventually I want to own forty-eight stations, twenty-four AM and twenty-four FM," she says. We are sitting in the control room, with its view of H Street, the picture window looking right out onto the street. She is a picaresque warrior, dressed casually, blue jeans and a sweat shirt over another, collared shirt. She could be going to work the checkout counter at a Wal-Mart. Her hair is tied back into a cinnamon-colored rope braid that dangles carelessly down her back, nearly to her waist. In her late 40s, Cathy is an attractive woman. One can see she was once a powerful beauty and still can be when she so chooses. She appears unaffected by this. I am reminded of Janie, the protean lead character of Zora Neale Hurston's novel *Their Eyes Were Watching God*. Janie seems to have come to life here, in 1992, at radio station WOL.

"Why do you want to own that many stations, Cathy?"

"Because that's all the government will allow you to own," she says. "The limit is forty-eight. I'll get there. Because it means thousands of jobs for African-American broadcasters who wouldn't get jobs elsewhere. There are so many qualified African-Americans in the communications field who can't find work because we don't have enough Black folks owning their own facilities in order to employ them. Even if a station has a Black format, if it is White-owned, top management nine times out of ten will be White, because it's a White corporation and they want their fellow White folks in there counting and looking out for their money. I feel the same way about my people. The best thing about being in business is it creates opportunities. But it's not just about jobs. It's the philosophy of the business, the direction of the business, the commitment to the community by the business.

"Listen, this is a true story: A junkie broke in here once and stole that big vase sitting right behind you. It's a collector's item from Mexico that an older lady had given me long ago. We had it in front, in the foyer. Well, this brother stole it. Three days later he brought it back to us because his grandma told him he was getting ready to bring eternal damnation on them. She said, 'That's WOL's vase! You take that right back over there to Miss Hughes, you tell her you did it, and you ask for her forgiveness!' Well now, this is unheard of, for a heroin junkie to bring back something he has stolen. He said to me, 'Miss Hughes, I don't know what it is about you out here on this corner, but my grandma ain't never complained about me bringing nothing else home before.' She had put her foot down, I think, because we try to help people. When you do the right things in life, good life and happiness come back to you.

"A lot of people marvel at some of the things that my radio stations get involved in. Well, that's a reflection of my own personality. Anyone who has known me for any length of time would not be amazed or surprised. They'd say, 'It's standard operating procedure for Cathy.'

"I'm committed to upgrading the lives of my people. That's

my—our—job. Frederick Douglass really issued the call, the challenge, which was to agitate. I feel the way blessings work from God is like this: The more you give, the more you receive, and the more you receive, the more you are obligated to give. It's like a merry-go-round. I don't want a small merry-go-round, I want a gigantic merry-go-round that is able to ride and employ thousands and thousands of Black people on it.

"I'm a broadcast entrepreneur. I started doing 'The Morning Show' out of necessity. I was paying minimum wage, see, and nobody else would do it. I refused to go strictly to a music format when I bought the station. I believe the more information you give to African-Americans, the more receptive and loyal they are to your media outlet."

As she would undoubtedly tell you in the inflected, afflicting, vibrating megaphone she calls a voice, Cathy Hughes has been called everything but a child of God from the time she was a girl in Omaha, Nebraska, when she was a slip-skinny tomboy with legs like pipe stems. Her mother nicknamed her Skeeter, which, as most everyone from the country knows, is a dialectal diminutive of *mosquito* almost anywhere within five hundred miles on either side of the Mississippi River. Her father, William A. Woods, was from Chattanooga, Tennessee, where his mother and father worked in relative serfdom and lived in probably the most famous alley in all Chattanooga—Blair Alley. It was a status symbol for a maid, a manservant, or a chauffeur to live there. Cathy's paternal grandparents also had side projects and businesses—she baked cakes, he worked as an auto mechanic. "Their own little entrepreneurial efforts," says Cathy. "The White family my grandmother and grandfather worked for didn't want them to have these side ventures, so they were smart enough to strike a deal." The deal was this: If the Woodses were at the White people's disposal twenty-four hours a day, then a trust would be set up to educate all seven of their children. That's why they had been working the extra jobs, to send their children to college, to get them that much nearer to a better life. "The White family not only agreed to the deal," says Cathy, "they also honored it."

All seven children were eventually college educated. Cathy's father, after a wild youth, would himself settle into a career in accounting. This was back in the days when most Black folks had precious little to account for, and when they did, they were instructed by the larger, racist society to never trust other Black people to count it for them. Society would count it instead, and much more properly and accurately. Mighty White of them, wasn't it?

Cathy's mother was Helen, an iconoclastic girl who went to her father's school south of Jackson, Mississippi, and later played trombone in the International Sweethearts of Rhythm. She was also stunningly beautiful. "My mother was an original member. My father worked for a bootlegger until my mother found out that the hearse he drove wasn't carrying dead bodies. She sponsored him until he could get going in a profession. He studied and became a certified public accountant, running Woods Accounting Service.

"But Black folks at the time definitely weren't going to let other Black folks manage their money. My father's first big accounts came from the Honorable Elijah Muhammad and the Nation of Islam, then from Muhammad Ali, and the Reverend Clarence Cobb and First Church of Deliverance. He taught me how to run a business. I was obligated to run a business. My entrepreneurial spirit came honest, as they say. I've got a double, triple, quadruple dose flowing through me. We never went and got jobs. We weren't raised to work for other people. We always worked for ourselves."

"The reason I'm an entrepreneur is my father was one, and his father." Cathy's mother's father, Dr. Laurence C. Jones, was one of the first Black Ph.D graduates from the University of Iowa. The school he founded is called Piney Woods Country Life School, 21 miles due south of Jackson. It was founded in 1909. It is still open today, on 2,000 acres now, K through 12, three hundred students strong.

"My granddad was touched by God. He took his degree and went to Mississippi, sat on a cedar log, and began teaching these Black kids to read and translate and conceptualize. His school is almost one hundred years old now, the Piney Woods Country Life School. We still send any number of kids there every single summer—"60 Minutes" did a piece on them, with Morley Safer. Grandpa was always an entrepreneur. They had a traveling band and a choir; they baked pies, whatever. Back in the '50s, there was a television show called 'This Is Your Life,' starring Ralph Edwards. I think it was the No. 1 show in America. They had never done a Black person before, I don't think, but some people who admired Grandpa set it up. But Grandpa hated publicity, you see. He'd almost been lynched before down in Mississippi for having the audacity to educate Black children. I think there was even an old photo somewhere with him having the rope around his neck. I swear this. But he told 'em, 'Please, I'm gonna show these colored children how to be clean around you good White folks,' and the White folks went for it, and he lived on.

"Anyway, Ralph Edwards was crying by the time the episode was over. Out of guilt, likely. But no. Edwards has been a great help to Piney Woods over the last thirty-five years. On the air he asked all his viewers to send in one dollar for the school, and one million dollars came by mail. This was in the '50s, remember. Grandpa took the money and spent it on making the school a permanent place and went back to being low profile. He didn't believe it was in the best interest of Black people to let the media into their lives at that time. We had no outlets. Our lives were being heinously distorted by other media. He thought they'd take his land, kill him, threaten his family, kill them too—all of which at the time they could do.

"I was born with a veil over my face," Cathy says. "Those who are into superstitions and psychic phenomena believe such people are blessed, or they feel such people are dangerous. If I had been born in the days of Joan of Arc, I would have been burned as a baby for being a witch. It is supposed to represent an extra eye, and extra sense. I dream big dreams and always encouraged other Black people to dream them too. I've always been able to accomplish things in my career by visualizing thought into actuality. I see it in my mind's eye. I feel it. I work and slave toward it. At a very early age I knew I would work for myself. I'm sure there are a lot of people I've met who are happy that I do work for myself now, because my personality is so strong. But I always saw myself in charge. I have 114 employees, and I look forward to the day when I will have 1,000 and possibly after that 10,000. And that's going to become a reality because I see it, I feel it, and I'm working toward it diligently. Vision is very important."

Cathy is part of Washington, D.C., in microcosm, and she appears to have loved every minute of becoming it. There are some Black people in Washington who will tell you they don't like her radio persona, though I must say if she's laughing I don't see how you can avoid joining her unless she's laughing at you; even then her laughter is likely to infect you anyway. Her voice tones are struck with an enthusiastic vibrancy, and she thinks. She *thinks*. Cathy's enthusiasm is enviable, contagious, quick as lightning. She is a tuning fork: You feel her by watching. She's gone from being a single mother to the owner of one radio station in one market to the owner of four stations in two markets. In the end, that's why we should pay attention to what she says.

"It doesn't matter to me whether a person likes me or not," she says. "People have called me on the air and said, 'I don't care what Richard says about you, Cathy, you're all right with me.' I tell them right away, 'That's a put-down, that's not a compliment, sir. You're telling me someone else is saying something negative, but you're okay. Don't tell me what someone else thinks. Tell me what you think.'

"I don't know, in terms of feeling it or internalizing it, that people disagree or dislike me. Because like I said that ain't my message. That has no value to me, whether they do or don't. I love it when people share their good feelings with me, but it doesn't bother me when someone confronts me because we're still exchanging, we're still growing from the give and take. I hear about this from time to time, about people being critical of me. Most of my friends have been broken of the habit of repeating it. I don't defend myself. The WOL family defends me.

"There was one incident where I had to intervene on behalf of someone who was attacking me. I was in a merchant's store, and he was cursing out a man who appeared to be blind. Because he had walked into the store and said, 'You all listen to that terrible Cathy Hughes.' The merchant was about to put the man out of his store! I said, 'No, please don't. It's okay for him not to like me.' And the merchant said, 'Oh no, he can't shop here.'

"Black folks don't usually come to your defense like that. I'm a voice to them. Many times my listeners disagree with me, so what they are being protective of is not me. I'm the symbol of the freedom of expression for some Black people, for my listeners. *That's* what they're protecting. I love that. That teaches us how to protect ourselves. That's what we've never done. We've never protected our peoplehood.

"Quite frankly, on the popularity issue, I have been concerned in this order: Am I pleasing to my Creator? Was I pleasing to my parents, my ancestors? Am I worthy of the respect of my son? As for everybody else—I love them very much *as people*, whether they like me or not. I'm unconcerned with it past that. That's why I'd never consider going into politics. I have never cared about popularity contests."

Tony Brown, the Black talk-show host at PBS, hired her at the age of twenty-five away from the campus of Howard University. By then, her only son, Alfred Liggins, was eight years old. She'd had him when she was seventeen. "Being a single mother didn't stop my entrepreneurial goals because I never got the two confused," Cathy says. "My son was always my top priority. I do believe in the law of karma. I'm not a real religious woman even though I do go to church. Not as much as I should, but I do go. But I am very spiritual. I believe that if you go with the natural order of the universe, the way God intended, you'll be all right. When God blesses you with a child, He intends for that child to be your top priority, and if you go against that, then things happen that you can't explain. Bad luck comes out of nowhere. I did the opposite.

"The only time I ever got fired was because my son got sick at school and I had to go home and see about him. I had to go. They said, 'Your son's with a babysitter, you're not a doctor, what can you do?' I knew I was not a doctor, but I was all my son had, and little boys, men too, revert back to infants when they get sick. Even if you can't do anything but be there and say, 'Are you feeling better?' that helps a child, or a man. And I understood that instinctively. I never regretted losing that job and never looked back. That happened to me in Omaha. That was one reason that I came to Washington.

"My son had a tuxedo by the age of seven, so he could accompany me to certain social events. He was my traveling partner. If I had conferences or dinners or workshops or seminars to attend, he attended, and that just became a part of the life-style. When I moved to Washington and became sales manager and then eventually general manager of WHUR-FM, it was the first time in Washington that a woman had managed a broadcast facility. I was an outsider to the Howard

University academic community, where the station is based, so they were very judgmental of me. I knew I had to be twice as good in every area, work twice as hard, twice as long—and I'm not a workaholic. I believe in doing the job right so you don't have to do it twice. I believe in doing it quickly, getting it out of the way. A perfect manager."

Cathy set up light housekeeping at the radio station. She had a sleeping bag and a portable refrigerator in a corner, along with a set of toys, games, and books for her son. She worked out a deal with a restaurant near the radio station to prepare dinners for her son. No television was allowed. "We had a disciplined life while he was growing up," she says. "And I took some serious criticism from some people who said I was depriving him of his childhood."

Well, the end result is that her son, after being raised in that environment, is now the twenty-eight-year-old general manager of his mother's four radio stations—in essence, he is now the boss of Cathy Hughes, host of "The Morning Show." She laughs that startling laugh. "Yes, he is, isn't he? He runs them, doesn't think anything of it, thinks that's what he's supposed to do," she says. "It's second nature. Because he's been there all his life. He laughs and tells people, 'I can do radio in my sleep. It's all I've ever known.'

"Not that it was particularly easy! When I got to Washington, Alfred was in the second grade, and basically my entire support system was a young man named Melvin Lindsey, who went on to be the on-air voice behind my 'Quiet Storm' concept that's been copied by so many urban contemporary stations. In weekend evening prime time, nothing but love songs. Because young people love loving and being in love and expressing it. Melvin was my babysitter. He's the one who would pick Alfred up after school and run across the street to get his dinner from the restaurant while it was still warm. That's how Melvin and I became close. Alfred thought Melvin was his older brother for a while. Melvin even lived with

74

me for a short period of time, because he was working for me almost around the clock. He was my first employee. I paid for his four years of college practically out of my own pocket. I needed a right hand. I wanted it to be a man.

"For so many years after Melvin became the voice of 'The Quiet Storm,' our relationship became a bit strained. Later, just before he died, he told me it was because he was gay. One of the hardest things he had to tell me was that he was gay—because he has spent so much time alone with Alfred. I told him, 'Melvin, honey, I know the difference between a homosexual and a pedophile!'

"He said, 'I never wanted you to feel uncomfortable in any way that I had been with Alfred.' I said, 'Melvin, I've known you were gay for years. That doesn't mean I'd think you were a child molester.' That was the furthest thing from my mind. Unfortunately, his fear that I would be homophobic cost Melvin and me many good working years together.

"When Alfred was eighteen, I put him out. He laughs about it now. It was time for him to go on his own, to go to college. I'd come to Washington and gone to Howard University, but I didn't graduate. There were certain opportunities that then demanded my attention before I could get that done, but by then I also had Alfred to worry about. I carried him to class and work tied to my body. An old man once told me that was an African tradition. I didn't have anywhere else to put him. I admit I was a little envious of college graduates, and still am. I had to come home, cook, and wash diapers. My father had two jobs when he went to college. You have no idea how blessed you are if you have a scholarship or a family with the means to send you to college.

"I sent my son Alfred to U.C.L.A. because that was where he wanted to go. I figured, 'Great, at last I'll have the house all to myself.' Except for that tinge of envy. I was giving him an opportunity I had not had myself. His second year, I stopped getting grades in the mail. One day I was reading the trades and I said, 'Durn, there's an Alfred Liggins producing a record in the record industry. What do you know about that?' My friends said, 'Is Cathy drunk? That's your son, fool!' He had done some work with Iris Gordy of Motown, and with Benny Medina, who was then a young, up-and-coming record producer.

"I went off!

"I said, 'Alfred, I gave you this opportunity. If you want to work, I'm not so vain as to think I'm Motown, but I'm a Black company. Unless you are going to marry one of Berry Gordy's daughters, you need to come back and work for WOL.' And of course he said, 'Well, I'm a man. I'm not a mama's boy. I'm not going to do what you say.'

"We don't go into business in my family because we want to. It's required. We have to. So I excommunicated him on the spot. I made it clear to him emotionally. He was out. My secretary would say, 'Ms. Hughes, your son is here.' I'd say, 'What are you talking about? You know I don't have a son.'

"And then one day Alfred came to me and said, 'I'm sorry. You're absolutely correct. If I can't work for my own mother . . .' My friend Carl Anderson had told him he had an obligation to try and help me because I was struggling with WOL at the time in a big way. They were trying to cut off my electricity. It got that bad. I was down to trying to keep my transmitter on the air. I had to sell that house I thought I'd have all to myself. Carl told Alfred, 'Be man enough to reimburse your mother.' Alfred told me he'd come back for two years and work at no salary. But then he was going back to Hollywood. That was eight years ago. I tell him, 'Alfred, aren't you due back in Hollywood any day now?'

"Now he's my president and general manager of WOL-AM, Majic 102.3 FM, and also WWIN in Baltimore. I had wanted to simulcast "The Morning Show" on AM and FM after we had done well at WOL and the opportunity came to get Majic. But the bank making the loan told me I was too controversial for the suburbs. The bank told me this. Of course it was illegal for the bank officers who were loaning me the money to try and control my on-air programming—it's illegal only if you're not a girl, or colored. I told them it was illegal, immoral, and unethical, and I was getting ready to go off—I'm ready to pop a cork. I thought, 'It won't matter what's on the air because I'm getting ready to kill everybody in this room!'

"But then Alfred stepped in and said, 'Just give me thirty days with my format, mother, and I'll turn you into my No. 1 listener on Majic 102.3.' And he did. I was amazed at what he knew about on-air programming. He did oldies and hits, Word for the Day, other things, and found a market among the thirtysomething baby-boomers and consumers. He knew I had created the 'Quiet Storm' format when we were at WHUR at Howard U., with Melvin. Alfred wanted to show me and Melvin Lindsey that he knew what he was doing on his own.

"Later he told me, 'I want to be in charge, be your boss.' I said, 'Excuse me?' He said, 'I want to relieve you of the operational stresses. You can concentrate on your show.' So for the last two and a half years he's been my boss. I'd rather work for him than anyone, though you know how talent is—once a year I have to let him know who's really boss.

"He and I have not lived together since he was eighteen, because it can be easy to allow a son to substitute for a man. I was never one of those mama friends. I've got no friends his age—particularly none I gave birth to. I never worked to be a friend. I wanted to be his mother, there when he needed me. We aren't friends. I'm still in charge."

"Was there more difficulty in being a woman or being Black?" I asked. "Or couldn't you make the separation?"

"I've always been able to make the separation," says Cathy, whose last name is Hughes because she was married to a radio broadcaster named Dewey Hughes. "It's always been about Black. And the difficulty is not in being Black. The difficulty is in how both White and Black people treat you if you are Black. Being Black in and of itself is pleasant. It's good just to be alive, y'know? But many people treat you according to your color. That's why I get so upset when Black men say things like 'Black women have it easier.'

"The first thing White supremacy deals with is the color of your skin. Gender is secondary. A lot of sisters learn to use their gender to get them certain privileges and certain opportunities. But all Black folks are oppressed. All Black folks are discriminated against. My problems with being a woman . . . let me say again I believe in karma, divine order, in the energy you project. I didn't believe my gender would stop me. I may have had fewer problems over the years because of this attitude, though I had some classic run-ins with sexual harassment that others would be devastated by.

"But the times I have experienced personal sexism to the point of remembering it, interestingly enough, have involved Black men. Because when I sit down at the negotiating table with the White power structure, I'm fully aware of all of the problems of discrimination that I must confront. So I come in fully prepared. The couple of times I've been caught off guard have been when a brother would say out of his mouth, 'Well, I don't think Cathy is best suited for this because she's a woman.' Or 'Cathy is too emotional.'

"I'm not too emotional. There's no such thing. It's wonderful to be emotional. That's not going to cloud my vision or my abilities. I love the fact I can get excited. I love the passion that comes with my African-ness. And to have a brother reject me based on that—I wish brothers would allow themselves to have and show more passion and emotion. But we as women help to condition them to believe that if they do that, it's a sign of weakness. Black mamas often try and make their sons hold up their emotions to protect them from the system. But I don't really think that's the correct way to protect them from the system.

"When I was getting ready to buy this station, my first, a prominent brother in this community said to me, 'You've done a great job at WHUR. Stay with that.' WHUR was No. 28 in this market when I took over, and when I left it was No. 3. By then the 'Quiet Storm' concept had gone nationwide. And I thought this brother was a friend, an ally, a mentor. He said, 'Cathy, you don't want to go into business for yourself and own your own radio station. That's too much for a woman to handle.' Not only did he put me down, discourage me, he told the people who were going to loan me the money that I was not a good credit risk. Is that sexist? Thank you! Yet he still doesn't see it. He says it had nothing to do with sexism. He says I'm too emotional, I get on air and curse somebody out or cry. But 99 percent of my obstacles have come from racism, not sexism."

What may be most fascinating and enviable about Cathy Hughes is the sincerity of her belief in the capabilities of her own people. At the same time, she seems to be able to sniff out a shyster in a second. Now, D.C. can be clannish—a pool of cliques where they like their women's hair straight and their men's noses up in the air. In D.C., Cathy Hughes could have sat out this ongoing contest of wills somewhere behind the Gold Coast, a queen bee ordering a hive in some inbred blue-vein stronghold, or lolling about as if on a lily pad. She could have done this and been disappointed either way with the results later on, or maybe not have been disappointed and maybe not deserve recrimination for her choices. Many who came before her are not to be blamed for living as they saw fit. But Cathy insisted on conducting her business right there where all the people could see her.

The people in the street had a wildly disparate view of her as one consequence. She calls them "the WOL family," then carefully pays attention to those who don't seem to object. She talks about herself a lot as part of her show, and shares some things about her personal life, and makes more than a few good jokes and bad enemies, but the lesson to be learned has nothing to do with personalities. She is a Black woman with a media outlet as a successful business. She is a power, a voice in a Black community, a person who talks openly about the odds she's faced, and what has given her strength to make it in spite of those odds.

People envy her for the strength she ascribes to her family. She'd been *obligated* to succeed. "Wasn't an option in my family," she says. People say she's likely done terrible things to people in her life. I wondered how that made her unique. It didn't, in fact. It was the business she ran that made her unique. Nobody ever said business would be anything but hard work. Nobody ever said it would be pretty.

"We're conditioned to believe that if you get to be financially successful, the community will be skeptical and won't feel you're loyal to them. I tell them. I talk about my Cadillac. The reason it's not a Rolls-Royce is because I believe in American-made cars. My relatives are working in Detroit. I keep trying to keep this on Black folks' minds. I'm trying to make Black folks realize that it's good for us to feel good about ourselves. I've never been disappointed.

"Every time I've needed something, Black folks have come through. When I said to the community, 'Let's band together and try to buy WKYS (the No. 1 station in the market), the critics came out in droves. They said we couldn't stick together, that Cathy was trying to get the people to foot her bills and buy the station for her. I couldn't legally do that anyway. My $25,000 was the first money that kicked off the fund. We eventually had $492,000 sent in by some eleven hundred Black folks, mostly in small contributions of $20 to

$100. Not one penny of that money was mishandled. That money sat on deposit in a Black bank, the Industrial Bank of Washington. We had an emergency contingency in case you needed your money back for a death in the family or something, during the year we were trying to get that station for the people. But in that entire year, not one person had an emergency that they brought to that account. Not one penny moved out. And in the end, when we couldn't do the deal, the money flushed clean back to the depositors. So everybody got their money back, and we said, 'We'll get 'em next time.' Those are the types of stories that don't get told about Black folks."

Some people make sullen faces when I mention Cathy Hughes. "Just look at her," they say. "She thinks she's something." They should hear themselves on the radio, to see how that would sound. Yes, undoubtedly, as she would remind you, as her grandmother said, Do tell, and Lord Ham Mercy. Look at her! Why even her legs got big! Isn't she something?

The warrior Cathy Hughes does think she's something. And she's right. If you're Black, you'd better watch out, or she'll have you feeling like you might be something, too.

"I thank God bitterness is not something I've had," she says. "I've had obstacles, and great blessings. You hear folks say, 'Black folks will disappoint you.' I find just the opposite. I'm amazed how much I've been given by Black folks. Work hard, get the job done, move on. I don't believe in lingering long over work. Get the work done, then let go and let God, and avenues, channels, and arenas will open up to you. I believe that. Believe it? I've lived it!"

Imagination

Imagine it is your own image flickering on George Holliday's videotape. Or can you? Imagine a balmy March night in Lake View Terrace in Los Angeles County, in 1991. Why do these four policemen surround you, shining harsh light into your eyes? Fool, you think, they don't need a reason. You've been drinking. You tried to escape from reality and found you could not. Your vision is blurred. Your eye is swelling shut. You are writhing on the ground. You feel pain. You feel you're being electrocuted. You are.

Two Taser lines are hooked into your skin, relaying heavy jolts of electric voltage to your heart and brain. The controls are held by one of the police. You can barely make out his nameplate. Sergeant Stacy Koon? Oh no. He probably had no reason at all to resent Black people, no reason to hate you, not with a name like that growing up among other White boys, eh? It begins to dawn on you now. Yes. You are Black. Your name is Rodney Glen King.

Three thick policemen, including officers Laurence Powell and Theodore Briseno, are clubbing you with three-foot aluminum batons. The beating is so sound, so brutal, so complete, it finally becomes pure atavism. One policeman, Powell, is particularly murderous in his application of the baton. He seems to hit you fifty-six times all by himself, as if to see how much it will take to crack your body like a hard-boiled snake egg. The beating continues unabated. Kicks are leveled at you once the police tire of electrocuting you and beating you about the head, face, and body with their clubs.

"Imagine." That's what Beatle John Lennon said. And everybody, especially White people, loved John so much, right up until he was shot dead, and even afterward, we're told. "Imagine . . . the world will live as one." You'd have to imagine it, because you sure can't look outdoors or in court or on George Holliday's video or anywhere else and see it, if you are lying there instead of Rodney King. If that is you, you realize that all you can do is imagine.

This is what the defense attorneys for the police officers said in court. Imagine if it had been you, poor jurors. Imagine if it had been your son, or brother, or father. Then what would you have done? Only White people were asked to imagine if *one of those police officers* had been their son, or brother, or father. That is the world according to the most powerful among them. This would make sense to them, since all but one of the twenty-three officers at or near the scene of this particular incident of imagination in L.A. County on the early morning of March 2, 1991, were White, and twenty-two were men. You could say the trouble started there.

Black or White, the police are notoriously cynical about the rest of us. This imperfect homogenization is one of the hazards of the job, which police seem to eventually take out on the rest of us. Police are not usually called in to break up weddings, so they can say they do not get to see the best in people. But White police can go beyond cynical when it comes to Black men. They go out of their way to find a Black man, looking there to see the worst in themselves.

In Miami, for a long time, an "NHI" call meant "No Humans Involved." It was a code meaning Black people were in need of some kind of law-enforcement assistance, which the Miami police were happy to provide as long as the assistance was a good beating. The police beat a Black man named Arthur McDuffie to death with flashlights in 1980, and McDuffie was a good man, or so the Black people who knew him said; the police were acquitted, even though they knew they had done it. The trial had been moved from Miami-Dade County to a Tampa venue. After the verdict of not guilty was handed down in 1981, there was a riot, or insurrection if you will.

You see, Black people almost instinctively know what these not guilty verdicts mean—they had nothing more to lose. They had lost everything but their lives, and what were those lives worth now?

Around the time of the Rodney King verdict, a writer named Richard Price told *Vanity Fair* that some police official in a New Jersey township told him that police didn't go into a particular Black neighborhood very often—they didn't need to, because what with AIDS, guns, crack, and crime, it was "like a self-cleaning oven." Price heard this while doing research for a novel entitled *Clockers*, which is certain to become a $30 million movie one day soon, perhaps directed by Martin Scorsese himself. It is a story about a young Black crack dealer named Strike.

Somewhere, some White person will read this and ask, "What is it that upsets you so much about all of this? And why are you lumping it all together like this?"

I was standing in an airport one day recently when suddenly I heard an argument between a young Black woman who was working at the security X-ray machine and a middle-aged White businessman. The man had muttered something only she could hear while she was going through his bag. She became very upset and said she didn't have to take that from him. She was a feminine-looking woman, even though dressed in the faded blue manwear of the airport security agent.

This White businessman looked at the other Black people working at this station and said, "She hit me! [She had not.] Where is somebody I can talk to here? I'm going to call the police!"

Don't tell me White businessmen do not use the police to attempt to strike dread into all Black people. Here was a female security guard being threatened by the presence of the police, even though she had done nothing to require their attention and was herself responsible for the law at her station. She had defended herself verbally. But the White businessman was letting her know that he knew her story would be of no account next to his. (I should say, in defense of these particular police, that once they came and I told them she never touched the White businessman, they believed me. One said, 'She doesn't look like the type.' But that doesn't change the reality of the White businessman who threatened a Black woman, then called in the police, the same police who can take care of business against a Rodney King; that does not change that man's lack of courage.)

Imagine, White people were told, imagine that you out-numbered Rodney King only four to one, thirteen to one, or twenty-three to one, depending on how you're looking at it, on the early morning of March 2, at 12:47 A.M. Imagine what this brute might be able to do to all of you once he tears away from those puny Taser lines like some kind of prehistoric creature or low-level primate, whom he resembles; overpowers the four policemen nearest to him, as a gorilla might do it; talks them out of one of their Glock 9-millimeter pistols with profane, vicious cunning; and opens fire indiscriminately into the balmy night. He might be able to kill all twenty-three White policemen nearby and several innocent bystanders before anyone can get off a round in return. After all, the Rodney Kings of this cruel world are quick, like animals; they move in blurs and feel no pain. They self-generate PCP in their veins. They are remorseless, crazed beasts. In fact, they have no civilized traits, which is why they all deserve beatings from time to time on general principle. Imagine if your son was faced by a Rodney King and outnumbered him only twenty-three to one. What would you have wanted him to do?

In late April of 1992, the jury in Simi Valley said, "Not guilty." And in saying this, they said much more.

There are a great many White people who shook their heads then and who know exactly what I'm talking about now. They knew that in this case, the police were guilty of something. Many White people came out later and said everything to support this, some even admitting they were briefly ashamed to be White after that verdict came in—not the best way of accentuating their displeasure, but good enough. It was not close enough to home for more than that to be said or felt.

Predictably, the city of Los Angeles, City of the Angels, exploded shortly thereafter. Any time you live in a society based on law, and the lawgivers are held above that law, then you have anarchy. The violence began when the jury in Simi Valley condoned the senseless brutality perpetrated on Rodney King by the police—the lawgivers, who are supposed to be employed to do the very opposite. And that was when violence was condoned. That was the unknown riot.

But you must be able to imagine in a certain way to see this. When Black people imagined—about their sons and fathers and husbands—they imagined them to be Rodney King lying on the ground, as difficult as that might be for White people to grasp. And there was no doubt about guilt in the minds of Black people. And if there was doubt in your mind then *you* were irrational, and no amount of so-called clear thinking and intellect and jurisprudence and interpretation of law could wipe it away.

It was White supremacy, completely, utterly that. It was the lack of regard in any sense for Black life, and every event that transpired both before and after the verdict proved it beyond a doubt. Not that it needed further proving to most of us, but there were some Blacks and Whites who felt reason to doubt its existence. Usually they were younger people, or older people with an agenda attendant to White supremacy over democracy.

Black people already knew that it didn't matter who the Black man was; Rodney King's criminality or lack thereof had nothing to do with the brutality. Some people, Black and White, said this brutality came because Rodney King had a criminal record, was on probation, and this and that. The Black people who said this said it to keep from losing their minds. The White people were attempting to salve what remained of their puny consciences, which they still attempt to prop up from time to time. But King's record meant nothing. The police didn't know anything of one when they beat him. And the only record Arthur McDuffie of Miami had was that of ex-Marine, model citizen, and businessman. And what of all the Black men who had been stopped by police, rousted, spread-eagled, handcuffed, beaten up, and otherwise demoralized in Los Angeles County in the two-year period prior to the Rodney King incident? Let's see—Joe Morgan, the baseball player; Jamaal Wilkes, the consultant and former basketball star with the Los Angeles Lakers; Wesley Snipes and Blair Underwood, successful actors; Al Joyner, a quiet, God-fearing man who was an Olympic gold medalist in track and field and is the humble husband of Florence Griffith-Joyner, the heroine of the 1988 Olympic Games. And those were just the publicized roustings. These people were humiliated by the Los Angeles police for being behind the wheels of cars the policemen who beat them and rousted them could not have afforded without stirring the suspicions of Internal Affairs.

But it was not class conflict; they were not stopped because of their cars. They were stopped because they were Black people driving those cars. Don't kid yourself otherwise. This was why: If you ain't better than a nigger, White man, who are you better than? So know your place, nigger, and get in it, nigger. Be ready to die at any time, nigger. It's in the rules. We can kill you and get away with it. You can look it up, nigger, if you can fucking read, nigger. I can't read that well myself, nigger, so you better not be able to read at all, nigger, not read better than me and hope to live.

When a White person tells a Black person he doesn't understand why that Black person was so upset about the not guilty verdict in the Rodney King incident, then that White person is the trouble, is dangerous both to Black people and to himself. That White person is one to be watched closely.

But the verdict in Simi Valley had to come back guilty, otherwise it meant that anarchy had already begun. It was of the utmost importance to understand that. Black people know better than anybody the importance of equality under the law. They know this to a painfully higher degree than do White people in America. Most White people have never had any reason to question the law—and especially no reason to question enforcement of that law, not with Black people around to take the worst of the American way.

Imagine this: Near the turn of the last century, a Black woman named Ida Barnett watched as the mutilated and burned body of the husband of her best friend in life was laid out on a cooling board, just inside the limits of Memphis, Tennessee. This had happened merely because this Black man was running a successful business, a country store that outstripped its competitors. The American way—only if you can't beat 'em, kill 'em, and that is the way many White men regard the American way when it comes to Black people. So this man was lynched and mutilated. His business naturally went downhill after that. But Ida Barnett, who later married and became Ida Barnett Wells, founder of the *Memphis Free Press*, never forgot. She was chief architect of a listing entitled The Red Record, giving dates, times, and places of lynchings of Black men by Whites in the U.S. The numbers reached past the range of three thousand when she stopped, out of an utter weariness. Rarely were any heinous criminals lynched. You had to go to many lynchings before you found one where even a minor criminal was being lynched. So Black people know what law means. If I outstrip you, and you can then kill me as your means of competing with me, then human accomplishment stops for your personal gain. Nobody gets better. I know I don't.

It was not personally comforting to people, this riot and insurrection in Los Angeles, caused by the verdict of not guilty brought in by the jury in Simi Valley, a largely White enclave outside Los Angeles proper. So why was the trial held there? What happened to Los Angeles County? It's still there, apparently. It just wasn't the place to hold the trial, according to the office of the L.A. district attorney. The difficulty was that the D.A.'s office usually works in concert with the police. A Black prosecutor, Deputy District Attorney Terry L. White, was appointed to the case. They figured it wouldn't look as bad that way, when the not guilty verdict was handed down—only in a world of personal imagination, gross miscalculation can run rampant.

Molotov cocktails spring eternal, but I didn't see many or any in this case. Stores went up in flames, and I wondered where all those fires had come from. There was looting and that was bad, but not nearly as bad as the S&L looting, on balance. Some buildings were left unscathed. Some Korean merchants were firing their own Glock pistols. People were setting their own businesses ablaze in hopes of getting paid by their insurance companies. There was widespread fighting and shooting. Most memorable, thanks to video, was the beating of Reginald Denny, a White truck driver who had the bad fortune to be at the corner of Florence and Normandie on Thursday, April 30, 1992. Everybody across America had been forewarned—if only they could have remembered the name of one Arthur McDuffie. I know I had no trouble remembering it.

I distinctly remember the Black female news anchor in far-off Washington, D.C., coming on air and saying, "We'll have a report on the Rodney King verdict soon." She said this rather breathlessly, and we knew there was no other verdict but not guilty coming in.

Reginald Denny was caught unawares, caught very viciously unawares. We all saw his beating many times on television during the next several days. I counted seven blows, and nearly all of them could have been debilitating, delivered by four young men, each of whom got in one or at most two. A final brick to the face really did the most brutal damage. They seemed to know what they were doing when it came to hurting people, rather like the police, but without all the trappings. However, after this brutal beating, it was some other Black people who took Denny to a local hospital. *Now* White people got interested in this, and the issue became earnest. This is what it took. Before this, the majority of them were more or less detached.

On the NBC "Today" show, the co-anchors, a White woman named Katherine Couric and a Black man named Bryant Gumbel, had different reactions, where normally they seem to get along like Siamese twins. Gumbel was busy trying to make a juror explain to him how she had reached a not guilty verdict in the Rodney King case. The juror said King had been in control of the situation and could have stopped it at any time—by just acting more White, one assumes.

Gumbel asked her if there was any time during the eighty-one-second beating where she felt Rodney King lost control. The woman juror said no, and Bryant Gumbel was left with the realization that no matter how well he spoke, in the end, this woman would never think him human, or even want him to be. After the show, it was reported that Bryant cried, and he doesn't appear to be the sort. He would get over it quickly, however. He'd already shocked the people on the set of the "Today" show some time earlier by saying the book that had most influenced him was *The Autobiography of Malcolm X*.

Meanwhile, Katherine Couric was very angry, not about the verdict but about the beating of truck driver Reginald Denny. It was horrible, an outrage, her twisted face said. Bryant Gumbel's face said yes, it was, but wasn't it the second outrage, Katie? Wasn't there an earlier outrage you're forgetting? Katherine's face did not appear to notice Bryant's face anymore. Twins no longer. The viewers of this program were shown the Denny beating in its entirety and the last five seconds of the Rodney King incident, when King was being cuffed and "helped" into the police car.

Imagine.

Some time after the people who beat up Reginald Denny were caught and held under a million dollars bond each, a couple of young Black people were heard from. First there was Sister Souljah, a rap artist whose given name is Lisa Williamson. Shortly thereafter came Ice-T, a rapper from south-central L.A. and, more lately, a succesful Hollywood actor with a beautiful wife and a home in Hawaii.

I had met Sister Souljah just before the not guilty verdict. She and I and Al Sharpton were together in a small room in a television studio on 57th Street in Manhattan, and we were engaged in our own private histrionics, for we knew we were about to be dangled in front of cameras to tape (I might as well admit it) a "Geraldo" show to be shown nationwide. All three of us had our doubts, not about each other so much as about what we were all doing there at the same time. I for one was not told who the other guests would be besides Sister and the Reverend Al, and a cute little Black boy and his mother, who were the victims of hate crimes.

It turns out the producers who worked for "Geraldo" had

pulled a fast one (surprise, surprise) and brought in some living fossilized remains from the Aryan brotherhood, the Klan, whoever—the kind of people I am never around, no matter what they call themselves. These White career racists were fighting a suit in court about their hate-mongering, using a First Amendment defense. We were helping to make them legitimate, whether we liked it or not. Once I found out, it immediately put me in a bad mood. I figured we were being used. Geraldo Rivera is a rather hard-charging professional telejournalist, which meant all bets about what was fair were off. He would love it if a fight broke out. He had been working out in the boxing ring for some time and was itching to clock himself a racist, plotting revenge for having his nose broken on-air in just such a confrontation a couple of years before this. At any rate, Sister got upset during the show (surprise, surprise). She's young. She has her rap down cold, but she's still young. I understood her rage. I advised her if she was going to do many of these shows, she should make sure she got paid. The people who would put her on their shows had their own agendas. So she should have hers. I found her smart and pleasant. I believed she had been given an opportunity to record by Chuck D, businessman of the group Public Enemy.

Some time later, after the riots, I began to see Sister Souljah on more shows—in a less circuslike atmosphere, but still among people with their own agendas. I can remember in particular an NBC "Sunday Today" show. They are gluttons for punishment over there, I suppose. Sister Souljah was on with Representative Charles Rangel of Manhattan, Senator Bill Bradley of New Jersey, and the network correspondent Garrick Utley.

Utley seemed thrilled to have Sister right there in the studio—not thrilled at all by her company, but perhaps by what she could do for him. He was about to be taken off the "Sunday Today" assignment and his "Sunday Night News" anchor assignment, so who knows what was going through his mind. Maybe Sister would say something truly outrageous and he'd get some great sound bites. Even if she didn't, he had some snippets from her video, the one where she said, "I am Black first, I am African first, and if my survival means your total destruction then so be it! They say two wrongs don't make a right, but it damn sure makes it even!" So Utley played this and looked at Sister and asked her if she meant it. For just a second that feminine part of her rounded her eyes, and then she went on and said, "Yes, I meant it."

Several things came to me there. First, I gained admiration for Chuck D, who had helped put her out there. Second, I saw that Chuck probably had done the music, because this song was from a group called The Hate that Hate Produced, a title taken from a news segment about the so-called Black Muslims thirty years ago. And if you substitute White for Black in the lyric quoted, you have the basis of White supremacy. It sounded like timely art to me, perhaps not as subtle as the language might get, but then what young person has ever taken the time to think of subtleties? Sister's name wasn't Sister Nun—it was Sister Souljah.

Interestingly, at this point Senator Bradley didn't take the bait from Garrick Utley. Instead he said there were certain languages different people used, and we still had to find a way to come together. Rangel agreed. Utley saw his career winding down further. His father had worked for NBC in Chicago once upon a time. He'd had a good run himself.

Some time later, Bill Clinton, then the Democratic candidate for President of the United States (but perhaps still no Bill Bradley), came out at a gathering of Jesse Jackson's Rainbow Coalition and excoriated Sister Souljah, who had said after the L.A. uprising that since Black people are killing Black people in the slums and ghettos all the time, maybe they should take a week and kill White people.

I will admit I questioned her subtlety again myself—rather foolishly, since I too make my living by pissing people off—until I saw her flesh out her views in an hour-long interview on Black

Entertainment Television. Where else? I saw a copy of her video, "Slavery Is Back in Effect," and again I saw the influence of Chuck D. The story line of the video was risky, excellent— Black people going about their normal lives, then being informed that, due to Black people scoring low on tests, slavery was brought back into effect by the U.S. government. Not all go quietly. It was fascinating stuff, as far as music videos go.

Bill Clinton, talking to middle-class White America, said Sister Souljah was no better than David Duke. But I can say unequivocally that David Duke has never made a video as entertaining as "Slavery Is Back in Effect," although he would have loved to be blessed to be that creative.

Bill Clinton made a real mistake (as opposed to a political mistake—as far as politics go, what he did was shrewd) in doing a number on Sister. I don't mean because Jesse got mad at him, either. The sitting president, George Bush, quickly followed by having his staff excoriate Ice-T for a song off a new album, a heavy-metal monstrosity called "Cop Killer." I began to wish for a famous politician to excoriate me. It would help product sales—a point Sister had not been loath to make when being interviewed on BET.

No politician has a say when Arnold Schwarzenegger kills cops a dozen at a time in a movie like *The Terminator*, or when Richard Gere plays a cop who kills his own partner in *Internal Affairs*, or when Axl Rose of Guns 'n Roses or Ozzy Osbourne or some other White artist calls for chaos and anarchy. Why not? They're artists first. They're Americans first. And if their survival means my total destruction, so be it. They aren't seriously questioned, let alone censured by politicians. *I am Black first, I am African first.* Where do you think Sister Souljah learned her stuff? In America, from Americans. And she doesn't even have to imagine it. The nightmare is far too near, all too real. And we're all bound up in it together. There is no waking up or getting away.

Why do you think they call it rap?

ABOUT PERSONALITIES

Where Once
Black People Laughed

Richard Pryor was a profane philosopher. I find myself still quoting him on occasion—the way some dramatists quote Shakespeare when they fail to add drama, the way some ministers quote the Bible when caught with their trousers down, the way some scholars quote the dead when they don't want to be challenged, the way novelists quote each other all the time. By comparison, Pryor's observations rang harshly against the grain of gentility. Odd how the harsh observations were the most hilarious, the most true.

This harshness of reality, Pryor's reality, was his uncompromised subject matter—until he grew older and less angry, less probing of his experience. Once toward the end of his effectiveness as a comedian, he said, "I don't get it anymore," and he meant his own anger. After that he became just another clown, aside from personal history no different from the Wayans brothers, who by then had badly parodied him.

Apparently, their thinking is that dressing up in rags and walking around with a rotten banana in a jar of pickle juice while picking imaginary detritus from one's nose is a commendable way to make the homeless laughable, funny in any sense once one had left the lower depths of elementary school. Or that moving as one imagines the palsied and those with multiple sclerosis (a malady that Pryor now suffers) move is a hilarious way to include the handicapped in the good, honest fun. There is a simpleminded cruelty to some of the humor of "In Living Color," the Wayans' hit TV show. At rare times it is funny. Most of the time it is retro-Fetchit—though the Wayans totally missed the undeniable grace and canny knowledge that the whole thing was a joke beneath Steppin Fetchit's syrupy movements a half-century earlier. Fetchit wasn't acting like that because that was the way he acted; he was acting like that because that was the way he had to act around White people in order to get along. So even as Keenan Ivory Wayans and Damon Wayans (the talented one) and Kim Wayans have mocked the Richard Pryors and Redd Foxxes, they haven't equaled them, haven't come close. They enjoy the fruits of past struggles and rest on other people's laurels. But this can be said for them—they work hard. There would never have been a show entitled "In Living Color" if it hadn't been for Richard Pryor in his best days, when he was in his zone, when his timing was strong, his vision sure, and the laughter came in pouring sheets—the days best cast from his most evocative character, the old man of Mississippi by way of Peoria: Mudbone. Mudbone's voice is eternal in my head, synopsizing, querying, warning, bawdy, baffled. He's easily the equal to any critic, editor, mimic-only comedian, or other second-guesser I've ever met.

•   •   •

Throughout that gray, ominous decade of the 1970s, the most trenchant observations on the directions, the meanings, and the underlying, unutterable frustrations of many American lives could be gathered most accurately from selected books of the New Testament and the piercing monology of Richard Pryor.

That Pryor was a stand-up comic wasn't beside the point. Only with humor can the hammer of repression and the anvil of guilt and misunderstanding be put down. Not everyone is susceptible to reason, but most people know how to laugh, especially those with noses for the truth.

The authors of *If I Stop I'll Die: The Comedy and Tragedy of Richard Pryor* have not missed this most telling point. The veteran novelist John A. Williams and his son, Dennis, a former *Newsweek* correspondent and an instructor at Cornell, in Pryor's argot, "booked the numbers, didn't need paper nor pencil." Their generations bracket Pryor's. Their sensitivities counterbalance their scholarship. They are aware and sound as clear as two bells. They show us Pryor's legacy being wrought from mind-boggling stand-up routines—the best in his 1975 album, *Is It Something I Said?* The authors note this album's cover shows Pryor about to be burned at the stake and relate that to his later immolation in real life. They pick out some of his best lines and put them in the context of his existence, only to see the lines fall flat. This is because the old Pryor didn't just deliver jokes. The material was unalterably his. Just listen to many of his monologues, like "Little Feets" from that 1975 album. "Little Feets" is undoubtedly his best work, a tall tale that defies retelling.

Why? Well, you could retell a Pryor joke: "If it comes down to dying in some [specific female anatomy] or being hit by a bus, which line are you gonna be in? I know which line *I'm* gonna be in. I'm gonna be in that loooong motherfucker."

But it was the delivery of the joke that killed you: Pryor standing there after the punch line, in that endless, imaginary queue, craning his neck to gaze ahead, turning to check the unending line behind him, patiently gauging his progress, moving forward one small step at a time, as the unsure laughter turned into an awed recognition and roaring ovation. No one else could deliver the material in the same dimensions, not even Eddie Murphy, who admits, "Without [Pryor], I couldn't have become Eddie Murphy."

MUDBONE: *Now why, outta all them good stories that boy told, you gotta go pick out a nasty one? That's just like a nigger, ain't it? Same thing that boy used to do. Just dare White folks not to like it. That Pryor boy told more truth than that. Although, come to think of it, some pussy every now and then, ain't much more to truth than that, is it? 'Cept dinner. And goin' to work. 'Course, look like to me you wouldn't know nothing about none of that. 'Cept dinner.*

The authors acknowledge Lenny Bruce as a pioneer in using forthright honesty as the crux of the finest humor—and meeting total societal resistance. They then acknowledge Dick Gregory and Bill Cosby as two of Pryor's progenitors and comic influences, who affected Pryor because they were where—not who—Pryor wanted to be: in front of the largest possible audience. The authors note Pryor didn't become a seminal cultural phenomenon until he became truly himself— storyteller, mimic, social commentator of incomprehensible prescience for his time, the ribald Stroker from Peoria. It was Pryor who long, long ago joked of a choke hold ("Cops, he broke. Does it say you can break a nigger?") used in Long Beach ("You in jail in Long Beach? Well shit, we ain't coming down *there* to get yo ass.") by southern California police ("*I am reaching into my pocket for my wallet*, 'cause I don't want to be no motherfuckin' accident.").

In describing the memorable characterizations of Pryor's oeuvre—the Wino, the Junkie, the Preacher, the Father, the Grandmother, Macho Man, Cockeyed Junior, Miz Rudolph—the Williamses slip only twice. They continually refer to his most vivid persona, the wizened old man, as "Mud-bones." His name was Mudbone. I was surprised how both-ered I was by this small error, perhaps as emotional as a cinephile might be if Charles Foster Kane were misspelled.

The second slip comes when the authors, to prove Mud-bone's wit, refer to a monologue in which Mudbone, now and long since of Peoria, Illinois, says he is originally from Tupelo, Mississippi. The authors put this as "Tougaloo." When a female voice in the audience asks, "Where's that?" Mudbone answers, "Near Onepelo." The Williamses have this as "near Woomaloo." Tch.

MUDBONE: *That's right, don't let 'em start calling me out of my name 'round here. You can do a lot, but don't do that. Ain't nobody can get away with calling me out of my name 'round here, nobody but Mister Gilmore, Junior.*

The true quality of the biography comes from the study of Pryor's personal crucibles—his battle with cocaine and his work in film. The authors offer a brief, slanted study of that industry; how from its beginnings it stood for years as exclu-sionary of Black people in the creative process and heinously manipulative of their images in the final product. Pryor ap-peared in some forty-two films, the majority of them bad by acclamation. The authors point to a history of racist Holly-wood screeds as the reasons for this apparent failure. But Pryor always had made racism his tool, and he undoubtedly would have done so in film had he the knack for it. But to put the master monologist into a collective endeavor like fea-ture filmmaking was like asking James Baldwin to write a book by committee. What really did you expect?

Pryor did have signature moments on film. His first two concert films were knockouts. The authors say 1978's *Blue Collar* and 1977's *Which Way Is Up?* are Pryor's keepers among his feature films and go on to explore the dynamics of his pairing with Gene Wilder in 1976's *Silver Streak*.

Blue Collar was about auto workers, corrupt unions, the pitting of poor Blacks against poor Whites. It was Pryor's penultimate dramatic turn. His sly performance in *Which Way Is Up?* is stunning, explosively funny. He plied three roles, a Mudbone spinoff, a Preacher spinoff, and the vulnerable Pryor as a farm worker attempting to scale classes. Some of the most hilarious lines, expressions, and improvisations on record are in this B picture. Chaplin would have recognized them.

A great deal of the worth of any artist is in how many sons he leaves ready to kill him, ready to outperform him. For Eddie Murphy and Robin Williams, Richard Pryor was an incalculable boon, a model. He was only slightly less so to others like Whoopi Goldberg, Martin Lawrence, Elayne Boosler, Sandra Bernhard, Marsha Warfield, Robert Townsend, Arsenio Hall, and all the brothers and sisters Wayans. Other renowned comics from troupes like the "Saturday Night Live" cast and Second City owe him less, but with the exception of Bill Murray, none of them has ever been as funny as Pryor was in the disquiet of the '70s. Jay Leno and David Letterman and especially Steve Martin are staid by comparison.

The genius of Richard Pryor was that he didn't need a writer to be funny, and he didn't need anybody's permission to tell the truth as he saw it. This is what he was once, the Pryor the authors have seen, heard, and understood. Pryor himself might now learn something of value about his life from this book about a master who played in a minor key.

MUDBONE: *Now, you know you really didn't think that book was all that good, did you, boy? Well, you shoulda told the peoples that! What's wrong with you? What? You say only a fool says what he thinks all the time? Well, sound like to me you must be trying to live to be ole. You don't get to be ole by being no fool. It's plenty of young wise men out here that's deader than a motherfucker, ain't it? Do what you feel like you gotta do, and keep some sunshine on your face.*

Mister Justice Thomas

In the late summer and early autumn of 1991, the Senate confirmation hearings for U.S. Supreme Court Justice nominee Clarence Thomas were held up on Capitol Hill in Washington, D.C. During these initially enervating proceedings, a week-long gathering of thousands of serious, well-dressed Black people also took place in Washington, on the last week of September. This large gathering is called annually by the Congressional Black Caucus, whose members were, in 1991, the nearly thirty or so Black elected members of Congress. Since there are more than five hundred members of the House of Representatives, not counting the ones who are asleep, the Black Caucus's most influential political role is responsibility for the annual coming together of the Black Caucus. There were no Black senators at all when this episode began, so nobody at the Black Caucus had anything directly to do with the confirmation on the Hill.

During this Black Caucus Annual Legislative Weekend, as it's called, there were many panels conducted in hotel conference rooms and at the Rayburn Office Building on Capitol Hill. And, in fact, some useful data might have been available—if you were persistent and looked hard. But for the most part, it appeared people came to the Black Caucus to network; meet, greet, and chat up other people; advance their own positions; and do some business. However, although nobody would ever openly admit it, they were also there to further the hunt for a suitable mate, or to impress or silence the mate they had by taking him or her "someplace nice."

People like to act as though they are always only thinking of work, of creating new legislation, running wings of the government, and commerce, and panels and commissions. But human beings are not so removed from the need to love and/ or procreate that they're not moved to act oddly from time to time. Women and men. White and Black. It scarcely matters where one fits demographically. People might deny this, but I believe it to be true. The agenda is intractable and above the law, an act of God if there ever was one.

An idea was pitched to the Black Caucus that since Judge Thomas's confirmation hearings were occurring at the same time, right next to the Rayburn Office Building, it might be a good idea if a few thousand of the revelers, er, participants in the Black Caucus went down to the Senate chambers and made themselves visible. This seemed like a good idea, since the consensus from the Congressional Black Caucus itself was that Judge Thomas would not do as a Supreme Court Justice. In fact, they had gone on record in opposing him. But the people of the Caucus and its weekend passed on going down to the Senate, where they might have been mistaken for limousine drivers. You'd think the Black Caucus could have spared a thousand people from the bar at the Washington Sheraton alone, but they were too busy shining the elbows of their suits while discussing the social investment in learning to do the Electric Slide.

If I'd had a nickel for every time somebody said, "Clarence Thomas, excuse me while I puke" at the Black Caucus, I could buy my way into the Senate. Usually his name was said with such utter disdain I wondered why I'd never heard of him before. A man this despised on the one hand, and supported on the other, had to be famous. I was told he was the perfect example of a sellout bum, of Uncle Tomming, of Oreoitis. That he was an enemy of affirmative action and possibly, even more heinously, an opponent of *Roe* v. *Wade*, which "allowed" women the right to do as they wished with their bodies. This explained Thomas's popularity with Congress and especially with the Republican administration, which are male dominated the way a Y chromosome is male dominated. The endangering of *Roe* v. *Wade*, a charged issue of procreation, was one of the hottest issues of the Caucus.

Nothing much came of it being an issue with the Caucus. Only senators confirm Supreme Court Justice nominees, and as I have noted, through some stroke of extreme ill fortune there were no Black senators at that point. Just a merry Black Caucus unwilling to take a stroll over to Capitol Hill and lightly grill Clarence Thomas. But there were some excellent parties, or so I've heard, even though no major legislation emerged from them. The activities of the Black Caucus week concluded. Attention moved to the other side of town, into the Senate chambers, an alternate universe.

You have to admit, until Black people got involved any Senate confirmation hearing was an extremely tedious affair requiring great concentration on the part of the person attempting to be confirmed and the confirmers just to stay awake. But now, Professor Anita F. Hill of the University of Oklahoma law school quietly accused Judge Clarence Thomas of sexual harassment. She said it began in 1981, when she worked as his assistant at the Department of Education, and continued later at the Equal Employment Opportunity Commission, known as EEOC. So the question ceased to be about whether Mister Thomas gutted the EEOC (the answer to that question is yes). The question became whether or not Clarence Thomas said provocative things to Anita Hill.

A group of one hundred people, ninety-eight of them White men (oh all right, Senator Inouye of Hawaii isn't White no matter what they say) decided this was more important to consider at length than how Judge Thomas had performed at the meat of his jobs. During Thomas's tenure at EEOC, all reasonable Black people and Latinos and Asian-Americans and women and seniors and the physically handicapped and all the other minorities, if that many folks can be called minority, began to see if you had a problem at your job that you felt was based on race or sex or sexual preference or advancing age, it was better to quit or bite the bullet than take a valid complaint to the EEOC, because nothing would come of it there. Management via employee harassment is a part of job function that many American managers seem to enjoy and consider their prime directive. How do you think America fell behind in all these areas of production in the first place? I'll bet you thought it was Black people's fault.

Soon Clarence and Anita became the new Kingfish and Sapphire Stevens of American television. Only the honeymoon was definitely over now that the Kingfish had gone to Yale and was nominated for the Supreme Court and had married a White woman, and Sapphire had gone to Yale and was teaching at a law school in Oklahoma and missing the Black Caucus. Anita Hill had to say words like *penis* and *pubic hair* and *Long Dong Silver* in public, on TV, and in the Senate chambers, for God's sake, for hours at a time! And Clarence had to act as though he didn't know what she was talking about when she said it, like he was born the day before yesterday! It's amazing, the things one must go to Yale to learn!

When you're a Black American, like it or not, professional or not, Yalie or not, you are the public sexual surrogate for an entire way of life. You live with it.

People had made up their minds about Judge Thomas before Anita Hill. Now they were not so sure, or were utterly convinced. But of what? Some who had been for him turned against him with a vengeance. Some who had been against his judicial policies found themselves more in his corner. Men disagreed with men, women disagreed with women, and in some cases men agreed with women. It was heavy stuff.

A couple I know were going through an acrimonious divorce at the time, but they decided to reconcile because they found they agreed on one thing, their views on the confirmation hearings: In the end, after much testifying by both Clarence Thomas and Anita Hill, and others on their behalf, after much pontificating and name-calling by senators who have harassed women like nobody's business, judging from the way they treated Hill, after Americans ignored baseball and football games and even soap operas to stay glued to these proceedings, after Clarence called it Kafkaesque and a high-tech lynching (I sort of believed him on both these points) and Anita said Clarence bragged on the size of his penis and asked if that information might affect her in some way (I sort of believed her too)—this divorcing couple realized that they *didn't believe any of them.* And if all these people in the Senate chambers were a good example of what was out there, then this bitter twosome felt they might as well hold their tongues and stay together.

How we got from deciding whether to confirm a conservative Black judge on a conservative, bone-White Supreme Court threatening to take away a woman's right to her own body, to discussing the sexual evil that many men (only Black men, supposedly) do is what we had to try and figure out.

These events had an effect on me, first of all because I live around Washington, D.C., and have to put up with these kinds of invasions of my privacy on a consistent basis, however that makes me sound. But compared to the life and hard times of Thomas, the Southern Black lad up from the poverty of Pinpoint, Georgia, who used an outhouse and felt rejected by Blacks and Whites, felt both Black and White people hated him for being Black down deep, I'd had a free ride. I myself had been a Southern Black lad up from Delta poverty of a kind I didn't know was poverty until somebody pointed out that the books at school might be missing their hinges at times. Or that the uniforms of the band and athletic teams were laced with darning whorls and stitch scars, when you could find tops and bottoms that matched without much difference in fading. I never went hungry. I put the lawnmower away in the outhouse, never used the outhouse for its intended purpose. As for all people disliking me, I prefer not to dwell on it that often.

I've tried to pull myself up by my bootstraps and have found that I seem to be too heavy. I actually lifted myself an inch or two before American people started pointing out to me that I was nearly as Black as my bootstraps, and didn't I find that to be a real hindrance, not being able to tell my hand from the strap? If I didn't find it a hindrance, they most certainly did. Interestingly, not all of the people who informed me of these very sobering facts were White. When Malcolm X once asked, "In America, what is a Black man with a Ph.D?" and then answered, "A nigger!" he was not only referring to the way White people learn to think. He was referring to the way all Americans learn to think, including, most horribly of all, Black people themselves.

Wasn't America in large measure constructed on the free labor and inventions of Black people, despite a blurring, stunting, and twisting of these accomplishments in the media? In the media, very often Black men were not very subtly portrayed as crazed lunatic walking phalluses for exhibiting precisely the same kind of clumsy behavior that gets White men called charming, dashing, and irascible good old boys.

Judge Clarence Thomas was nominated to the U.S. Supreme Court by George Bush, then president of the United States and chief representative of a conservative power structure. Justice Thurgood Marshall, the esteemed barrister and our first and (until Thomas) only Black Supreme Court Justice, had once muttered to the effect that he'd try to outlive everybody. But now ill health had forced him to retire. At the press conference announcing his retirement, he sounded an ominous chime: "A black snake is just as bad as a white snake." (It would not be discursive to mention Malcolm X, who once said that when your children are being bitten by snakes, you don't stop to ask which ones. You rid yourself of snakes. This man now dead twenty-six years seems inescapable.)

Justice Marshall was considered a living legend by Black people, including himself. He'd successfully argued *Brown* v. *Topeka*, against the Board of Education of the small town in Kansas in 1954, outlawing school segregation in law, if not in reality. Reality came limping in later, and in far too many cases it was not a very pretty sight.

Justice Marshall had himself gone to Lincoln of Pennsylvania and Howard universities, two colleges of that type where most Black people had to go if they wanted to learn— so-called segregated schools, predominantly Black universities—once upon a time in America. Marshall had been turned away by the University of Maryland. So Marshall had a clearcut, defined battle to win, a battle of inclusion.

Some people, usually White but sometimes Black like Clarence, call the historically black schools obsolete now that we have integration. So, in a sense, Justice Marshall had helped run his own people out of business. Integration remained only a theory. People put it into practice and then usually kept their eyes closed. It was not put into real practice. You see, it was the *White* schools and institutions that were integrated, sort of, skimming off the best five percent of Black talent and then ignoring it. Black schools were not integrated by Whites for the most part. For the most part, they were abandoned. Some people sensed this would happen. In 1955, Zora Neale Hurston wrote:

> I had promised God, and some other reasonable characters, including a bunch of bishops, that I was not going to part my lips concerning the United States Supreme Court decision on ending segregation in the public schools of the South. . . . The whole matter revolves around the self-respect of My People. How much satisfaction can I get from a court order for somebody to associate with me who does not wish me near them? I regard the ruling of the United States Supreme Court as insulting rather than honoring my race.

Malcolm X put it this way in a speech at Harvard on December 16, 1964: "I believe in the brotherhood of all men, but I don't believe in wasting brotherhood on anyone who doesn't want to practice it with me. Brotherhood is a two-way street." In the year of his retirement, Justice Marshall questioned whether Malcolm X had had any effect on the condition of Black people in his life—much less a similar effect to his own. This served to prove that even the most honorable of justices should try and get out more often. On the other hand, I understood. Justice Marshall did go unappreciated by historians and presidents and other policy makers and by the population at large, in many ways. Here is one litmus test of that theory: When it came time to make a movie about him, it was a made-for-television movie.

Justice Marshall was the last real opponent of capital punishment on the High Court and a defender of *Roe* v. *Wade*. The court itself had long shifted to what people call the right, the conservative side. President Bush could have nominated anybody he chose, and there was nothing the senatorless Black people could do. Bush was unlikely to nominate anyone who was particularly liberal. He decided on Judge Thomas, who is quite obviously and irrevocably Black.

I had decided to more or less accept that before Anita Hill came up. I mean, what else was I going to do? Call up a senator? Also, I'm quite tired of Black people not wishing each other well because they don't believe self-improvement possible. How often we, of all people, find ways to say, "I don't like him (or her)," when talking about other Black people. We don't have this luxury, even if that emotion is very well founded. Often it isn't. Not liking each other is perhaps Black people's greatest internal problem, worse even than the Black Caucus, as difficult as that might be to believe.

At the same time, many other "minorities," especially women of all colors—who were waking up to the fact that they were not a minority—watched the reactions of Black men carefully. On the face of the matter, nobody reasonable and Black supported Clarence Thomas. If he'd been White, he never would have made it past the concession stand. And everybody knew it, too. Remaining neutral about him smacked of treason. So did being for him. So did being against him. Enchanting.

Thomas's judicial record was not as lustrous as Justice Marshall's. Many Black and White people felt he didn't measure up to Justice Marshall in any way, shape, or form. And these people were probably right in the end. Some of the disparity was a function of time and opportunity. Justice Marshall was in his eighties. Judge Thomas had only just made it to the age of forty-three. He had a lot of catching up to do just to get respectable, to get clean, and would never emerge from Marshall's long shadow.

Clarence Thomas's battle would not be as clear-cut as Justice Marshall's had been. After inclusion comes what? Influence? Action? Patience? Different forms of exploitation to be divined? Thomas went to Yale, where he was informed by the attitudes, comments, and body language of some of his White peers and instructors that he'd been let in, and that he'd better stay busy struggling with his bootstraps rather than learn about law. It wasn't natural that he should learn, anyway. Better he should cook, or box, or groom horses. Don't laugh; I've had my share of White people say this to me, especially when they found out I was good at something. Some Black people said it might have been better if Clarence had gone to Lincoln. But George Bush went to Yale, and he makes judicial appointments. So who can say?

Anita Hill went to Yale, too.

We are left with what black historian Carter G. Woodson once said: "In my opinion, Harvard has ruined more Negroes than bad whiskey." What's that to do with Yale? Oh, nothing.

Before Professor Hill came forward, I'd call someone merely to inquire about their health, and that person would say, "I'm fine, except for Clarence Thomas. He disgusts me."

"He does, or the way he thinks does?" I'd ask.

"You know what I mean."

There's no reasonable reply when someone says you know what they mean. The best course of action is to act as though you do know, then remove yourself from their presence. Then I'd call someone else to arrange a meeting in hopes of doing some work, and that person might say, "Yes, that would be fine, if people would stop bothering Clarence."

"You like him, then?"

"Didn't say all that. Just wish they'd leave him be."

The people I had normally agreed with because they are supposed to have my best interests at heart, White liberals and other Black professionals, were against Clarence. Then there were a lot of people I didn't know and frankly didn't want to know, people who are conservative and no doubt even more who are quite racist, who wanted Thomas confirmed posthaste. Even arch-conservative Senator Strom

Thurmond wanted Judge Thomas confirmed, to the extent that we could tell what Thurmond wanted, speaking as he does with those marbles in his mouth. I enjoyed the beauty, the life-affirming pinch of the irony scarab. The arguments were good arguments, with merit—solid debate material if ever I stepped in it.

The White liberals and Black professionals said Judge Thomas's judicial thinking, what little there was of it, was all wrong, all wrong, especially being silent on *Roe*, acting as though he'd never heard of it. Black leaders didn't like how he had ignored them, and their call for him to become a champion of affirmative action and give them audience. He wouldn't stamp their Head Nigger in Charge papers for them. Some Black friends of mine said that to be on the Supreme Court, Clarence should have been sharper, quicker of wit, more eloquent, and should have had a broader legal base for interpreting the Constitution: In fact, he should have had a greater body of work in general. They said he embodied White-implemented affimative action that would rather put in place a mediocre, malleable Black wonk than the true, brilliant Black talent. I asked, "You mean you don't automatically get to be brilliant by osmosis just because you go to Yale?"

I have few conservative and no racist White friends (that I know of), so I can only speculate what they thought. The conservatives probably thought Clarence was a man they could work with. Racists thought him a good boy.

"I know Clarence," said Maudine Cooper, a Washington lawyer, a Black woman, on Kojo Nnamdi's talk show, "Evening Exchange," broadcast on WHMM in Washington—the television station at Howard University. "And he wouldn't be in the top ten of Black judges I would have nominated to the Supreme Court, even from the Republicans. But it was George Bush's choice, and considering that, from Bush, I really wasn't going to get anyone any better than Clarence."

Maudine shrugged. She had expressed my sentiments exactly. Even before Anita Hill there was something stopping my knee from jerking in the direction of Clarence Thomas's behind, too. I think I had hope for him. I'm in the habit of forcing myself into hoping for Black people. I read he had once listed one of his heroes as Malcolm X, but then I had read that in the pages of *Time* magazine, so who knows?

I do know about doublethink, however. This is the necessity of a southern Black lad—and a northern one too, if he has any brains—to think twice before he acts and speaks. His first instinct is to think as any intelligent person would think. But then he has to think of what the White person he is communicating with might be thinking. I cannot explain this any better than Richard Wright did in his book *Black Boy*, copyright 1937, still relevant in 1993:

The climax came at noon one summer day. Pease called me to his workbench; to get to him I had to go between two narrow benches and stand with my back against a wall.

"Richard, I want to ask you something," Pease began pleasantly, not looking up from his work.

"Yes, sir."

Reynolds came over and stood blocking the narrow passage between the benches; he folded his arms and looked at me solemnly. I looked from one to the other, sensing trouble. Pease looked up and spoke slowly, so there would be no possibility of my not understanding.

"Richard, Reynolds here tells me that you called me Pease," he said.

I stiffened. A void opened up in me. I knew that this was the showdown. He meant that I had failed to call him *Mister* Pease. I looked at Reynolds; he was gripping a steel bar in his hand. I opened my mouth to speak, to protest, to assure Pease that I had never called him simply Pease, and . . . had never had any intention of doing so, when Reynolds grabbed me by the collar, ramming my head against a wall.

"Now, be careful, nigger," snarled Reynolds, baring his teeth. "I heard you call 'im Pease. And if you say you didn't, you're calling me a liar, see?" He waved the steel bar threateningly.

If I had said: No sir, Mister Pease, I never called you Pease, I would by inference have been calling Reynolds a liar; and if I had said: Yes sir, Mister Pease, I called you Pease, I would have been pleading guilty to the worst insult that a Negro can offer to a southern white man. I stood trying to think of a neutral course that would resolve this quickly risen nightmare, but my tongue would not move.

"Richard, I asked you a question!" Pease said. Anger was creeping into his voice.

"I don't remember calling you Pease, Mister Pease," I said cautiously. "And if I did, I sure didn't mean . . ."

"You black sonofabitch! You called me Pease, then!" he spat, rising and slapping me till I bent sideways over a bench. Reynolds was on top of me demanding:

"Didn't you call him Pease? If you say you didn't, I'll rip your gut string loose with this fucking bar, you black granny dodger. You can't call a white man a liar and get away with it!"

I wilted. I begged them not to hit me. I knew what they wanted. They wanted me to leave the job.

"I'll leave," I promised. "I'll leave right now!"

They gave me a minute to get out of the factory, and warned me not to show up again or tell the boss . . .

I hoped that Judge Thomas might grow into the job. With a lifetime appointment to the Court, I hoped that he would act according to his true conscience, the conscience of a right-thinking man of intelligence and sensitivity, of a man born and raised in America, who knows the general thinking hasn't been right in the past and something must be done about it occasionally, within the law, today and tomorrow.

In the past, a couple of other Supreme Court justices had proven this possible—and they were White. Though there was plenty for me as a Black man to dislike about Clarence's train of thought, I did not oppose his appointment. It is a joke for me to say senators breathed easier because I was silent. But as Cathy Hughes said at the time on her show on radio station WOL: "I'll take a Black man on life support before I'll take a White conservative Bush nominee."

I believe this is why I didn't oppose Clarence now that I've had time to think about it. I sort of like it when I don't know why I feel the way I do about something right away. It is the challenge that makes me think. Soon I had a headache. And I'd have to say it was ninety-eight White men of the United States Senate, and not Kingfish and Sapphire, er, Hill and Thomas, who gave it to me.

Anita Hill was minding her own business when she was contacted by someone from one of the offices of the ninety-eight White men. Just whose office it was might come out later, but it definitely had to be one of the ninety-eight White men, I'd say.

I imagine Anita was pitched this way: "Say, Anita, there are charges of sexual harassment against Clarence. Your name has come up. It probably would be better if you talked to the FBI about this. If you stay quiet, then we'll have to take somebody else's word for what happened. You should hear what *they* say. We've heard it wasn't pretty. Just thought you might want to know. Now, of course, it's your choice whether or not to cooperate with the FBI people. That's up to you. You went to Yale and everything. You're not a Black Panther, are you? Ha, ha. So it's up to you. And we just want you to know, if you do tell us the truth, it will be strictly confidential. No one will know what you told us. If you've been harassed, Judge Thomas will withdraw his name for nomination to the Court. Think about it."

Anita didn't have to think too long, not with the FBI or people who looked like the FBI staring at her like fish, not blinking. So she told her story. And then somehow the story was leaked. Suddenly she found herself between a rock and a hard place, having to come to Washington to testify before the Senate and on television to as many Americans as possible.

Anita testified that Judge Thomas bragged about the size of his penis and that he talked to her about an X-rated movie with a lead character named Long Dong Silver. And that once in his office he told a joke with no punch line, the one about what a pubic hair was doing on a can of Coca-Cola. She said she suffered an upset stomach from having to put up with this, which surprised no one. She sighed and seemed to have to clear her throat before she said "penis," and this is a woman with twelve brothers and sisters. Surely she had heard the word before. She was utterly convincing. But then, after all, she is a lawyer and paid to be convincing. I take my cues from bell hooks on matters like these as pertaining to women, and hooks seemed a little displeased with Anita's televised performance, or so hooks said in an open forum. hooks had wanted Anita to be more forceful and honest and truthful, saying, and I am paraphrasing her, "Look, this man did harass me very much, just as most of you harass most of us, but I was his protégée, as most of us start out, and we agreed on political issues, so I had to suffer it as most women do." bell hooks said, "My girl forgot she was on television," meaning, I believe, that there was no need for doublethink: Anita had the mike and could be frank with us.

The ninety-eight White men took this ball, so to speak, and ran with it—especially Senator Ted Kennedy, the person Judge Thomas was looking at when he answered Anita's charges by saying the full scenario was Kafkaesque. The judge thought, how can any of these men sit in judgment of me in this matter? Why aren't they smiling like they did when I called my sister a welfare queen, when they realized I hated myself with such a groaning passion? How can they do this to me?

Senator Kennedy's loudest pronouncement during these

proceedings was to imperiously state that they had nothing to do with race: "This is one African-American charging another," he said. Which sounds like a convenient thing for a voyeur to say: I'm not peeking, that window was in my way. This had nothing to do with race? Ha, ha. Change the heritage of the players and the scenario totally changes. Make Hill Black and Thomas White and the whole thing never comes up. There is no investigation. She can't even get a case, because White men have always been able to go to the quarters to touch Black women at their leisure. The senators would have brushed it off their shoulders like dandruff. Make Anita Hill White and Judge Thomas Black and he is not confirmed by a two-to-one margin among these senators, who wonder how a Black man could have the audacity to say such things to a White woman. Black men have been killed for saying less than "Hi, dear" to White women. Why, Thomas had better not say anything to his own wife in the future. Make Anita Hill and Judge Thomas both White and the whole matter might have been pursued, but in closed session, if it had gotten that far, which I doubt.

Senator Arlen Specter accused Anita of perjury.

Senator Orrin Hatch accused Anita of lifting her tale from *The Exorcist* and from various court cases. Later on, this precise man accidentally called her "an alligator."

Strom Thurmond mumbled something no one understood.

All the Republican senators on the Judiciary Committee took gleeful note that Anita had followed Clarence from job to job with nary a whimper. He had helped her get jobs teaching at Oral Roberts University and Oklahoma University, and besides, wasn't it now ten years after the fact, and wasn't the statute of limitations involved here? What took her so long? Why, Clarence had been confirmed by the Senate four times already for various other positions. Where was she and her preposterous story then?

The same group of ninety-eight White men who had insisted Anita come forward were now pillorying her, positioning her as a woman scorned. She had left messages for Judge Thomas in the years in between, from eleven to twenty phone messages, said the Republican senators, some of them including the precise hotel room number where she was staying. Her last message was congratulations on your marriage— implying that you can't write down sarcasm, showing how little they know about writing. All these men who knew they had done many things more repugnant than what Judge Thomas was supposed to have done scoffed at Professor Hill. They also knew that an Angela Wright, another former coworker, had made some of the same accusations against Judge Thomas. It was the most two-faced proceeding since Judas at the Last Supper. "What kind of woman is this?" the senators asked. And what manner of men?

I was in California, trying to escape the Black Caucus and the Senate peep show. I couldn't get away, as usual. I can never get away. So I live with it. In the *Los Angeles Times*, Sam Fulwood III wrote: "Just as African-Americans failed to find common political ground when Thomas was nominated, many are torn by the new focus on the sexual harassment charge. But aside from the conflicts, there are issues of common concern. . . . Hill's charges will affect relationships between black men and black women and . . . will give new life to old stereotypes about black sexuality."

He was correct in gauging the reaction, although I knew the old myths about Black sexuality didn't need new life. They were constantly fed by the media and had never, ever stopped growing until they burst from their sheaths in many minds. Not four years before, a fifteen-year-old named Michael Donald had been killed and hung from a tree in Mobile, Alabama, merely for walking on the sidewalk with a White girl his own age. Many similar cases occurred from Mississippi to Maryland to Massachusetts. Jurisprudence had its day in the Michael Donald case however, and a conviction was won for this wrongful death in the same Mobile, Alabama. Such were the powers offered Judge Thomas.

Back in L.A. I stopped to talk for a while with L. P., a White woman who, despite her intelligence, works in TV and film (similarities between cinema and politics, Hollywood-Burbank and Washington, D.C., are so many and varied it is barely necessary to mention it). L. P. was adamant, had no doubt at all that this was sexual harassment because she had experienced it to the point of distraction, and she was sure most women had experienced the very same thing. I told her I believed this was very true—the last part at least. And I couldn't know it the way she knew because I'm not a woman, but I had the similar experience of racial harassment. I've also experienced sexual harassment, though I didn't tell her this. Some women can be excellent sexual harassers—the theory being that those who have been oppressed can oppress, depending on the power they wield and their state of mind. There was no point saying I had once or twice been harassed, because whatever harassment I'd experienced I'd gotten away from easily. I told her I didn't believe it was cut-and-dried in this case, however horrible that made me seem. She allowed as how I had a right to my own opinion but held firm that the issue was bigger than the specifics of this particular case, although the case was grim enough. She asked: "When is it a woman's time?" I pointed out that because of this the workplace might never be the same, but at the same time I wouldn't hold my breath. If it was like racism, it was not something one hearing would abolish. Men weren't likely to change that fast. But women were 53 percent of the population, weren't they? It shouldn't be too hard to figure out. The best revenge would be seats on the floor of the Senate.

I began to get uneasy, though. So I called M. J., who has worked with me for years in spite of people telling her nothing would ever come of this dubious association. She's a marketing specialist, a Black woman. We'd had a vigorous debate over the Judge Thomas issue long before Anita came up, and M. J. had offered by far the best argument against him in purely political terms. It was as simple as *Roe* and affirmative action, and how could a man like Thomas be dumb enough to be against either one of them? Where did he learn that, Yale? He should know poor women could not afford safe abortion should it be made illegal. He should have known he would never have been invited to Yale or into the Republican Party, for that matter, if it hadn't been for affirmative action. Corporations had an economic stake in the diversity of their staffs, M. J. said. Because if you don't hire me, then I don't do business with you. Affirmative action therefore was an economic fact of survival.

Besides that, she said, White men had gone creative-soft, having been given most everything they had. Productivity had been declining precipitously among American businesses because of this: there was no doubt who the managers had been. To make matters worse, White managers then stole everybody blind with things like the S&L scandal, the B.C.C.I. scandal, and the junk bond insider-trading scandal. We the taxpaying people had been bilked out of billions of dollars, most of which were in Swiss, Argentinian, Japanese, and South African banks by now, depending on which of them could keep the best secret. M. J.'s argument was quite sound indeed—sort of a welfare argument in reverse. The David Dukes of America had better hope they never run into her.

My weak countering argument to her had been that Judge Thomas had long ago put his finger to the breeze and had done what was politically expedient. Once he was confirmed he could shed the false garment of denial and see things logically. M. J. didn't see it quite that way. We had done business with many Black people who never seemed to trust us even though we almost never failed to make them money. We had long ago discussed the intransigence of this patented self-hatred among Black people, admitted it, and gone on.

Now I called on her again, very tentatively this time. Over the years, M. J. and I have openly, laughingly discussed many behaviors involving human relationships, including sex. Yet now, I didn't know how she'd feel about this issue. I asked her if it would be better to fax her from now on.

She laughed. "They're both holding back," she said. "And you don't do that to a Black man who has helped you."

J. S. called me next. She is a Black feminist so sharp she can skin the average man without him knowing he was cut. "What she should have done was tell him they wanted her to testify, and she wouldn't—as long as he eventually helped get her a judgeship on the Circuit Court of Appeals," said J. S. "This isn't a case of a woman scorned. A woman thwarted. She was on his coattails. Sure, it was harassment, and that kind of harassment goes on every day. Men do it."

Some women, too, I thought, but I didn't say it because I didn't want to sound like a White person saying, "But Black people can be racist, too." What I had gotten from women had not been sexual harassment; rather it had been sexual invitation, sexual teasing, or sexual banter. They didn't have the power to harass me unless they had the power to force themselves on me in some unpleasant way.

"The feminists will line up like ducks. In the end they want their own power," J. S. said.

I had to agree, although my plan, had I been Anita, would have been different. I could have understood, even if we'd had a past, teaching Clarence a lesson, but I wouldn't have done it over the microphone in the Senate. I would have told them it was all in the record, and if they wanted to say it over national television they could, but I wasn't going to do it. Bad enough I had to tell in the first place. It's not the kind of conversation you want to repeat in front of company. Anita knows she was raised better.

J. S. told me about her friend, a ten-year former cop in the New York City Police Department, who took disability in part because the harassment was so severe. This woman didn't believe Hill either, because harassment was debilitating, as she saw it. I told J. S. that this issue would galvanize women, but there were only two of them among the hundred in the Senate. At that, they were doing better than Black people.

The Black women I knew—not all of them, but the ones I did business with occasionally—almost unanimously held their tongues on this one, and anyone who knows these women knows they don't hold their tongues unless they want to.

"They were both set up," J. S. said.

"They were used," M. J. said.

"When is it a woman's time?" asked L. P.

I was back in Washington by the time the senators voted 52-48 to confirm Judge Clarence Thomas to the Supreme Court. That's far closer than any vote ever on a potential Supreme Court Justice. The die was cast on smoke, mirrors, and hope. It had been a good debate. Some people said Judge Thomas could not have gone through what he went through during these hearings and not be a changed man once he sat on the Court.

I knew that if the preceding forty-three years hadn't done the trick, the last ten days wouldn't. All along I'd hoped that he would change because he would have the power to change. How could he be so slyly sexually adventuresome and then be against abortion? Would you like every woman who responds favorably to a joke about pubic hair on a can of cola to have your baby? That would be the height of hypocrisy.

On November 1, 1991, Clarence Thomas was confirmed as the junior and youngest Justice on the U. S. Supreme Court. No cameras were allowed into the swearing-in, which seemed odd to me under the circumstances. That very weekend, Professor Hill was given the Ida B. Wells Award by the National Coalition of Black Women. Ida Wells was a journalist, the recorder of lynchings. I could sympathize with Anita Hill. I could understand. Perhaps what she had gone through might begin to galvanize women politically. But what I could not do in any sense was find a link between Anita F. Hill and Ida B. Wells, other than the fact that they were both Black women.

I spoke to G. K., who is a White female editor at a house with the nerve to have published one of my books. "So it's everybody for himself?" she asked.

I told her I hoped not. Justice Thomas could not be so forgetful, so stupidly arrogant as to help overturn *Roe* v. *Wade*. And if he did (as he would in the summer of 1992), even as a Catholic on a religious argument (his likely cop-out), then I hoped both Clarence and I would be struck dead on the spot, him for losing his soul so easily and me for daring to hope that he would not. G. K. said, "No, better still, just impeach him." Best piece of editing I've ever had, if you don't mind my saying so.

Justice Thomas then began to vote as though he would enjoy being impeached. But a Black woman named Carol Moseley Braun was running for U.S. Senator by then, against Republican Richard S. Williamson. She'd already upset Senator Alan Dixon, one of Anita Hill's old tormentors, in the Illinois Democratic primary in March of 1992. Carol Moseley Braun was elected as the first Black woman United States senator in history on November 3, 1992. She was joined by three White females on the Senate floor—two from California, the Honorable Dianne Feinstein and the Honorable Barbara Boxer, and one from Washington state, the Honorable

Patty Murray. Some measure of responsibility, however small and unintended, for their newfound power and position must be given to, yes, Justice Thomas. As the old folks say, the Lord works in mysterious ways. The day could come when there are fifty-three women on the floor of the Senate. Men must welcome this time and dare to hope that women will not use power to do to us what was once done to them.

Some of My
Best Friends

The best writers I know of are dead, which may prove it pays not to become too good at this most peculiar art.

For me the best writers are, in no particular order, DuBois, Dickens, Twain, Wright, Dumas, Baldwin in essay form, Fanon in polemic, and Hurston when she was feeling good about herself. There are any number of others I won't bore you with here. I'm not sure they're the best in an objective sense or if they got the best posthumous distribution. I should say they are my favorites among those I have had the opportunity to read. Even then, most of the best stories I have ever read were composed by none of them.

Just as I know my favorites, I am aware there are many living people who write well, and better; they write about things worth reading. Writing well is one thing, inspiration another, being widely read yet another. At times the whole enterprise seems to resemble nothing so much as a back alley crap shoot among a bunch of drunks under dim light.

Suffice it to say there are many good writers alive today (although honestly they are outnumbered by more than a thousand to one by those who are not good writers and maybe don't know it yet: They suspect, but don't know). There may even be a great ten thousand writers still alive, who knows? This period may be considered a Renaissance one day. It's not for us to say; our great-great-grandchildren will decide.

If I were merely throwing out names of living writers I could say Peter Taylor, Ishmael Reed, Octavia Butler, John Updike, Jamaica Kincaid, Norman Mailer, Wole Soyinka, Gabriel Garcia Marquez, Charles Johnson, Gunter Grass, Anne Tyler, Naguib Mahfouz, Susan Sontag, Gore Vidal, William Least-Heat Moon, Anne Rice, John Wideman, P. D. James, Don DeLillo, Lorene Cary, Walter Moseley, Albert Murray, Darryl Pinckney, Samuel Delaney, and bell hooks. There are several thousand or so of them in the heavyweight classes, and more than that in their own lighter classes.

It would be nice to eventually join one of the lighter classes, especially posthumously. I respect the dead writers much more than the living. Living writers do not intimidate me. But I know I could not be a liver spot on DuBois's aged hand: I couldn't be a piece of lint on T. S. Eliot's least-favorite sweater. But I am among the living, and the next line I write might be the one to inform me that I am a writer.

I've never had any hope of becoming a writer on my own. I've needed help from my friends to even gather enough fortitude to make the broad attempt. In writing, as in other battles, one needs friends, because a good measure of writing is commiserating about what went wrong with those who can relate and sympathize and help you out.

You're a writer? Then you do have my sympathies.

"Oh, I'm a writer too!" a woman once said to me after dragging from me the fact that I got by as a writer. Her voice was so joyous, so sure. I told her I doubted she was a writer because she was a little too happy about it. Don't misunderstand. I wasn't being cruel. I was trying to help.

Getting to be a writer is hard work, and that's putting it mildly. It wears you out, to say nothing of those around you. At first it seems as if it will all be very pleasant. There is a glimmering in you, a way of seeing things, the ability to turn a phrase in a pleasing or illuminating way, and that rush after someone says he or she was amused by what you have written. Then comes the intoxicating dream of turning these attributes and compliments into clear sustained writing, much I suppose as an alchemist wishes to put a lump of lead into a box, mutter an incantation, and remove gold. Most writers begin self-assuredly, then develop increasing doubt and finally even paranoia after they've made enough pathetic attempts.

Luckily, the first requirements usually appear when you are young, full of pep, zip, and naiveté. For if you knew what was in front of you after that, you'd likely go lie down on some railroad tracks and be done with it.

Starting out with a glimmering is like an apprentice plumber who has a solid 3/4-inch open-end wrench and good intentions of letting the water flow freely at his command—toward his purposes. But he has nothing else in his toolbox. He can fix a leak here or there—write a good letter, or couplets, or a story not unreadable. There are only three categories of writing: the Beautiful, the Readable, and the Unreadable. The vast majority of all writing that is ever done falls in the latter two categories. Soon the initiate finds there's more to this plumbing than one tool and good intentions. The rest is experience, rote, trial and error, one step forward, two back, two forward, one to the side. It becomes a circuitous hunt for the seamless transition, the right word, the ability to re-create what is complex and do it simply. Writing becomes a realization that water is perhaps the most difficult element to control in volume.

Writing is also like building a house. A clapboard shotgun A-frame is not the same as a brick outhouse is not the same as a granite pyramid is not the same as a marble temple is not the same as a stone cathedral. But they are all built from the ground up, and one bad angle, one weak joint, one wrong compound meant to bind even the finest materials and greatest lines and highest intentions causes the whole structure to crumble—no matter how honestly planned—under the weight of a single pair of eyes.

For me the perfect analogy for writing is hitting a baseball. If you're patient enough to get your pitch, and you know what to do with that pitch, and you don't try and hit it too hard, and you swing level, you have a chance of hitting the ball as well as it can be hit by you. Even a person who is not a home-run hitter might be able to hit the occasional home run and feel even better about it than the home-run hitter. The home-run hitter is expected to hit home runs all the time, and sometimes the pitcher won't allow it. As a hitter you have to pick your spots. You have to wait for your pitch and then turn on it and hit it straight into the bleachers and trot around the bases like it's no big deal.

Writing and waiting can take up a lot of your time. It can break your will because there's always that little dark corner in the head of a writer, or would-be writer, where is hidden the fact that even good writers can write bad books, or weak books, or books that don't come off. Even with a full toolbox, one must have a job to do, something to say that has meaning, a design, however modest or grand. And just because you're dedicated to writing and put in the time with it doesn't mean you'll be able to implement your design, achieve your design, as well as you might like.

A friend taught me this. I admit I was skeptical of him at first, but I eventually found what he said is true.

• • •

I often give White people a hard time in print—quite deservedly so, as the more honest of them will admit. Yet some of them are among my best friends because they helped me to be a writer. The help often came disguised as cruelty.

First I must tip my cap to all those White people along the rock-strewn way who have insisted to me that I could not write. I can only assume they divined my personality and knew that anytime you want me to do something, insist to me that I cannot do it, tell me it's beyond my ken, scoff at my efforts to pull it off. That's the best way to make me more committed to it. So to these many men and women I offer thanks.

I must also thank Paul Horgan, even though I never knew the man. He may be dead. He could certainly use rest of some kind. If he is alive, he's been writing steadily for more than seventy years. Try writing anything for just a couple of days and perhaps you'll begin to get an inkling of the magnitude and feel of this work ethic. The first piece of his I learned of was called "Last of June Brides Makes Exit in the Heat." It was first published in the *Albuquerque Morning Journal*, in 1922, while he was temporarily the society page editor. The last piece of his I read was contained in a book entitled *Approaches to Writing*, published in 1973. In between—well, if you're an aspiring writer I do not want to depress you. Suffice it to say that for fifty years he wrote constantly, and he was good, and last but not always least he was White, so he was published almost as often as he wrote.

My mother gave me *Approaches to Writing* in the far-back autumn of 1975, while I was a copyboy at a small newspaper in California. Inside, she inscribed this note: "To get another view, not to be chewed and digested." Naturally I chewed and digested it. My mother knows me well.

The first item from the book I remember was a story Horgan related about Charles Dickens. He quoted Dickens answering a lady who was hitting on him (Horgan called her "importunate"):

> "I hold my inventive capacity on the stern condition that it master my whole life, often have complete possession of me, make its own demands upon me, and sometimes, for months together, put everything else away from me. . . . All this I can hardly expect you to understand—or the restlessness and the waywardness of an author's mind. . . . It is impossible to command one's self to any stipulated and set disposal of five minutes. . . . The mere consciousness of an engagement will sometimes worry a whole day. These are the penalties paid for writing books. Whoever is devoted to an art must be content to deliver himself wholly up to it. I am grieved if you suspect me of not wanting to see you, but I can't help it; I must go my way whether or no."

Now, a normal person would just have said, "No thank you," and let it go at that. So you can see what loony-bin writers must skirt by comparison, not to mention the rigors that the people who hit on them must suffer.

Horgan then related another story. I must pause here before I continue all this horrendous name-dropping of people I don't even know and explain something: Name-dropping (and, worse, word-dropping) is not good writing. There is a school of immature writers who think juxtaposing words and phrases like *agitprop*, *bollix*, *demimonde*, *deus ex machina*, or *roman à clef* next to names like Dos Passos, Steinbeck, Flaubert, Camus, Sartre, Proust, Spike Lee, Bergman, Kurosawa, or Madonna constitutes an acceptable form of writing. It most certainly does not. Some sense must still be made.

Horgan told another story about French novelist Gustave Flaubert writing a letter to his friend, the writer George Sand—who was really a woman named Amandine-Aurore-Lucile Dupin Dudevant, to show you how much typical sense writers make of themselves occasionally: "Dear George," said

Flaubert, speaking to the woman. "You don't know what it is to stay a whole day with your head in your hands trying to squeeze your unfortunate brain so as to find a word. Ideas come very easily to you, incessantly, like a stream. With me it is a tiny thread of water. Hard labor at art is necessary for me before obtaining a waterfall. Ah! I certainly know the agonies of style."

Now there is good sense being made, and not an *agitprop* can be found anywhere.

During my earlier years of forced labor as a newspaper copyboy, I noted a number of Horgan sayings that were equally educational to me, such as:

"Creative writing, the essential act of literary art, cannot be taught entire. You cannot teach anyone to be an artist. He either is or is not an artist by nature and endowment. You cannot insert talent into anyone else." And: "Becoming a writer is mostly a matter of continuous work to be done alone."

And: "The key to readability is rhythm."

And: "The artist should look for form in everything—nature's forms, those of all the arts, those of the performing athlete, in which energy precisely meets need."

And: "Everything has been said; but not everything has been said superbly, and even if it had been, everything must be said freshly over and over again."

And: "The ear must always be satisfied by what the pen has silently written. Always read aloud. The ear will often correct what the eye misses."

And: "A writer may be as arrogant as you please in his personal life, but if he is not humble in respect to his work, all is lost. A true writer is as humble under his successes as under his failures."

And: "A writer who loves his art more than his own work

as part of it will never begrudge a fellow writer the praise due him."

And: "The artist's *real* hardship: daily communication with others, in *their* terms."

And finally: "We need a word somewhere between *talent* and *genius*."

By this point I'd figured the word was not *copyboy*. So I worked my way up to cityside reporter at the newspaper and struggled for a while at that, writing in a tight, furious, ragged, and imperfect circle. One day a man named Jim (not his real name), the sports editor, pulled me aside and gave me the first in a long line of good assignments. Jim is a White man. Not that he ever pointed that out to me in any context at all; he was just Jim, a man with a voice as deep as a bear's grunt, who moved like a boxer, an ex-dancer, lightly, weight on his toes, and who smoked and laughed huskily through the rings. Jim had a temper, and he wasn't that good a writer himself. But he was fair. He could recognize good writing and talked to you as though you were merely the next person and not Little Black Sambo trying to make tiger pancakes. As sports editor, Jim had replaced another White man named Gene, whose voice was even deeper than Jim's, deeper than a tugboat horn hidden in the morning mist of San Francisco Bay. Gene loved to watch Willie Mays play baseball. Before Gene retired and left for the hills, or in this case the Sierra Nevada, he gave me a copy of the *Atlantic Monthly* magazine that contained a well-crafted short story entitled "Hoop." Gene looked at me, then said emphatically, "You can do this."

So I must doff my hat to both Gene and Jim. But I must doff it again for another White man named Frank, who was the Sunday features editor at the same small newspaper. He had a mustache like a manatee's and looked very askance at the changes in the world which tried and crowded his niche. He once told me a story about a close relative of his who had ordered a vasectomy done on himself because he'd found out that one of his ancestors had some measure of discernible African blood. He didn't want to pass the stain along to his potential heirs, Frank told me while smiling smugly. I smiled back at him and said, "Good." I believe that threw him off, so he went on to a different inspirational tack.

I had begun to compose a story about a major league baseball player with the San Francisco Giants named Larry Herndon, who had grown up on the other side of my home town. We used computers even back then, so I had stored this story in the "advance" file of the system, with no by-line because it was incomplete and no would-be writer dares sign his unfinished work. Frank was always searching for stories to fill his Sunday "bulldog" edition, the edition of the Sunday newspaper you get on Saturday if you are unlucky. In his desperation for stories that would be deleted eventually once the real Saturday news came in, he pulled up my piece without by-line from the computer system. He decided against using it because the daily features people would probably want a good feature with a local angle like that. Later, after the finished story ran as a weekday feature under my by-line, Frank took me aside and assumed a paternal tone. "Lookit, fella," he said, his arm around my shoulder. "I saw that piece a week ago in the advance file in the computer system. I know what you did. And I can understand. Writing is tough. But some sharp-eyed editor from the syndicate will see it, and then you'll get into trouble."

It dawned on me what he meant. "You're saying what? That I stole that story, plagiarized it?" This was utterly ridiculous because of the personal nature of that particular piece. Slowly, I felt myself turn angry. I told him, "I don't have to do that." Then I stormed away, shocking the slot man of the news copy desk, a nice White man named John, by saying,

"That idiot accused me of plagiarism!" Later on Frank complimented me on pieces I'd written. For all I know he may otherwise have been a decent sort of man. Frankly, I don't lose sleep over it. I know how he helped me.

Before we get off plagiarism, let me say this: Mark Twain once had to write a letter to Oliver Wendell Holmes in apology for having unconsciously lifted a long foreword from something Holmes had written. Holmes brushed the incident off because he believed that all writers are the sum of all they've done or seen or been or read, and there are times when strange things happen.

I've been appropriated many times, and said not a word about it. In a way, it's a compliment. You wish people would give you credit for saying it first, but as a writer, how do you know where your effort came from in your own head? I value that experience with Frank in that I do not let that fact of assimilation allow me to be lazy and take the easy way out and transpose other people's thoughts on purpose. I also thought the charge against Rev. Martin Luther King by scholars at Boston University that he had plagiarized in his doctoral dissertation was strange, because academic writing is pure plagiarism. So much plagiarism goes on in academia they need appendices to record the bibliographies. And that's in each and every book. Apparently they feel if you can't look it up somewhere, why bother writing it down?

After a few years at the newspaper I was offered a chance to try my luck at magazine writing, and again I must thank a White man named Ned, an excellent writer who chose to specialize in sportswriting. He was engaging, told a good story, loved his job, and gave me a recommendation to work at a popular magazine in New York. I shall not name this magazine because I'm in enough trouble in publishing as it is. Ned's other recommendation was even better. He said there was a young writer there I should meet named Carl. Ned said Carl was pleasant company, my age perhaps, a White man, Italian and Scot, something like that, who knows? Soon after, I met him in Washington, D.C. We were there for an event. I had leased a new car, a small BMW. I picked up Carl at a hotel, along with a couple of other employees from the magazine. I don't know what came over him, but as we were driving across the 14th Street bridge at night, he looked up at the Washington Monument, with its two tiny blinking red lights high up on its face to warn away aircraft. Carl said, "Haw, it looks like the Grand Wizard of the Ku Klux Klan." Not knowing what else to do until I could get rid of Carl, I looked over and said, "It looks like an obelisk to me."

Upon my arrival in New York, I met more friends who would help me write—as soon as I learned how to read them. In the ensuing years, I knew I was doing well when I would come in and none of my colleagues, my writing peers, would speak to me. I knew I was doing poorly when they would welcome me in the halls with slaps on the back and other hail-fellow-well-met gestures. It took a little time to figure this out. And it took a little time to adjust my writing to these new demands as well. At magazines, the editors take their titles quite seriously. They decide to become Editors, whether they have the eye and taste for it or not. This is one of the hazards of becoming a writer. You have no choice about who is going to ride you in the race.

One editor named Geoff sat and talked about one of my early stories. I think he was a pretty decent man, a fairly good editor. Finally, he said, "Wiley, whatever you do, you can't baffle your editors." Now that was worth remembering, and it was kind of funny, so I laughed and thanked him. But I also told him, "I hear what you're saying, Geoff, but many of those lines I wrote would've knocked you off the couch laughing if you had thought James Thurber had written them." The actual editing at the magazine was fifty-fifty. Often I was helped. Just as often I was hindered, the rhythm destroyed, the key to the readability of what I was writing lost.

Another editor, named Stanley, later told me, "In five years, you'll be more clear, a much sharper writer." Only being a Black man, I didn't know if I had the years to spare. There was another writer at the magazine at this time, a White man. I'll call him So-and-So. A few years before, when I was working at the newspaper, I had gone to Pittsburgh on a job. There'd been an elegant soiree, and I'd been invited. When I showed up, I was the only Black person there who didn't have on a red jacket and a tray of hors d'ouevres balanced on his fingertips.

After an hour or so I went to look out of a bank of gigantic windows. A White man came over and inquired the nature of my profession. I answered, "Writer." He paused, then stuck out his hand and said, "Hi, I'm So-and-So, from Such-and-Such magazine in New York." He meant to impress me. It was only after I'd come to New York to work at Such-and-Such magazine and met the real So-and-So that I found this man in Pittsburgh had lied to me for the fun of it because it would never come back to haunt him, or so he thought.

I almost didn't make it past the first year at the magazine and undoubtedly wouldn't have, had it not been for one of my best friends, a White man named Bob Creamer. I was having a difficult time of it. I've always been able to do a bit of good writing in spots, but early on at the magazine, it was coated in dross. The story was "in there, somewhere," as the editors liked to say. Eventually their disdain and my discomfiture with my inability to create what they wanted began to take its toll on me because I had to divine who was telling me the truth and who was telling me I was a nigger.

Things began to get out of hand in my mind, and my brow stayed furrowed. Each story seemed to be so important to me— so important, as it turns out, that I barely remember any of the early ones now. At one time they were so important.

One day something happened. A story of mine was changed

radically. Not edited radically. Changed. There was nothing to be done about it but brood, so this I did in my small office. My brooding became agitation, the agitation became rage, and I began to physically shake. I think I frightened an older, White editor, a precise man who was named, fittingly enough, Jeremiah. He moved like a tabby and was semiretired. He came by my office, looked in at me, shrank back somewhat—he was a genteel White man—and said, "Ralph, you can't let this happen." It was the best he could do for me, but small consolation. How could I *not* let it happen? I was at my wits' end that day. I walked down the long hall determined to do something. If I quit, that would be something. I still believed I could write, but I no longer believed I could write there.

At that moment a white-haired Visigoth emerged from a conference room, looked at me, and bared his huge teeth. This was the whitest White man I'd ever seen, none of this pink stuff, this olive tint, this bone coloring, I mean *white*, so white as to seem alien, not of any earth I knew.

"Gosh!" he said, eyes gleaming, as he pointed to a copy of another story I had feebly handed over to the editors. "This is one of the best examples of clear writing I've read around here in a long time!" There was nothing specious or sarcastic in his manner or I would have been pricked by it immediately. His voice seemed detached from its owner—it was vibrant, lively, quick, not particularly deep, and ending on an uptick, ready to spin a story at a moment's notice.

You must understand, it didn't matter to me whether or not what he said was the truth. It did not matter that he was White. It was that he offered an educated opinion that favored me. I was desperate for any life preserver. I was astounded it would come from this man who seemed to be a cross between Ichabod Crane, Rumpelstiltskin, and Marley's Ghost. His name was Robert W. Creamer. His friends called him Bob. He was a writer. Even though I was ignorant of this, of everything except my own mood, I think I recall mumbling a rare, low, indecipherable "Thank you."

Creamer was nearing his retirement from this magazine, but he still came in often, and I found myself gravitating toward his office just to chat. He always seemed pleased to see me, and we'd talk about things that had little to do with the job. He told me stories about growing up in New York state, just north of the city, in Tuckahoe. I thought I remembered him saying there had been but one Black student he could remember in high school, and that he'd never paid that much attention to him.

Actually, as he corrected me later, he remembered most all of his Black classmates and their stories. But it seemed as though I remembered him speaking once as if there were only the one Black student, the one he didn't get to know as he might have liked. The Black kid's name was Richard. Creamer described to me how he had looked, how he'd once been slightly plump, warm and jolly and intelligent when they went to Tuckahoe High. How he'd grown lean, untrusting, unsmiling, curt. How that bitterness may have been due to experiences as a Black serviceman in the World War II American army. Creamer remembered these things, and I wondered what makes up a bed of empathy in a human being.

Once Creamer left the magazine, he fell into the habit of writing letters to me on a semiannual basis, seeming to have just the feel for what a would-be writer might need at different stages. Just before he left, he offered me two observations. The first was verbal—and a rare chastisement of sorts. "I suppose you won't have the problems the rest of us have, word repetition in the texts you write, occasional problems with clarity, ennui," he said, his normally placid countenance hinting at the clear sternness in that quick, fascinating voice. Later, he sent me a note that said, "Just try to hit simple line drives up the middle, nice and clean and straight, and the home runs will start coming again." We had the habit of speaking about writing using moldy baseball metaphors, and he knew I wanted to consider myself a home-run hitter in that context. The thing of it was, he didn't discourage me. And he was a very good writer himself, very good indeed, so good I need not heap any more praise on him. There are very few writers as good in the way Creamer is good. His style is simple on its face, straightforward. He writes lucid, accessible prose, with conjecture, rejoinder, common sense, and insight. He was not given to ostentation or pronouncement. He writes as if he doesn't have to prove that he is a good writer, or that what he says is true. All he has to do is tell his story, and you make up your own mind.

I was somewhat taken aback that he'd used his skill mostly for writing about baseball. He seemed much too good to limit himself to merely that. But then I considered two things: first, what Paul Horgan had said about the artist studying all forms, including the athlete, who brings his energy to precisely meet need. Secondly, perhaps this was not limiting to Creamer at all, merely what he wished to do. He could not see history or reality from my eyes, and feel something missing from them, something close—in the end he was a White man in America, and the real urgency of having to prove not that you can write, but that you *exist*, and that you will fight for that existence, was mercifully absent from his life, so he could go on to do other things. For Creamer, simple baseball was good enough.

He has three books about baseball that are among the best ever written about that particular pastime. He also knew enough about jazz to write about that. The point is, I read him, and he was an extremely good writer by my eye. And this was what made his counsel so valuable to me.

A peer counseling and praising me would not have been the same, nor would an older person who was not a good writer by my own measure. What could they know of it that I could use? But Creamer became my friend because he was a good writer who took the time to recognize a younger man equipped with a wrench and good intentions. He took time even though he had nothing at all to gain from it other than knowing it was the thing to do. If it hadn't been for his honest counsel, I don't know if I would have stayed at the magazine as long as I did. And if I had left one millisecond before I did, I would've regretted doing so for many years. Creamer steered me straight, but only in the direction I really wanted to go, and that is what a true, honest friend tries to do for you, I think.

Creamer had a son named Bobby who worked at the magazine one summer after Creamer retired and near the end of what turned out to be my intemperate tenure there. Creamer had asked that I stop by and say hello to the young man, and I made a point of doing so—too great a point, I'm afraid. I located him and immediately began telling him that if it weren't for his father, I would never have made it at the magazine, how his father was a great man and a great writer. Immediately, from his reaction, I felt my error. A young man wants to be his own man, not merely a reflection of his father. It's hard enough just being a decent human being on your own without carrying around anybody else's work. I tried to defuse what I'd said by mentioning that magazine work was probably not what young Bobby wanted to do at all, which showed his greater good sense. I told him he should have fun that summer and then get on with whatever it was he wanted to do on his own. He smiled. I felt better.

So in the end I must give the higher thanks to Bob Creamer over Paul Horgan. Over the years, Creamer has written letters to me that have the feel of something more, something larger than a collection of random meanderings. Earlier I offered you sayings culled from Paul Horgan's lifetime of work, and they helped me understand this peculiar art better. But Creamer, in the course of a few letters merely tossed over his shoulder with his left hand, gave me more direct advice and knowledge and theory and the stuff of disagreements. And it

meant much more because it was specifically directed to me.
I felt I was his friend.

This is Creamer:

"As I no longer will ever go into a McDonald's (unless, like
Mark Twain's remark about Mrs. Thomas Bailey Aldrich, I
was on a raft at sea with no other provisions in sight), I swore
I would never go see a Spielberg movie again. Nonetheless, I
went to see *The Color Purple*, and flinched every time a line
of people was outlined against a sunset. . . . Yet I couldn't
help feeling, god, what a movie this could have been if someone like Luis Buñuel made it."

And: "There's an awful lot of bullshit written about the
glorious old days."

And: "A good editor is like a good jockey or a good caddy
or a good second; he (or she) can't run or golf or box—that's
you doing that, kid—but he or she can draw your attention
to the best part of the track or the right part of the fairway
or the way the opponent drops his shoulder."

And: "Never mind all that humble crap. You're right, a
good writer knows he can write, so why feel humble? Maybe,
though, it's something akin to not being conceited (which is
false self-praise). There is something I think of as the humility
of confidence; when you're sure of yourself you don't have to
run around making sure people are impressed."

And: "After all, you said a writer has to be arrogant. Maybe
it isn't so much arrogance as confidence—*you're* sure you're
doing the right thing, even if the critics miss the point and
people don't buy. And if someone writes an admiring letter
that praises you for things you were trying to do (and apparently succeeded in doing) you should nod your head and say,
'He is right. A perceptive man. I'm grateful to him for knowing. I thank him for telling me.' "

And: "Your beautiful new baby arrived at my house this

week, along with a nice note from the editor, Amy Hertz, and it looks great. God, you must feel good, perhaps a bit like your wife after parturition. Lots of work, lots of pain, lots of anguish, but what a lovely result."

And: "The bookstore manager seemed impressed that I had ten or twelve people buy books and ask for autographs in the hour I was there—'Usually it's only two or three,' he said, which I know is true, since I've done other signings where throngs of people managed to slip by without buying a damn thing."

And: "All great writers shift around, do different things. I'm not really an admirer of much of Updike's fiction but I am in awe of his production, his diversity, his accomplishment. James Joyce wrote poetry, a play, and in his early years—up to *Finnegans Wake*—wrote essays, commentaries, reviews. Twain wrote off in a thousand different directions. . . . The main thing is: You are a writer, and writers write, all the time, in any way they want. Nabokov was always writing something, shooting out a critical tirade, trying something different . . .

"When selling becomes more important than writing, *then* you're in trouble. You're the best judge of your writing. Oh sure, it's gratifying to have someone tell you what you know, but *you* have to do the writing, and you have to do it the way you want to do it. You have to get comfortable and let it rip."

And: "As I type this I think of my three-year-old granddaughter, who can move from a dead stop to full flight in, oh, maybe a tenth of a second, or effortlessly from doing absolutely nothing flick a hand out and pick up something she has no right picking up and which you would have told her not to pick up if the whole action wasn't done and completed before you (me) could blink."

And: "I knew you were a good writer, but good writers can write bad books, weak books, books that don't come off."

And: "I have written to order almost all my life. Only rarely have I written completely for myself. Some of that stuff stinks—it's precious, self-conscious, derivative—but some of it is the best stuff I've done. And I wish I had the economic and psychological independence to have written that way, or to have tried to write that way, all my life."

And: "Your letter cheered me tremendously. I always knew you had talent but I suppose I never really *knew* before that you were a writer. That should be capitalized. WRITER. I mean this in the sense that writing isn't something you are going to do some day when you have time; it's part of you now; it's part of your life. I find myself envying you that drive, that need, that almost compulsion to write all the time, every day, to put something down on paper or in the machine. To keep turning it out. I think of the way your talent keeps sharpening and growing, the urgency and the strength the writing develops. I think it's great. I'm in the stands, rooting, with the wonderful feeling that I don't have to worry about you getting down on yourself, quitting. Everything you write may not be as great as everything else you write. That doesn't matter a damn. The important thing is the writing, and you're doing it, and you'll never stop. You, sir, are a writer, and I bow in admiration."

A serious and honest man must be secure in himself to write such things to another man, and if you start throwing White and Black in there it really gets improbable. I hope to write such things myself some day. I won't be able to say that I didn't have help from any eerie-looking White men, however. I cannot be prepossessing enough to tell that lie, the way many White men have done concerning eerie-looking Black men in the past. When people call me prejudiced and say I only see life in race-colored glasses, when they say I'm too honest for White people, if not a bigot myself, I say, "Nonsense. Some of my best friends . . . are honest."

Strange Fruit

(John, Jodie, Jonathan, Jeffrey,
Jack, and Mike)

The United States of America is a place where the citizenry, both native and naturalized, learn to think and act as if they want nothing to do with me or my kind if they want to get ahead, even though Black people nurture them, empower them, profit them, turn over to them our best ideas, give them a stylish resiliency they seem to utterly lack otherwise. Yet we are said to have nothing to do with this. Occasionally there is an anodyne reference to some small contribution we must have accidentally made. For the most part we are blamed for slowing down the process, stealing it, or raping anyone near it. As a result many of us are tortured and exploited. This can be frustrating at the very least, and there are few ways to discuss it lightheartedly.

So it seems important to let all know who I am. I am a

card-carrying, classic, out-of-wedlock-born, diamond-balled Black bastard and occasional son of a bitch, figuratively speaking, who knows how to work on a nerve when he gets hold of one. My father had a plate in his head. He wasn't married to my mother when he impregnated her. She could've aborted me and would have had every right, except a legal one, to do so. She didn't. I went to "segregated" schools all my life, lived colorfully on a fault line in California, and worked mindlessly as an automaton in New York City. There is nothing in my past to offer much salvation except a bunch of strikes, four at least. Not only am I out, the person behind me has a strike on him too. When I was a boy, oblivious to my impending doom, my relatives took good care of me in hopes I might turn out. Only they gave me half a chance.

The United States of America isn't all bright smiles and bands and cheerleaders and feature films at matinee prices with 3-D glasses; it is not all Boy Scout troops, Girl Scout cookies, the *Reader's Digest*, white hats, blond heroes, and black villainy; it is not all nobility, gentility, and a willingness to help one's fellow man find the right way to the Greenwich Country Club. It is not as they say it would be for everyone if only my people would not cast a pall over all these wonderful proceedings. The idea behind America may be in the end its saving grace, if it is to be saved. It needs saving, for here is an underlying stain born of an assumed power. Men— all men, but specifically White men—grow up with an implicit belief that they are born to wield power over others weaker than they. And if these men find they have no power, then they must find the weakest of all and wield what they can. Monsters are thus created.

And who are these monsters? Well, first of all, I realize I will be castigated for even looking at this side of American life. Why am I not concentrating on inner-city crime, welfare cheats, soulless drive-by shooters, or touchy athletes beginning to sense their obsolescence? I will be told how angry I am, how my anger makes me unreasonable and paranoid and delusional. Just tend to yourself, people will say. I merely intend to give all their due, know what is possible. *Magna est veritas, et praevalebit*—truth is great and will prevail. So, who are these whispered monsters? Let us turn over Plymouth Rock and see if we can find out.

In our capital city, Washington, D.C., there is a neighborhood, an entire quadrant of this small Federal colony, called Southeast. It sits east by southeast of the brown Anacostia River and due east of the Potomac. It is populated by many peoples, especially Black people, a sizable percentage of whom lead bittersweet existences at best. Every day, through precious little fault of their own, they are cheek by jowl with poverty and crime and weakened but still effective and quite unavoidable illegal narcotics and their pitiless traffickers. Yet many of the people in Southeast live dignified lives in spite of this. It is human nature to overcome hardship. Southeast is a place, some say in speeches, where no human being should have to live in such conditions. But I have lived there and flourished.

In the middle of Southeast, off what is now called Martin Luther King Avenue, there is a large mental hospital called St. Elizabeth's. It is made of brick and set back into large, open grounds, surrounded by a twelve-foot black iron fence. I remember a summer when I was fourteen and relatively carefree. I was walking by St. Elizabeth's, on what was then called Nichols Avenue. I was on my roundabout way home from summer-school class at Ballou High, where I was attempting to get credit for accounting while studying it minimally; or perhaps I was on my roundabout way home from my summer job of buffing the floors and cleaning the latrines of that same high school. I do remember being carefree. In fact, I was whistling a rhythm-and-blues standard, "The Way You Do the Things You Do." Then I noticed a White man standing inside the iron bars of the fence. I could plainly see through the iron bars that he had exposed his genitals. I walked into the street, then to the other side, averting my eyes while he made pitiful noises. I quickened my pace and soon was home, where I was so safe I never had to consider safety. The man's behavior was beyond my experience. I never forgot it. A few weeks later, one of the men that I worked with in the custodian's department at Ballou, a mentally slow Black man of about thirty-five, asked me if I knew what a pervert was, and if I might be one. For the first time in my life I snarled at someone who was almost a perfect stranger. "Nooo!" I hurled at him, somehow knowing instinctively this word had to do with the man behind the bars. And it had to do with the man in front of me not behind bars. It had to do with something I hadn't been told by my family who gave me half a chance. Up until that time I'd no idea what a pervert was. I began to lose my innocence, but not so horribly as some have.

Today, in 1993, there is another White man, named John Hinckley, who is in residence at St. Elizabeth's Hospital in Southeast Washington. You may know Hinckley as the person who shot Ronald Reagan and James Brady in 1981. At the time, some people mentioned a parallel between Hinckley's actions and those of a movie character named Travis Bickle in the 1973 picture *Taxi Driver*, written by Paul Schrader, directed by Martin Scorsese. The Bickle character had wanted to assassinate a candidate for president but was soon seen in the media as a hero because he ended up, quite by accident, shooting some people who happened to be engaged in a ruinous prostitution business.

Also in this film was a child actress named Jodie Foster. She portrayed a twelve-year-old whore, and Hinckley, it's said, became obsessed with her. The assumption was that Hinckley was obsessed with Jodie Foster, and so still might be in 1993, many years after the picture was made. There are people in the media who never fail to bring up Hinckley's obsession whenever they talk about the adult Jodie Foster. I don't believe Hinckley was obsessed with Jodie Foster at all. He was obsessed by her depiction of a twelve-year-old prostitute. Once she became a strong woman he had no use for her as a fantasy. This, apparently, was his ultimate fantasy—an underage sexual receptacle that he could have for the taking of its innocent weakness. Something he could be a god to, and use, and command, because he was a usurper. Of course, no life is actually like that, not even for American White men, so when this fantasy is brought up short by the real world, this would-be powermonger takes what he has the power to take—vulnerable women and innocent children. Once that is done, this vicious and horrifying life cycle is set. And repeats.

Jonathan Demme is a movie director, White, which leaves a lot of room for other traits. I have not met him, but I've been intrigued by some of his work, especially two of his films I have seen, *Something Wild* and *The Silence of the Lambs*. Film directors are attempting to re-create reality in their own fashions—as Picasso once said, "art is the lie that tells the truth." Usually, their efforts do not fully succeed. Their films do not ring true. Many directors do not always enhance the genuine suspension of disbelief they seek. But Demme knows how to stage things so they look natural, realistic. This is a complex technique to master, this creation of reality. Harder still is to reflect, within this re-creation, the hidden realities, the universal themes.

I like the way Demme thinks, as he exhibits it on the screen, and I'm usually hard on White people in this light, harder than I am on Black people. When it comes to making images, White people have to be twice as good to go half as far in my mind. This is because the images they have created have been dangerous to me and the collective image of my people. White people made *Birth of a Nation*, their seminal example of picture making, proposing a collective instrinsic criminality of Black men (which does not exist) when it is they, collectively, who committed the crime. And so, whenever their collective guilt surfaces, it seems to manifest itself as further punishment against us.

Most big-box-office jawbreaker movies and the men who make them are toeing the bottom line. Not Demme or Scorsese. Their exposition of these hidden realities has been thorough, keen, acute, and unblinking. They constantly show us to ourselves naked, and we wish to be clothed.

Something Wild was written by E. Max Frye. It is a picture about a man in New York City who is observed stiffing a small lunch check by a woman with a few quirks of her own. The story is about indulgence having its ultimate price. It was the mounting of the story that I found to be so striking and impressive, and that was mostly because of the way the Black people made their appearances in the background. As I have said, Demme is a White man, so it logically follows that most often his main characters (in this case Melanie Griffith, Jeff Daniels, and Ray Liotta) are White. There has never been anything wrong with that. But usually when Black people show up in films where White people are the protagonists, Black viewers see right away that these makeshift Black people are out of context, not in focus, false and bizarre and not like any real people that they know. And if Black people do not see this, they slowly become whatever it is they are watching. You can see and understand the relative importance of a Jonathan Demme, who keeps introducing these tangential Black characters in the most believable places, doing and saying the most believable things, living life as we might see it lived in reality.

Some years after making *Something Wild* Demme came upon material based on Thomas Harris's book *The Silence of* the *Lambs*, about two serial murderers, one of whom, Hannibal Lecter, a brilliant psychiatrist, is a cannibal. The book was turned into a screenplay by Ted Tally. Then Demme made this utterly believable picture about something so bad it cannot be discussed. Not just child abuse, but the full life cycle of the horror.

This tale was well told and simply drawn. As far as I can see, there might have been only one discernible flaw in it. The title refers to something experienced by the heroine, Clarice M. Starling, who is an FBI trainee, and her motivation for obsessively seeking a serial killer. As a child, she had run away after she'd heard and seen lambs slaughtered when she was living with her late mother's cousin, and her cousin's husband, on a Montana sheep ranch. So she feels obligated to try and save the female victims of a serial killer called Buffalo Bill, so named because he skins his female victims, as it turns out, to make himself "a woman suit." Bill was an abused child.

LECTER: *"Our Billy wasn't born a criminal, Clarice, he was made one through years of systematic abuse. Billy hates his own identity and he thinks that makes him a transsexual, but his pathology is a thousand times more savage."*

The narrative would have been made even more believable if the heroine had been abused by the husband of her late mother's cousin—and had then seen the slaughtering of the lambs. That is nit-picking, perhaps.

LECTER: *Did the rancher make you perform fellatio? Did he sodomize you?*
STARLING: *No. He was a very decent man.*

Starling was portrayed by Jodie Foster, who apparently knows how to pick 'em when it comes to her movie roles. This was perfect counterpoint to her original portrayal of the exploited innocent in *Taxi Driver*. Now Foster would herself hunt down the exploiter of innocence in *The Silence of the Lambs*. The film won awards and, even more impossibly, actually deserved them. And once again I noticed Demme's subtle knack of adding these believably well-placed Black peripheral characters to his backgrounds. For the second time—the first was in *Something Wild*—I noticed a small photo of Martin Luther King, Jr., on the walls of places where Black people worked and White protagonists did business.

Some people said they couldn't stand to watch this kind of picture or understand what was good about it. Such atrocities were not to be realistically admitted, much less understood. Better to have made a lighthearted musical set in Paris or, better, on a sound stage constructed to look like a café in Paris. The actress Bette Midler, speaking specifically of Scorsese's work, told writer Rita Kempley of the *Washington Post*: "So who wants to go to the movies to watch that? I want to go and see some sequins!" To some, even some artists, art becomes a lie that hides the truth.

A few months after the box-office success of *The Silence of the Lambs* in the spring of 1991, a Black woman named Glenda Cleveland called the Milwaukee Police Dept. and spent long, agonizing minutes trying to convince the police dispatcher to call for a unit to investigate what she was certain were wrongdoings at 924 North 25th Street, in number 213 of the modest Oxford Apartments. "There's this young man, buck naked, he's been beaten up, he's really hurt!"

Hours later, three of Milwaukee's Finest delivered an unlucky, fourteen-year-old son of Laotian immigrants named Konerak Sinthasomphone back to the man in apartment 213, and they did it with smiles, in all likelihood. Perhaps one of them even winked. The boy was bleeding from wounds in his hand and lower torso. He was also naked and crying, talking as if drugged, in a foreign tongue. And the police made sure he went back to blond, blue-eyed, ruggedly handsome Jeffrey Dahmer, where the young boy would be safe.

The officers didn't even run Dahmer's name through a criminal records check. Imagine, if you are a Black man, being stopped for a minor or a phantom traffic violation and not having your name run through a criminal records check, at the very minimum. Inconceivable, is it not? Imagine how many times police cars have followed you and not stopped you, staying in your rear-view mirror while they ran their check on your license plates. Had the three officers done any of this, they would have seen Dahmer was on probation for a 1989 sexual assault conviction in Milwaukee. The victim in that case was Konerak Sinthasomphone's brother.

Soon, a distraught Glenda Cleveland called the police again. As a dispatcher told her everything was all right and the situation had been checked out, this Black woman kept asking, "Are you sure? But, are you *sure*?"

Some days later, a young man named Tracy Edwards managed to escape Jeffrey Dahmer's room of horrors. After this young Black man breathlessly reeled off his story a few times, the police decided to maybe look into it—"it" being apartment 213. There had been complaints from other tenants before about the smell emanating from this apartment. These other tenants were Black, too. Dahmer had explained it was just rotting meat in a broken freezer. Milwaukee is one of the most segregated cities in America. No doubt believing Black people were for the most part malodorous anyway, the police felt, "What could they know about it?" Maybe those Black people complaining about the smell emanating from a White man's apartment were smelling the tops of their lips. Oh yes. Black people have a hard way to go in Milwaukee. Black people are but 5 percent of Wisconsin's population, yet were 55 percent of the murder victims between 1984 and 1990. White unemployment was 3 percent. Black unemployment was 20 percent. Apparently conditions were so commonly bad, so much a part of the accepted fabric, that a White man, even a Jeffrey Dahmer, could come among Black people and commit the worst acts and not be noticed because no one notices what happens among Black people. It doesn't matter. It is said to affect no one but them.

His Black neighbors complained about the power saw Dahmer would run into the wee hours of the morning. One man, next-door neighbor Vernell Bass, asked his wife, "What's he building in there?" Dahmer was already on probation, but his probation officer had stopped visiting his apartment because the officer's caseload was too heavy. Imagine, if you are Black, a probation officer cutting you such a break. The Milwaukee Police, no threat to the reputations of Interpol or Scotland Yard, finally groped their way to his apartment, where to even their horror they found seven human skulls, four heads (three of them in a freezer), a blue fifty-seven-gallon drum of acid with human remains, including those of Konerak Sinthasomphone, and more than one hundred grisly photographs of Mr. Dahmer's other dates (see Hannibal Lecter's appraisal of Buffalo Bill). Dahmer soon confessed to killing seventeen potential lovers and dinner guests. He drugged them with Halcion, killed them, then dismembered them. He was born in Medina, Ohio, and had taken his first victim near there. He took a few more at his grandmother's house near Milwaukee. That he had been abused as a child seemed to go without saying.

In the film, Clarice Starling mentions to Jack Crawford, her boss at the FBI, that serial murderers tend to kill within their own ethnic groups. Dahmer had broken the pattern. Twelve of his murder victims had been African-Americans. Demme had long since turned to other projects. Milwaukee slept on. Meanwhile, many media personalities came out and said they had been sexually abused as children: a former Miss America; Roseanne Barr Arnold, the most popular female comedian in the country; Oprah Winfrey, the most popular talk show host. It was a tabloid Thanksgiving. Also on the front pages at this time: the impending rape trial of William Kennedy Smith, an aspiring physician and one of the noted Kennedy clan. The trial was revving up in Palm Beach, Florida. But, in spite of admitted sexual relations with a woman named Patricia Bowman (she said they were forced), Willie, as the young Smith was known, was acquitted.

In the fall of 1991, I went to Las Vegas to seek a brief audience with one man whose public reputation was far worse than William Kennedy Smith's—and promoted more along the lines of a Jeffrey Dahmer. I went to see a man of whom a White acquaintance of mine had quakingly asked, "Aren't you afraid of him?" I answered, "No, not particularly." I had met him several times before. The man in question was the former heavyweight boxing champion of the world, Mike Tyson. He had lost his title to a Buster Douglas and was in the course of trying to gain a match to get back this singular title, now temporarily in the hands of one Evander Holyfield.

In the meanwhile, Mike Tyson had become known as a "serial buttocks fondler" in the mass media (I'd never heard of one before). At the time he granted me a brief audience, he was under indictment, five charges, stemming from an alleged rape in his Indianapolis Canterbury Hotel room during the week of Black Expo '91. The charges had been levied by a participant in the Miss Black America Pageant conducted during that week. Desiree Lynn Washington was this woman's name. It is not my idea to give her name, but she insisted on it being made public later, after Tyson was convicted. Back then, Tyson was looking at sixty-three years in the pen. Dahmer was looking at the same stretch in a spot like St. Elizabeth's. Kennedy Smith, as previously noted, walked.

I drove alone to Las Vegas from the L.A. basin. Traffic was murder on Interstate 10 East all the way out to I-15. I lost some of the traffic there, swung left toward the San Bernardino Mountains, and began a steep, winding ascent on a highway that had runaway pits on the downhill winds, pits designed for trucks that might burn out their brakes and go out of control. I thought of John, Jodie, Jonathan, Jeffrey, and Mike. Soon I passed the mountains, shed the desert towns, descending into Death Valley. It was October—still warm. This barren world of rock domes, dry creek beds, and sandy flats seemed to turn to rust as the sun set.

Five members of the Washington Capitals hockey team were seen with a young woman who apparently had the bad sense to hang around them too long. She said she was gang-raped at a restaurant in Georgetown in 1990. The five hockey players were White, and she was said to be a light-skinned Black woman. The papers made a bit of a fuss about it for about a week or two until the charges against the hockey players were somehow ameliorated. One of them had had charges of indecent exposure in front of prepubescent girls ameliorated earlier in his career in another city. Then for about a week or two more, the sorry state of athletes and nookie, and whether or not there was any legal difference between skeezers and fine young women, became the subject of much editorializing. Then the matter was dropped.

A similar scenario occurred later in New York, in the borough of Queens, when three White members of a St. John's University athletic team were accused of raping a young woman, who happened to be Black. This was another woman with the bad sense to hang out around these jocks. Their case went to trial. They were acquitted. Case closed.

This follows a pattern you can follow back to any lynching tree. Black men are literally and figuratively lynched because of this White guilt over what White people know goes on for and with themselves. Black men take the rap for it, in media, in law, in society, and in the criminal justice system. Black men take the rap for all of the male chauvinism, for all the societal sickness, while White men commit the more heinous acts, then wave their hands in front of our eyes and say, "Nothing happened. What happened was aberrant; in fact, a Lecter in art, a Dahmer in life should get cult status, if you examine it intellectually." And we all nod our heads and say, "Boy, aren't White men smart!"

Mike Tyson you should know. He was the heavyweight boxing champion of the world. He might be again if he can get out and stay out of jail. At the time of his trial there were six lawsuits against him, accusing him of everything from using suggestive language to being that loathsome "serial buttocks fondler." "Serial buttocks fondler," you know, the kind of stuff that Sam Malone, the Ted Danson character on "Cheers," pulls every week and gets tons of laughs for doing. But now, at twenty-five, Tyson was looking at sixty-three years in prison, and he was being judged guilty by decree. People pointed at his "record." First, trying to steal a kiss from a parking lot attendant in L.A. a few years before, then barely cuffing a parking lot attendant who had come to the woman's aid. Then Tyson had grabbed a few derrieres in ensuing years. What a perverted freak.

I can recall several years ago talking to a couple of editors from a publishing house in Glasgow, Scotland, that was planning to publish a book I had written about the so-called sweet science—boxing. We were discussing some past champions, and they mentioned that Sonny Liston had visited fair Scotland once and while training in the gym there had pinched a local woman's behind. "You know, Ralph, that sort of behavior is frowned on in Scotland," one of the editors burred. I chuckled with them and said, "You know, friends, that sort of behavior is pretty much frowned on everywhere. But a heavyweight champion must wrongly figure he has some kind of special dispensation, some fistic immunity."

And so too do powerful, White men. The mayor of Washington, D.C., Sharon Kelly, came out in 1992 and said that even her behind had been pinched—not by Tyson, indeed not by any Black man, including her own husband, but instead by one Jack Kent Cooke, the Croesus-rich owner of the local professional football team, the Washington Redskins. Nobody said or did anything about this but wink. Pigmentation and dollar immunity were the mitigating circumstances, no doubt.

Tyson had been married to actress Robin Givens. It was said that before their divorce he had beaten her within an inch of her life. One of his publicized heinous acts, according to him, was landing "the best punch I ever threw" on Givens. Apparently, he didn't hit her hard enough to keep her off the cover of *Life* magazine or out of the stores on Rodeo Drive. If he was such a beast, why did she marry him in the first place? For money? For fame? For love? Certainly we cannot speculate for love. She was in and out of there so fast all Tyson was left with was windburn and male braggadocio. Robin Givens actually hit Tyson under his heart. Broke it.

In Indianapolis Tyson had been an honored guest of the Black Expo and hung around the Miss Black America Pageant contestants. The entrants posed with him in their bathing suits, giggling, trying to appear alluring. I recall walking through the lobby at the Century Plaza Hotel in Century City, California, some months before this, during the Miss Universe Pageant. I was walking with a male friend of mine, and we were in business suits. We had appointments elsewhere. Some "contestants" appraised us quickly. My friend nudged me and said, "Did you see that? She just looked you up and down, from your shoes to the top of your head, like she was appraising!" I hadn't noticed. But I did notice the tables of older White men who sat and waited to have conversations with men who may or may not have had anything specific to do with the Miss Universe Pageant. "You know what's going on, don't you?" my friend asked. "Man, I think they are going to cut deals for the company of some of these women." I shook my head, scarcely believing him.

Much later on, one of the Miss Black America entrants ended up in Tyson's hotel room at two o'clock in the morning. From there the tales differed. But in the media, Tyson was seen as heinously as Jeffrey Dahmer ("but aren't you afraid of him?"). An editorial cartoon in the *Orlando Sentinel* pictured a couch potato looking up from his easy chair and newspaper at a wife carrying a basket full of his dirty laundry. "Think there's any chance of them putting Jeffrey Dahmer in the same cell as Mike Tyson?" the couch potato, a White potato, said. Indeed, if both Dahmer and Tyson had been in two different hotel rooms and you had to enter one, a reasonable American would choose to enter Dahmer's.

If you think my sympathies lie with Tyson, you are correct. First of all, he is a boxer. What this means is he is slowly being destroyed for the pleasure and leisure of voyeurs. And second, the sick, twisted pathology that publicizes what the White viewing public believes to be a Black male sexual-psychopathological blot must end. Black men cannot take the rap for male chauvinism, and Tyson is not the first twenty-five-year-old man to want a little nookie at 2 A.M., nor will he be the last. As to whether or not he raped anybody, that is what they made courts to try and decide—not newspapers and magazines and television shows. We know what most of their minions think. We know what makes good (easy) copy. And much of that was written prior to his trial. This much was assured. Clearly Tyson was convicted on his image in the media. The demonized "monster" had to be guilty of abusing the deified "God-fearing girl." I was certain Desiree Washington would not have been portrayed as God-fearing if she had come to Willie Smith's hotel suite in the dead of night with a skimpy, sequined outfit on and proceeded to go into the bathroom and remove an intimate item from her person, and then proceeded to recline on his bed in the bedroom portion of the suite. They had been together that day, when Tyson proclaimed a not-necessarily-salubrious interest in her. They had been together earlier that night, when they had been seen kissing torridly in his rented limousine. Simply from the facts, there was much to reasonably doubt here—only Tyson, "that beast," must have done it. It was the only sane thought in America, where one learns that Black men do all the evil that must go punished. As Mae West once said, "Who's harassing who?" Where was a court of law for judgment of this chilling demonizing of only Black men? There was none.

I went to the cheapest hotel I could find on the Strip, which was Circus Circus beyond any doubt, checked in, and dialed Tyson's number. We set a meeting. I told him that I didn't want to interview him, per se. I only wanted to talk. What seemed like the next moment, I pulled up at the sentry station at the front of an enclave of manicured residences not far from the Strip. The guard was hidden in a kiosk, anonymous behind the darkened glass.

"Yeah."

"To see Tyson."

"Name?"

"Wiley."

He called it in for verification, and a few seconds later the black and white barrier lifted and I was driving along the inner roads of the complex. Not knowing the exact address, I drove slowly past the golf course, where a few senior citizens were washing their golf balls and wrapping up the day's leisure. A car came up alongside. Inside was a Black man who smiled pleasantly and told me to follow him.

Tyson's home was not much different from the others in this set-aside from the outside world. Four cars were parked in or near the driveway, the most conspicuous being his top-of-the-line German model. I got out and went to the door, offering perfunctory salutations to his seconds. One of them saw me inside. We went up to closed double doors. "He's in there," said this man, who opened the doors, then left.

Tyson sat there calmly in the middle of a large couch far across the room. A wide-screen television was tuned to C-SPAN. The Thomas-Hill affair. Tyson seemed pleased to see me, or perhaps anybody who wasn't on his payroll. I went to him and smiled at him and we shook hands. I sat next to him on the couch and pointed to the television. "So. You must be a glutton for punishment, Mike." No hint of discomfort on his part. "I just like to keep up," he said. "Good to see you again. Been watching you. You a strong brother."

"No, Mike. I'm not strong. I only have the strength of the strong. It's the people who respond to me, one way or another, who give me strength."

He paused. "I know what you mean. What do you do without it, though? The positive?"

"What do you mean?"

His face clouded and he looked over at the screen, past the cluttered table filled with boxing magazines and the newspapers and some fruit and a pile of legal documents. He looked at the weird glowing light from the television, the blue-grayish radiation bathing his face, causing it to appear ashen and distorted. "Why can't we leave the other alone to live, you know what I'm sayin'?" he said. He seemed to want a definitive answer from me, and I had none for this.

I looked at him sitting there, an unfinished work of bronze. I myself had once called him in print "a nineteen-year-old engine of destruction." Here he was, with a body that had been painfully, scrupulously sculpted into its current state of muscularity and awesome skill. There was no dishonest way to become what he was. I realized that through all that pain, he had not fully learned the most painful truth of all.

"I know you've got a lot on your mind."

"People are working. Lawyers are working. I can't believe it. You know what I mean? Can't believe it. I made myself clear. She came to see me. I didn't drag her. She came to me. She didn't have no problem until I wouldn't walk her downstairs. I was tired. Told her to take the limo."

"You're not like everybody else," I said evenly. We were sitting close and I looked him in his eyes. Fear? Fear what? What would he do? Hit me? If he did, would it disable me more than what I was hit by every day in this reality that prejudges me at face value? In God's name, what did White people make themselves see when they looked at him?

"You may still be a young man," I said, "but you can't act that way. You cannot be one of the boys. You can't let people touch you. You can't touch them. You are the heavyweight champion of the world—and you're a Black man."

A great sadness settled over us, or seemed to, and I believe it had to do with this reality which denies the humanity of those who must then learn to exemplify the best of what it means to be most human, and still continue to live in the face of this reality that they will never be seen as human because it is not convenient. Tyson dropped his head but then quickly turned that into a look away, the muscles in his neck distending. He was too proud to drop his head for long. Someone would have to beat it down.

It didn't matter that he was a scholar of his craft. He would often watch a contemporary boxer and say, "He resembles so-and-so," say, the middleweight Gene Fullmer or some other fighter out of the past, and be so correct no one would disagree with him. But in his studiousness about the fighters of the past, he didn't give enough note to Jack Johnson's railroading over the obsolete Mann Act, the "white slavery" act, even though the White woman who was his companion on a trip from Chicago to Wisconsin expressed sincere desire to be there before and after the fact. Sometimes you do not even need a Desiree Washington—a White woman will do for symbolism even without pressing charges. Tyson knew of Jack Johnson's fights inside the boxing ring, but he neglected to study how he had been beaten down outside of it. Jack Johnson had been everything Tyson is—some kind of nightmare to White people, a scourge of their conscience. Jack Johnson had a legitimate relationship with a woman he cared about turned into a legal crime for which he became an expatriate, and eventually it cost him his title, his innocence, his livelihood. Tyson knew Muhammad Ali, but he'd forgotten Ali was convicted for refusing to be inducted into the army via the draft, barred from the ring for three years. Tyson forgot Joe Louis was "sentenced" to fight past his prime to pay off back income taxes on fights he had taken as "exhibitions" for troops in World War II. They'd counted the house on Joe, then stiffed him on the check, and then asked him to pay taxes on it.

Tyson had named his son D'Amato, after his first manager, Cus D'Amato—"White" and Italian. But this would not be nearly enough to make people forget Tyson was Black, or that he employed a Black manager and promoter, Don King, who was or was not completely nefarious, depending on whom you checked with most lately. Tyson also had declared himself "a conscious Black man." White men like their Black fighters unconscious. He could never let himself forget that, because no one else ever would forget he was Black. Their eyes had to be his mirrors. He was a young man with no time to be young. Idealism of any sort did not become a man in his position. Practicality was his only choice or real defense.

Tyson had an active mind and had often given people what they wanted in their conversations. If you wanted it lurid, he could conjure it, having grown up in the bloodhole belly of Brownsville in Brooklyn. It goes without saying he was good copy, but I wonder how much truth about who he is, who he *really* is, got into print in the American media.

It goes without saying that Tyson can be a dangerous man.

He was the heavyweight champion of the world. He gets paid to be dangerous by a society encouraging the display of violence. What is Dahmer's defense? Willie Smith's?

I left Tyson a book. He pressed on me a copy of a speech purportedly given some three hundred years ago to a gathering at the James River in Virginia by a White plantation owner who came from somewhere down in the Caribbean. The document concerns the systematic control, dehumanization, and mental and physical oppression of slave property. It points out the efficiency of controlling slaves through divisions of age, skin coloring, and gender—geographical divisions upon the land. It could have been written today and by someone who was not White but trying to make a point.

I told Tyson I had seen it before, but he insisted I keep a copy. It wasn't me who needed it. Desiree Washington needed a copy. I wished Tyson well, wished him a life beyond bitterness. I shook his massive hand again and left. Without turning I could feel him standing still behind me. Then he called out to me. "Come back and see me one day. Come back and let's talk." I said I would. Circus Circus was the pits.

Tyson is in the pen now. Strange fruit hanging from a different tree. Yet the strangest of all walk among us—as long as they're free, White, male, and twenty-one. The greatest of these qualities is the freedom. I wonder how it feels? I am trapped and can only say, "Nooo!" and hope my scream is loud enough to discourage the monsters and keep them back until I am strong enough, powerful enough to fight my way free. Powerful enough to slip the noose from around my neck and put out the fire on my flesh. Tell my side of the story.

A Brief on the
Meaning of Being:
Muhammad Ali

Inside the rings of twentieth-century iconography, Muhammad Ali doesn't have to take a back seat to anybody. He was for a time the most famous person in the world. This is a dubious distinction when standing alone. Ali was also the most photogenic of the famous, the most accessible and natural, possessing the best chin of many of his contemporaries and near-contemporaries like MacArthur, Lindbergh, Einstein, Louis, Chaplin, Hitler, Stalin, both Dukes (Ellington and Wayne), Joe DiMaggio, Jackie Robinson, the Beatles, Frank Sinatra, Marilyn Monroe, Marian Anderson, Gandhi, Martin Luther King, Elvis, Michael Jackson, Reagan, Mandela, even Madonna or Oprah Winfrey herself. But for me (and you too, perhaps), Ali is also among the most relevant icons in the annals of human competition. He also goes beyond the twentieth century. Then the others in his firmament have names like Ulysses, Osiris, or Simon Bolívar—figures drawn from history and mythology, not recent, palpable fact.

By comparison, who is Howard Bingham? Muhammad Ali's photographer, friend, and, as it turns out, historian. Others from LeRoy Neiman to Red Smith to Malcolm X to the Honorable Elijah Muhammad to Howard Cosell to Ferdinand Marcos to Don King to President Jimmy Carter captured Ali briefly, in their own fashions and agendas. They were unable to know all of him or hold him still. They couldn't break Ali's appointments with his times. If they were wise, they helped him attain his destiny. No one tempered that red-blue flame from his lamplighter's inextinguishable wick; no one could change that glorious myth of Mr. Unchained Power and Glory himself, the myth of Muhammad Ali, a man who could light you up in more ways than one, pilgrim.

Ali assumed mythological proportions even as he was being surrounded by people who were mythic in their own rights, or who were accustomed to being close by—the confidants of myths. Mythmakers and mythbreakers. But any mythology is most important to the creative energies of those who are captivated by the telling and re-telling of these myths. I know they haven't hurt me, the myths of Muhammad Ali—the myth of the good-hearted sentinel. In the cold universe of Good, Bad, and no in-between, Ali was not merely of the Good, he was the champion of Good, its last line of defense, the keeper of a red-blue flickering flame. Other words you might read about him come from some of those talented mythmakers who knew Ali as someone within their own constellation, a man they could touch, hear belch, and catch drooling while he slept. They knew he was just a man, only that, just another human being who could be cruel or afraid or who could cry. A man who would grow old and halt one day. A man who'd often done that which he would one day regret.

I never knew Ali in that way when I knew him first and best. For twenty years, in that too-brief epoch of idealism that stretches from the ages of nine to twenty-nine—for me the years between 1961 and 1981—I knew him as an infallible icon who won even when he lost. He was infallible in the sense of never giving up on himself, on the power of self. Because he never did this, he never allowed me to do it either. I was an impressionable twelve-year-old when he wrested the world heavyweight championship from Charles "Sonny" Liston before exclaiming, "I'm pretty! I'm a bad man! I am the greatest of all times! I shook up the world! I shook up the world!" To me his ascent was easily as dizzying as Beowulf's over Grendel—even more so. Beowulf didn't photograph as well or take rematches this century, for starters.

I was fifteen when Ali said, "I ain't got nothing against them Vietcongs" and gave up the title of world heavyweight champion for such a curious set of circumstances—his own principles! I went into exile with him, ignoring most other prizefighters. When he came back three years later, in 1971, I came back with him. We were both older and different now, somehow, fighting on something more than merely youth.

Later, when I was aspiring to be a journalist and writer and a man of at least some principles, I would type RALPH WILEY IS THE GREATEST SPORTSWRITER IN THE WORLD, BAR NONE over and over again on the IBM Selectric typewriters hanging ponderously over tables, like Everlast heavy bags, in my places of training. I pounded and pounded them, improving my speed and accuracy, willing myself into a state of confidence my abilities did not warrant. After I came close enough to this curious goal to stop worrying about it, I had to give a lion's share of credit to the youthful Muhammad Ali. What had been a boast to him had been a kept promise to me. Like the time he punched his tongue out from the corner of his mouth, feigned a scowl of irritability, and scribbled, "Me. Whee!" Only poet Marianne Moore seemed to really get it at the time.

You must understand how much this was, coming from a man whose recent descendants were slaves, then illiterate sharecroppers, held fast in their forced ignorance, held there by fear and terror, held there with no rights a White man was bound to respect. They were people who had whiled away time at labor by singing "Nobody Knows de Trouble I've Seen" or "Soon Ah Will Be Done with the Troubles of the World" before hearing the report of a pistol, or the crack of a neck, or a flesh-rendered scream, cutting off what would remain of such a hopeful lyric as "Me . . . Whee!"

I also know some of the people who were photographed with Ali, like Malcolm X, know them as part of the essential myth, captured by the camera of Howard Bingham. And then who is Bingham? A quiet man who seemed to be everywhere Ali was; the one who never had to stop everything to take a reading from a light meter before he could get the shot he came to get. Bingham got the shot as it happened instead of staging it. In the high court of Ali, Howard Bingham was one of many singers of songs—just a shooter, as they say in the trades, just a flexible, reliable shooter giving impression and form to the Ali mythology to which I am so indebted as an artist.

Muhammad Ali is best described as a beautiful man. He is one of a few famous men of history who can be accurately described in that way. He floated above with us down here on the ground, either admiring him or hating him for being so handsome, so manly, so confident and fluid and principled and attractive to sensible women and men; loving him for being so lucky and so damned *right*, as it seemed in the end, right and lucky and good for having the wings we didn't possess. The rest of us seemed apart from him somehow, even as we surrounded him and touched him and tried to take some part of him with us, and give some part of us to him in hopes that he would take it with him back to the Sun, make it like him. He always seemed much more grand, so much more admirable than those around him, and it didn't matter who they were. When he was seated with a group of equally proficient Black athletes like Bill Russell and Jim Brown, it was Ali who stood out. Not that he was bigger, faster, stronger, smarter, or more accomplished than the rest of them. It was because he was Muhammad Ali, and he belonged to the world in a different way, because his sport had meant facing fear and death and ferociously beating them both back to become heavyweight champion of the world, that man who is without peer, that man all men and women can relate to, at some level, no matter what their national sport might be.

Ali went beyond sport. There was nowhere he seemed very uncomfortable, nowhere he seemed out of place. During lulls with sportscaster Howard Cosell, Ali was mutedly transcendent, even though Cosell had the vocabulary. Ali always seemed to know what was most eloquent about him. First the rapid-fire vocal delivery of his youth, his mother-and-country wit (which can be captured with a camera after all, captured in the faces of those of us who heard him). Then through mobility, that quick, muscular ballet he performed on those magnificent legs. Then Ali's eloquence came through his hands. He became obsessed with magic when he got older because he was accustomed to performing legerdemain in the ring. He had always amazed us and himself with what he could do with only his wits and his bare hands.

Finally Ali's eloquence came through his expressions, his ways of facing us. He never seemed out of place, but he always seemed more in place when captured with children. He was more natural in a more loving setting than the boxing ring. Myth and the progeny of myth. I don't think you get the true feeling of the enormity of Muhammad Ali as a mythic figure until you see him alone, or see a photograph capturing him alone. It was when Ali was alone that *he* captivated *us*—boxing, smiling, talking, thinking, moving, joking, winning, defending himself, then defending the collective self, making up the myth as he went along. He is best known alone. As we can see from his photos, even when Ali was alone, Howard Bingham was with him.

A few brave writers have tried their luck with Ali's life and times. The latest attempt is by Thomas Hauser, a prolific New York author whose best-known book, *Missing*, tells about the disappearance of an American journalist following the 1973 CIA-supported coup against Salvador Allende in Chile, and his family's efforts to find him. You may remember the movie adaptation, directed by Costa-Gavras and starring Sissy Spacek and Jack Lemmon. I hoped Hauser's *Muhammad Ali: His Life and Times* would be as thorough and brilliant as the champion in the ring himself.

Before Ali, you had to be crazy, as Jack Johnson was labeled, or docile, as Joe Louis has been portrayed, to be a Black man with a public profile in America. But today you don't have to be crazy or docile to be the Black heavyweight champion of the world, although you still are probably going to be portrayed that way. But that need not stop you. You don't have to be crazy or docile to be a successful Black person in America. Ali showed us. He showed us you could speak your mind, walk your walk, and be honored, appreciated (disliked perhaps, vilified certainly), but above all respected. If that were all Ali showed us, it would have been plenty. He also showed us very quick hands, great heart, and artistic grace within a most inartistic milieu.

In 1964, Charles "Sonny" Liston, malevolent proprietor of fists the size and density of small tombstones, was unbeatable. From 1968 to 1975, Joe Frazier possessed a left hook like the wrath of God. George Foreman, the destroyer of Frazier, was undefeated, among the most devastating punchers of the century. "I don't worry 'bout hittin' power," Ali said at thirty-two, before knocking out Foreman in Zaire in 1974. "I usually fix it so there's nothing there for them to hit."

Ali fought these opponents and a war to win hearts and minds at the same time. And won most contests. Jack Johnson was champ. Joe Louis was champ. Black neighborhoods grew hushed and intent and still as reports of their conflicts came over a crackling radio. But afterward, win or lose, nothing changed. If we went beyond that neighborhood and a White man wanted to push us off the sidewalk into the mud on general principles, he could. If he accused us of staring at his mug-ugly cousin or if we tried to run a small business that might offer a little economic independence, we could be hanged with impunity. We couldn't drink the water we drew. We couldn't eat the food we grew and cooked. For centuries of labor, we took in not a dime. We thought we were ugly and dumb. We were ashamed. We were trapped in a corner with a murderous system of bigotry banging away at us.

Now we can do normal things freely, arousing only a resentful suspicion instead of angry, teeming, murderous mobs. Who do you think gave us the temerity? A few people come to mind: the good man Martin Luther King, Jr., Fannie Lou Hamer, Emmett Till, those four little girls who were killed by a bomb in a Birmingham church. But who really changed it for all of us, and made it so now many White men will cross the street to avoid us? It may not be enviable to be feared, but it is preferable to being lynched.

Why that change? Because a man born Cassius Marcellus Clay, Jr., on January 17, 1942, in Louisville, Kentucky, sat and talked to Malcolm X in 1964, before Malcolm's assassination, and before Clay shook up the world by winning the title from Liston? Malcolm advised Ali, "Be peaceful, be courteous. Obey the law, respect everyone. But if someone puts his hands on you, send him to the cemetery." We learned nobody resents that response save a wolf who intends to make you his meal. It's not necessary to change the White man's mind, according to this new perspective. You *can't* change his mind about us. Instead, we have to change our own minds. We've got to change our own minds about each other. We have to see each other with new eyes.

Within the span of a few years, Clay achieved an astonishing range of accomplishments for a man who was, in the ways of books, uneducated. He showed us that anything was possible with belief in self. Changing his name to Muhammad Ali, he became a Muslim and aligned himself with Elijah Muhammad's Nation of Islam for a time. He employed a Black financial adviser. He wooed and married four women: Sonji, the first hot number he met; Khalilah, a handsome, religious woman who bore him four children; Veronica, a voluptuous siren who knew she was beautiful and who bore him two children; and finally Lonnie, the girl next door.

During his career Ali has lectured on college campuses, retired three times, won the world heavyweight title three times, made Howard Cosell's career, brought hostages home from the Middle East, starred in a movie of his own life (*The Greatest*, 1977), and tried to get a shoe-polish factory and an automobile assembly plant off the ground.

To stay out of the Vietnam War, back in 1967, Ali declared himself a conscientious objector on religious grounds. This bold act caused him to be stripped of his world title, an action repudiated a few years later by no less than the U.S. Supreme Court. Ali was once asked by television host David Susskind if his religious objection to war was sincere. Ali pointed out that he had divorced his first wife, Sonji, because she wouldn't wear her dresses below her knees, and that he was in the process of paying her a five-figure annual sum in alimony. "If that ain't sincerity, I don't know what is," Ali concluded.

In the years between 1964 and 1981, Ali became the most celebrated personage in the civilized world. In Mecca, Malcolm X uttered the name Muhammad Ali. An excited crowd, speaking Arabic, gathered around him, mistaking Malcolm for Ali. In Cambridge, Massachusetts, young White Harvard students debated with Ali, holding their chins and nodding when he made a good point.

Ali fought on four continents. People from New Zealand to Zanzibar knew him and what he stood for. It was possible for him to speak out against war or racism and stay pretty. White people cheered him, too. They were just as drawn to him as the world's people of color. Truth knows no color; it appeals to intelligence. Even today you can witness many Whites giving testimonials about Ali's appeal in commercials designed to sell subscriptions to *Sports Illustrated*. Back in 1965, *Sports Illustrated* ran an article co-authored by former champion Floyd Patterson entitled "Cassius Clay Must Be Beaten"; the article's subtext was "Why I can't let a Muslim be champion." Patterson refused to call Ali by anything other than Cassius Clay. On November 22, 1965, Ali boxed Patterson silly while asking him, "What's my name?" Eventually Patterson had to agree: Muhammad Ali.

As the young man who stopped Liston, Ali was God's gift to boxing. The faces of the White men in the audience were sober as Ali jumped in the air after beating Liston in Miami on February 25, 1964. Some of them didn't like the immortal words he uttered, words that to him were both boasts to sell tickets and ultimate truths: "I'm pretty! I'm a bad man! I shook up the world! I am the greatest of all times! God is with me! If God is with me, then no man can be against me!"

Ali showed it didn't matter whether anybody liked it. As he stood over the fallen Liston in the first round of their rematch in Lewiston, Maine, on March 26, 1965, his picture was taken by Neil Leifer and Bob Gomel for *Life* magazine. Ali was at his most magnificent as an exemplar of manhood.

He was 6 feet 3 inches and 211 pounds of a full, perfect human symmetry. He stood up on his toes, his powerful shoulders thrown back, looking down at the fallen hulk—this is the sort of pose that Michelangelo might have sought. Belief in such possibilities is what impressionable youth still seek.

Recently it was rumored that Queen Latifah, the rapper, is one of Ali's daughters. The rumor is false, but you can look at Queen Latifah and see how it got started. She does resemble Ali—she's pretty, and she carries herself with unmistakable pride. One of Ali's real daughters is pursuing a career in stand-up comedy, and two of Malcolm X's five daughters have recorded with rapper Big Daddy Kane.

In February of 1991, Ali, soon to be fifty, took a flight from Detroit with members of the Walter Camp All-America football team, including Tripp Welbourne from Michigan and Todd Lyght and Raghib "Rocket" Ismail of Notre Dame. When an attendant told Ali his seat in first class was ready, he responded in his now raspy voice that no, he'd stay in coach with the fellows. Ismail noticed that Ali was watching him, just as Ali had once, many years before, noticed Malcolm X watching *him*. Then the once-swift Ali spoke to him, in spite of his slurred speech, an effect of Parkinson's disease brought on by all his years in the ring.

Later, Ali took Ismail away from a group of laughing young men and mumbled, "N'mattah what we do, we still niggahs, ain't we?" And then, Ali smiled.

Jack and Joe would not have smiled. So this is Ali's legacy: an unshakable belief in the ultimate dignity of self; a winning smile, irrepressible joy, and great promise in the knowledge that being called a nigger need not stop a full life's journey. Not anymore. He *rocked* the world.

Spike Lee &
Denzel Washington &
Malcolm X

Who was the real Malcolm X, and why would Spike Lee stake both their reputations on a film about him? Malcolm X was known as a firebrand, an orator of raw power, like Frederick Douglass, or Pericles, or others history has remembered less kindly, if at all. For me, and I can only speak for myself, this was partly his essence, one of his gifts; his final legacy was much greater.

I am a devotee of Malcolm. I was born 240 miles downriver and a lifetime past the East St. Louis massacre of 1917. Few lessons had been learned from it at the time of my birth in 1952, the year one Malcolm Little was released from the penitentiaries of Massachusetts. As I grew up, around me Till, Evers, Chaney, Goodman, Schwerner, Liuzzo, King, and so many more who were nameless and faceless were killed, while I was held safe from such murderous and efficient hatred only by the gracefully closed ranks of my own people.

So when I heard the voice of Malcolm X, on the book page, on vinyl records, and eventually on videotape and film, talking about self-sufficiency, self-respect, self-help, self-love, and self-defense, he had a rapt audience in me, for I had heard of so many Black people, and people who had tried to be fair to Black people, who were killed; the only bloodcurdling screams I'd heard were the inhuman ones dubbed over Johnny Weismuller, mouth agape, as he portrayed the Great White Ape on all those jungle movies playing incessant double matinees every weekend of my childhood.

Influenced? Why, it was my sanity that Malcolm X rescued from the pyre of fear. Only later I sensed how he had influenced other Black Americans, and therefore America itself, because we are among the most influential people living here whether we know it or not.

Now Malcolm X would influence film. In the end, his truest legacy was to convince Black Americans to look homeward, inward, and above all, to accept and try to love what we found there, and to do this *by any means necessary*. Yes, he was gifted with a power to bend the wills of crowds without them wholly knowing how; power to turn them to knowledge as he saw it; an uncanny ability to gather their emotions, using the spoken word as image. Uncontrollable emotions, he controlled. Indecipherable feelings, he explained. Unspeakable memories, he recalled. Thus his human potential was unleashed, his flaws briefly overcome. The power to speak out was part of Malcolm's legacy, his face breaking into a glittering, knowing, crooked grin—one not unlike Spike Lee's.

He was born Malcolm Little on May 19, 1925, in Omaha, Nebraska; grew up in Lansing, Michigan; and remembered both places for the efficacy of their hell-raising night riders.

After placement in foster care, Malcolm thrived academically in an otherwise all-White grammar school, where he voiced a desire to be a lawyer; instead he was advised by a faculty member to try carpentry, a good trade for a *nigger*, which Malcolm later recalled as his common nickname there. In time he moved East, and on the streets of Roxbury and Harlem he became an initiate, then an intimate, with drugs, alcohol, numbers-running, and steering amiable whores to johns. He peddled reefers, rolled sticks of marijuana. Then he was a burglar and thief. The latter two vocations helped land him in the penitentiary in 1946, at the age of twenty, where he did seven years of an eight-to-ten-year bit on fourteen counts of burglary and possession of stolen property. In prison he changed his life. Inside the Charleston and Concord, Massachusetts, penitentiaries, he converted to devouring books (to the point of developing astigmatism) and then to Elijah Muhammad's Lost-Found Nation of Islam. From then he was Malcolm X, dropping Little, the "name of a slavemaster." It was then he found his courtrooms, at lecterns across the country. He became *the* lawyer—one with twenty-five million clients. He railed against the harsh treatment, brutal and often based on Jim Crow, of the "so-called Negroes" of the United States. His devout, ascetic life and oratorical brilliance lifted him to prominence in the Nation of Islam, then beyond.

Whatever Malcolm X was, Spike Lee and Denzel Washington, auteur and actor, descendants of slaves, forebears of filmmakers, are part of his legacy now, twenty-eight years after he was shot down at the Audubon Ballroom in New York City on Feb. 21, 1965. Washington and Lee, two men with no last X, with surnames from pages of White American history, are changing things while capturing universal themes in *Malcolm X*.

It won't be any academy that decides if Washington deserves the highest award for his portrayal, or whether Spike Lee did the right thing this time. History will judge them shortly. History and first-run box-office receipts, of course. But the stakes here are much higher than any projected gross of one holiday release.

"Malcolm was a proud man," says an intent Lee. "Denzel *became* Malcolm. We didn't have to say what this means to our—not careers. Our *lives*. We didn't say, 'Yo. Watershed.' We *know*."

"Spike loves that man," Denzel Washington says. His eyes, steel-hard, coolly survey me. "And it could be argued that he *is* that man, in his own way. Malcolm lived a concentrated dose of life. Took over everything he did, you know." Denzel seems in character. I wonder out loud: Has Washington-as-Malcolm X heard of that old Asiatic saying, "If you want to discredit a man . . ."

"Let him live," Washington says, finishing the idea.

Spike Lee has landed at the Los Angeles International airport with the work print for *Malcolm X* in his hip pocket. It is late morning, April Fool's Day, 1992. Lee spent the previous evening watching the New York Knicks lose to the Chicago Bulls at Madison Square Garden in New York. He spent the night before that at the Oscars in L.A., where he seemed as stiff as an ironing board in his tux, promethea-moth white tie, and fresh shave, mispronouncing Thailand as "Thigh-land" while presenting the Best Documentary Oscar with pal John Singleton. Considering the venue, "Thighland" was good wordplay. Only Spike wasn't playing. He'd had a root canal that day, and, sadly or not, nobody was confusing him with Billy Crystal in the first place.

Lee doesn't give great conversational patter. He has a knack for dropping a t here and there, a small flutter-by of a stutter at times, the slightest of speech impediments. He calls his own speech pattern "cryptic." Lee calls the White limousine driver "sir" and carries his own bags. He is polite. He offers a wicked smile while spanning the United concourse in a long, low stride. Spike walks like he's in a movie because we've seen him walking like this in movies, but this is just the way he walks. The Rodney G. King verdict hasn't happened yet. The Anbesol has kicked in on Spike's gums. The print he's screening on the Warner Bros. lot is 3 hours 50 minutes long. The sound is bad. Lee is thinking past the screening. He knows what he'll have there.

"Been working hard," he says. I fumble with a tape recorder. "Barry [editor Barry Brown] and the editors have been working round the clock to get us ready for this screening. This is for Terry Semel and Bob Daly, the big cheeses at Warner Bros. Today is D-Day. The bond company said we were going to have a copy ready by February 28, which was crazy. We didn't finish shooting until the end of January. They've been coming up with arbitrary-assed dates."

A month or so before this, Spike had shocked the life out of me by casually calling up out of the blue one day to ask what my writing schedule was like for the rest of the year. "Busy," I said calmly, my curiosity raging, "but not that busy."

I had been trying to do something with Spike for years and had been unsuccessful. I'd met him at his office, shaken his hand, sent him my books and an awful spec script I had composed, and written letters to him about his films and scripts. When *Sports Illustrated* sent a good writer, Rick Reilly, and not me, Ralph Wiley, to do a feature on Spike, that was one of the last straws I pulled there. Bad enough Rick Reilly got all my mail.

So I'd been working on an article about the production of *Malcolm X* for the movie magazine *Premiere*. Spike smiled broadly my first day on the set—like he'd been waiting for me to approach him with legitimate ends of my own before warming up, such as he ever warms up. He apologized for not stopping to talk, which I assured him was not necessary. He was working.

A couple of months later, Spike sent me a photo card. It was late February of 1992. The card said, "Dear Ralph, I want you to work with me on my book *By Any Means Necessary: The Trials and Tribulations of the Making of Malcolm X While Ten Million Motherfuckers Are Fucking with You*, by Spike Lee and Ralph Wiley. Peace, Spike Lee."

I called his executive assistant, Desiree Jellerette, in paroxysms of laughter and bonhomie. "Tell Spike I love it!" My enthusiasm would level off in the face of the grind of the work and the obscenely close deadline. It was a tough job, to open that seal around all of Lee's complexities, from his voice through his moods by his personality to his stunning creativity, and we didn't have much time to open it and close the book.

Now he stares dead ahead, trying to maintain his composure after it becomes clear the limo driver is confused, if not lost. Nothing upsets Spike more than a bad driver. He doesn't drive.

"Say, do you know where you're going?" Then, to me, "We're going to have to come up with more funds. I don't want to lay people off. We're too close. We projected the film Saturday at a place on Seventh Avenue. Denzel came in. We've got a great film here—if we handle it right. It's still a battle. Friday, they laid off the editors."

Lee had wanted $33 million to make the movie. Warner's never offered more than $20 million, plus an initial $8 million or so from Largo Entertainment for foreign rights—$28 million in all. Lee went ahead and made his movie. By Thanksgiving 1991, the production money was virtually gone, with a month of shooting in Africa still to come. That kicked off a struggle with Completion Bond Company (and its president, Bette Smith), which asserted financial control over the project when its overages exceeded $5 million. Lee had already kicked in $2 million of his $3 million fee; it still wasn't enough. Five days earlier, with the movie still lacking a score, Smith, who is Black, shut down postproduction work on *Malcolm X*. "Spike, you don't know who your enemies are," Smith had told him. "I'm looking at one," Lee cracked back.

"There is no need for me to be (in the editing room) every single fucking minute, and that's been Bette Smith's contention," Lee says. "She's trying to get into my shit about teaching class and saying I'm never in the editing room. That's not the case at all. I'm there when I need to be. The bond company's whole thing is 'Look, we ain't payin: The contract says this movie is two hours and fifteen minutes, and that's what we're paying for.' Warner Bros. is saying, 'We can't pledge additional money until we see the film.' Anyway, I don't want to lay people off. We're too close. We're going to have to come up with some more funds."

Lee's small, curving left hand does not hesitate, jabbing the cellular phone the way a raptor's talon would stab a rabbit. "It's time," he says as he punches numbers. "I called Bill Cosby, told him I was in trouble. When I got back from the Academy Awards, a check was there. I called Oprah. She'll help. Michael Jordan. He said yes. Warner Brothers and the bond company want to pull the plug on me. Hello? Lon Rosen's office? I want to get a message to Magic Johnson. This is Spike Lee . . . Hello, Magic?"

It had been a war since Lee took over the project in late 1990 from director Norman Jewison. "*Any* director who wasn't an African American faced almost impossible odds doing *Malcolm X*," Lee had said. First he had to choose among original scripts written (and rewritten) by James Baldwin with Arnold Perl, Calder Willingham, David Mamet, David Bradley, and Charles Fuller. Then came the disparity between budgets—Lee's and Warner's. Then Lee received warnings about the nature of his vision from Louis Farrakhan and others in factions of the old Nation of Islam. Lee had a load and no time to stumble under it.

Terry Semel hit the roof after one of Lee's strafings, at Gustavus Adolphus College in Minnesota, on how Warner's has a double standard for him and the White boys. Lee thinks it's a ploy. Semel and Daly are heading to Japan. A screening has been moved to April 1. Lee thought he was working on an April 6 date.

Lee's rants are calculated to keep the light bright, hot, and on him. "It's harder to do somebody up when people are looking," he says. "If I get done, people will know." Lee complains about Dan Aykroyd's $45 million budget for *Nothing but Trouble*, and about David Fincher, a first-timer out of music videoland, having $50 million to play with on *Alien 3*. It's not like Lee doesn't know the other half of the conversation. He's heard it enough. He never made a film with $32 million. His highest budget was $14 mil, for *Jungle Fever*. And all his films combined—counting the seminal *She's Gotta Have It*, *School Daze*, *Do the Right Thing*, *Mo' Better Blues*, and *Jungle Fever*—didn't gross $100 million, total.

Lee can then say he's never gotten the screens—*Jungle Fever* got the most, something less than seven hundred. His films average well over 200 percent profit. Some question if *Malcolm X* is guaranteed box office. Those who put up millions like the guarantees firm. "Especially on demand when you're Black," says Spike. "They can't see the forest *or* the trees then." Until *Malcolm X* rolls out to more than eleven hundred screens, the Black director with the highest-grossing film is Sidney Poitier, with 1980's *Stir Crazy* starring Richard Pryor and Gene Wilder, a benign artistic nonentity that nonetheless took in $93 million domestic.

At 1 P.M., the limo finally slinks through the gate at the entrance to the Warner's lot, past the white-columned executive office building on the right. "Ha! The plantation!" cracks

Lee as the car wends its way back toward Building 71, Screening Room 5.

It doesn't matter when I catch him—Spike's always looking at ten different ways to do a million things at once and seems to function better this way. If he moved more slowly, I could get away with calling him mercurial. He has many viewfinders in his eye—and he'll need that compound eye soon. It's a week before Christmas, Dec. 18, 1991. Shoot Day 69. At his platform desk in his Brooklyn office, Lee is on the phone with Tracy Chapman agreeing to shoot a video. He's already talked with Prince, agreed to do another. Next to Lee's calendar (film class at Harvard, 1-31-92) is a card from Whoopi Goldberg, an Annie Leibovitz photo of Whoopi reclined in a tub of milk. The inscription: "So Spike, are we ever going to make love?" Spike's answer, "Hell no!" is as intense as the one his character Mookie threw at the Jehovah's Witnesses in *Do the Right Thing*. I'm pretty sure Whoopi was joking, too.

Before long, he joins the *Malcolm X* crew in an old manse at 603 Park Avenue, shooting burglary scenes.

I'm watching now as Lee is looking over a *New York Times* piece on Al Sharpton and a shot is set up around him (Sharpton enjoys a cameo in *Malcolm X* as a streetwise impresario—a real stretch). Spike is also on the telephone while simultaneously beckoning for cinematographer Ernest Dickerson, who is bleary-eyed. His wife had a son, Ernest III, the night before. His directorial debut, *Juice*, hits in a month.

"We're using color and light to accentuate different moods of Malcolm's life," Dickerson says. It sounds like a refrain he's practiced. "Before prison is warmer, more idealized. Prison is very blue, very cold. After prison, no filtration, the light is hard and clear, as he is the Spokesman. Toward the end, in Mecca, when he makes yet another conversion, the clarity is softened—we're trying for a look showing an awareness of knowledge."

"The lights over those blond heads, Ernest, what about the bounce?" Spike asks. Then, into the phone: "Money? Didn't I just give you a check? This day-before crap ain't working! How much?"

Denzel Washington is talking to costume designer Ruth Carter about socks. "But these are thinner," he protests. Carter wants to replace them. "Well, these are staying. I guess there goes your Oscar," says Washington, smiling a daunting smile. Carter doesn't say anything, but she appears to want to. In February of 1993, her costume designs and Washington's acting gain the only two Oscar nominations the film will receive.

Washington grabs Lee away to confer on mood. "My question is this . . ." I think I am in the process of getting off on the wrong foot with Washington, unintentionally. Some of the more mischievous among the crew have been asking me, "Are you Denzel's brother?" Spike's brother David, the unit photographer, came up to me and began talking pleasantly until I turned around and he saw I wasn't who he had thought I was from behind. The actress Kate Vernon, portraying Sophia, young Malcolm's White girlfriend, had to look a long time as I stood in one corner of a room in the mansion, and she still wasn't quite decided whether I was him or not until I spoke to her and assured her I was not.

I may resemble Denzel Washington, only he is younger, more handsome, smarter, much, much richer, a million times more famous, and, in all probability, the way my luck is going, a better prose writer. Denzel, being quite observant, only knows someone is around whom people are talking about in some relation to him. We never do speak on this day. I'm shy. I know *Islam* is the Arabic word meaning "submission." In order to do my case study on the man portraying

Malcolm X, El-Hajj Malik El-Shabazz, I must learn to submit. It's not easy. Maybe later.

Debi Mazar, playing Peg, younger sister of Sophia, pops a mint and says, "I couldn't keep playing neighborhood shits the rest of my life." She was cast in both *Goodfellas* and *Jungle Fever*. "This is more. Feel it? This is history."

If so, then Lee might agree with James Joyce's Stephen Daedalus in that history is a nightmare from which he is trying to awake. In July Lee was petitioned by the writer Amiri Baraka. At a Harlem rally on August 3, 1991, Baraka publicly criticized Lee for taking on the project, oddly enough calling him "part of a retrograde movement in this country" and *"petit bourgeois."*

Baraka questioned Lee's motives and his ability to do this particular story justice. This from one who is considered by many a cultural voice—and father of a longtime Lee book collaborator, Lisa Jones. This fell in line with criticism Lee has received in the past from Stanley Crouch of the *Village Voice*, Armond White of the *City Sun* in Brooklyn, and syndicated columnist Carl T. Rowan, all of whom, at one time or another, for one reason or another, have considered Spike Lee anathema to their causes.

"How many Black people ran to criticize Malcolm at one time in his life?" Lee asks. He was once asked by Henry L. Gates, the Harvard professor, about such criticism. Gates quoted Baldwin: "When White people criticize me unjustly, it makes me stronger. When Black people do, it makes me want to cry." Lee repeats this and admits, "There is a difference. What hurt is that you never heard one peep out of Baraka when Norman Jewison was going to direct this film. Didn't say shit." Lee's artistic integrity is questioned, but he has the films on the wall, so to speak. This does not stop the criticism—in fact, his productivity fuels it. "Just because you're Black, you can't take the attitude you're beyond criticism, or being trashed," says Lee. "I think for the most part Black people have been too lenient on Black artists."

Brave words. In August 1991, after the Baraka episode and before shooting began, Lee was given his walking papers by his girlfriend, the model Veronica Webb, over sushi at a Park Slope restaurant. "As I was putting a piece up to my mouth," he says, "she said, 'I don't love you no more.' " Webb, who had been cast in a bit part in *Malcolm X*, kept her job.

The day her scenes were shot, tabloids screamed trouble. Lee's father, Bill, was busted for possession of heroin in a park in Brooklyn. "He'd been doing it for years. Not shooting but snorting. I told him to get help," said Lee. "He didn't listen. When they caught him, he said, 'I'm Spike Lee's father! Spike's my son!' He gave me up to try and not spend the night in jail." There were no newspapers in Lee's sight on the set the next day.

Some days later a young Black woman named Shona Bailey, who was to be an extra in the large Harlem rally scenes, was murdered in the basement of the building where she lived on 135th Street, and after the police found her datebook with *Malcolm X* written in it, that made the tabloids, too (the N.Y.P.D. has yet to make any arrests in her case). Then a car with a brick tied to the accelerator came hurtling toward the Harlem set during one of the mass crowd scenes, and although no one was injured when the car crashed against a curb, Lee was loopy from the confluence of events.

"But Spike hasn't let that affect his work, which is what is amazing about him," says his co-producer and friend, Monty Ross. "Malcolm belonged to the people, the have-nots, the miseducated, the uneducated. Spike knows if it's not picture-perfect, it could do more harm than good. People need to see this film made right."

In the Park Avenue apartment, Malcolm and a character named Shorty tiptoe through five or six takes of an interior scene in which they burgle the bedroom of a rich Brahmin.

Malcolm was so bold he'd take the diamond ring right off your finger as you slept—and that's what he does here. The ring comes off, sparkling in the "moonlight." Lee cackles after every take, a child with his fingers in the cookie jar, all the trouble worthwhile.

Lee has a saying: "He [or she] didn't *come correct*," meaning someone wanted to have a dialogue or discourse with him or about him, or criticize him, to spin off him in some way, and didn't approach him in the proper manner according to Lee's program. A Black writer and editor named Judy Simmons said, "I couldn't understand Baraka's point on this one. When did he become sole proprietor of the legacy of Malcolm X? Spike has problems as a filmmaker, as an artist, hell, as a Black man in America, I'm sure. That's what needs real examination." In 1992 the *New York Times* ran an item questioning why Lee was teaching at Harvard without a college degree—but the problem was he has *two*: a B.A. from Morehouse and an M.F.A. from New York University. Some would rather Lee *be* Mars Blackmon. The *Times* retracted. Few other critics have.

But this is why his saying, "He didn't come correct," is so revealing: The saying bespeaks one key to Lee's success—his association with the world around him, the world he lives in day to day, and not his association to a world of cultural critics. The critic's world is the *study* of the art of re-creation of the day to day. The criticism usually re-creates nothing of itself.

By heeding not the critics but the world as he sees it with his own eye, from close, from within, Lee has kept a finger on the popular pulse. To "come correct" is not only Lee's saying, but a popular saying among young people, yes, *especially* the young Black people of Spike Lee's demimonde; and they eventually serve as his authentication. He does not travel with a retinue. He is right there on the street, among the people. How he manages to maintain contact is something every Black artist should envy. James Baldwin put it this way, writing about Lorraine Hansberry in the preface of *To be Young, Gifted and Black: An Informal Biography of Lorraine Hansberry*, recalling his feelings after her great critical success with the play *A Raisin in the Sun*:

> This country's concept of art and artists has the effect, scarcely worth mentioning by now, of isolating the artist from the people. One can see the effect in the irrelevance of so much of the work produced by celebrated white artists; but the effect of this isolation on a black artist is absolutely fatal. He is, already, as a black American citizen, isolated from most of his white countrymen. At the crucial hour (of creation), he can hardly look to his artistic peers for help, for they do not know enough about him to be able to correct him. To continue to grow, to remain in touch with himself, he needs the support of that community from which, however, all of the pressures of American life incessantly conspire to remove him. When he is effectively removed, he falls silent, and the people have lost another hope.

Spike Lee spreads work and credit around, starting with his family, spreading outward through the neighborhood, to fellow alumni of Morehouse College, to the larger Black community itself, to, finally, what would best be called the progressives. He cast sister Joie in four of his movies, and father Bill scored and wrote music for his films until *Malcolm X*, when Spike sensed it was time to shift and did, to jazz composer Terence Blanchard. Dropping his father as scorer of his films might seem punitive, since Spike does not get on well with his stepmother, a Jewish woman in dreadlocks named Susan, mother of Arnold, Lee's six-year-old brother, or half-brother, as you like it. Lee's brother David remains the official still photographer on all of his films. A Morehouse grad, Scott

Sillers, is Lee's company comptroller; another alum, Court-
ney Counts, helps run the Spike's Joint retail shop in Brooklyn. It would be hard to name a Black American actor of note
who hasn't auditioned for him—or at least turned down an
offer to audition from him. And the actors who've used their
work in his films to springboard to greater success number
nearly as many Italian Americans as African Americans.

What Lee does best is see things coming and delegate. I
think this is why he sought me out to collaborate. Perhaps he
caught the references to Malcolm X in one of my prior books;
I've composed six book-length manuscripts—an experimental
novel, a book of short stories, a nonfiction book based on
boxing, two books of essays, Spike's book, and they all mention Malcolm X at least once. Did he catch this in his quick
study? Or was it some future project he was interested in
doing in which I might be useful to him? Of this I was certain:
Lee didn't call me because he liked my sweaters. He'd sought
out Washington years earlier when the latter was in a play,
Checkmates, on Broadway. Spike made Denzel's acquaintance, made *Mo' Better Blues* his vehicle in 1990, and
aided his own position to become director of *Malcolm X*.
Washington, nothing if not his own man, was signed to the
property at Warner's before Lee came on. This is why criticism bothers Lee—it can upset his plans. It is not the fact
Stanley Crouch dislikes him that so bothers Spike; it's that
Crouch is influential with trumpeter Wynton Marsalis, making it more difficult to get Wynton on Lee's Forty Acres and
a Mule Filmworks & Musicworks referral list.

"If I had to say Spike was better at anything, it would be
producing," says line producer Jon Kilik, who has been with
Lee since *Do the Right Thing*. "He's amazing. He'll say, 'Let's
get Stevie Wonder.' I'll say, 'We can't.' And we'll get him. He
knows what he wants and who he wants to do it. He has an
accurate dollar figure for that item and a running total in his
head. As a producer myself, I admire the hell out of him."

"Marketing. I'm proud of that," Lee says. "As far as the performing artists go, I'm the best at marketing, except for Madonna. She's the champ." Speculation among some Whites that he is a racist can become so loud it drowns out conversations among some Blacks that he is a wannabe *Mister* Uncle Tom working in an elite art form. "[Spike] talks about having final cut," said Henry L. Gates once. "One way people attack [him] is to say in the final analysis, [he] doesn't really have final cut."

I ask Lee about this. He says, "Martin Scorsese is No. 1, because he once told them he'd shoot them all in the head if they messed with any of his movies, starting with *Taxi Driver*. And for his pure cinematic sense. The way he sees the world in visuals. I admire that. Oliver Stone helped me by giving me data on how *JFK* was treated by Warner Bros. I love his work. Jonathan Demme got propers for *The Silence of the Lambs*. But I don't think there's a director alive with the pure visual sense of Scorsese. Nobody can fuck with him when it comes to visual skills. I read *Raging Bull*. Didn't think it was so hot a script. I saw that movie and said, 'Uh-oh.' Hadn't seen what he could do with it visually. I hadn't seen the additions he could make."

It is Lee's additions that some people worry about. How well does he tell stories? How well has he told this one in particular where so many hackles have been/will be raised? Lee has reason to be confident with X. His two most topical weaknesses have been:

(1) A universally decreed "choppiness" in some of his film narratives. A Spike Lee joint is a lush pastiche of images. Brilliant, hot, never-before-seen-on-film, wonderfully ironic images, but a montage of them nonetheless, lacking an easy-to-grasp thread. It was the desire to see more and more coherent (or conventional) sections of these rare Black real-life images that drove the interest in Lee's movies, more so than

any accepted dexterity with what happened to the characters and their stories.

(2) His treatment of women in that framework.

In the case of *Malcolm X*, the problems were solved for him. The script is based on a proven narrative, *The Autobiography of Malcolm X*, written with the late Alex Haley. Haley saw a portion of a rough cut weeks before he died. He pronounced it "extremely powerful. Denzel Washington is . . ." Haley shook his head.

Denzel Washington is Lee's ace in the hole—clearly now the best Black actor of his generation in what he considers the role of a lifetime. Morgan Freeman, costar with Washington in Edward Zwick's *Glory*, found Washington's intense research and his ideas "intimidating." Washington played *Richard III* in New York's Central Park, a Caribbean Xavier in *The Mighty Quinn*, South African Steve Biko in *Cry Freedom*, Reuben in *For Queen and Country*, Delta Demetrius in *Mississippi Masala*—using five wildly disparate inflections of the same language—and brought them all home. The late theater impresario Joseph Papp wanted Washington to play *Othello* with Meryl Streep. Denzel Washington is a driven man, with talent.

Within the Nation of Islam in Malcolm X's days, women were stationed behind men. One of the finest performances in *X* comes from Angela Bassett, as Malcolm's wife, Betty Shabazz.

So it was what Lee did with the story itself that would count. He had the openings. "Baldwin's script was great except for the last third. Didn't know how to handle Elijah Muhammad," Lee said. The Honorable Elijah Muhammad is played by Al Freeman, Jr., magisterial in a role of subtle internal conflict. The conflict is portrayed through Albert Hall. An easily discernible villain is often pivotal within the structure of a universally accessible narrative. Hall is feral as

Baines, the man who helps convert Malcolm in prison, then is at the root of a betrayal.

"I think what we ended up with on film was what Malcolm said himself," says Lee. "At first he believed when things happened like his house in Queens being firebombed, that it was all the Nation of Islam, but toward the end, he said, 'I'm going to stop saying it's all the Nation of Islam.' He said he'd trained them himself. He knew what they were and weren't capable of doing. For example, they couldn't deny him entry into France. That happened."

Lee does not roam too far afield from Malcolm X's public disclosure of the sexual improprieties of Elijah Muhammad, and how that fed into the frenzy of some members of the Nation of Islam against Malcolm X, or other facts of his life. Watching the print, I recall thinking, "It's all there," and my loyalty is to the effect of Malcolm; to what he thought was possible for Black people, especially those who were incarcerated or disenfranchised or otherwise left back—a chance to overcome that, or anything, by dint of an intractable discipline, inexorable talent, belief.

It will always be Spike Lee who started the '90s boom of Black cinema. Reginald and Warrington Hudlin, John Singleton, Julie Dash, Charles Lane, and Carl Franklin have come up since. Lee remains the one they admire for what he did and must top because he's in the way.

"It's like when Jackie Robinson broke into the big leagues," says Lee. "Some of the ballplayers in the Negro Leagues didn't like it very much. They said, 'I'm better than Jackie.' And they probably were. But what did they expect Jackie to do? Quit? In the end you have to please yourself."

Once I heard him talking on the phone with someone who must have been close to him as a friend, and he seemed to be upset, as if he'd been cuckolded in some way, in a general loose sense, by a collaborator or peer or lover—someone close.

"John Singleton wouldn't have done that to me," he said. Whatever "that" was seemed to have distressed him, but I did not want to hear about it this way, particularly since he had not invited me to do so. But I could hear the pain and understood what people were capable of doing to each other. When *Esquire* magazine ran a piece on him entitled *Spike Lee Hates Your Cracker Ass*, two months before *Malcolm X* was released, the title made him almost despondent. He had never buckled under these kinds of mild disappointments. I began to wonder how they affected him. I knew they didn't shape him—at least not yet. He railed against "the cult of personality" and seemed to wonder why the writer of the *Esquire* piece, Barbara Grizzuti Harrison, wrote about how he had made her uncomfortable, how she hadn't "liked" him. We all know how difficult it is for White people to "like" us when we are not thinking the way they think we are supposed to be thinking. Harrison had wanted Spike to stamp her Good White Folks papers for her.

"And I wouldn't do it," he said. Several times she wrote that he had yawned in her face. He denied it, saying he had been "raised better than that."

At the same time, he called and congratulated Tina Brown, editor of *The New Yorker*, for running a long case study entitled *The Children of Malcolm* by Marshall Frady in the Oct. 12, 1992, issue. It was elegantly wrought, told with an executioner's chill and bloodthirsty flourish for questionable detail. Example: Frady called the Nation of Islam religious orthodoxy "a kind of intellectual *Fantasia* that rivaled, in its fabulous loopiness, the racial anthropology of *Mein Kampf*." No doubt that is at least almost true. But parting the Red Sea with a stick, raising the dead, virgin pregnancy, and a blond, blue-eyed Jesus living well below the Mediterranean makes perfect and divine intellectual sense. Right. Frady took subtle pains to then suggest Malcolm X might have set fire to a house in Queens with his wife and daughters sleeping inside,

as his father had done (implied/proven?) before him. I think
this kind of revision confuses Black fathers with the Ku Klux
Klan. One day it will be Rev. Martin Luther King, Jr., who
bombed the 16th Street Baptist Church in Birmingham and
killed four little girls in 1963—one of the incidents that caused
Malcolm X to become his most incendiary self. He always
ignited through oratory. Frady's thorough work was more
ably deconstructed by Donna Britt in the *Washington Post* on
Oct. 20, 1992. But whatever it was, editorially speaking, it
was also seventeen glossy pages in *The New Yorker* including
the cover, so Tina Brown got her call from Spike.

The final genius in what Lee created with *Malcolm X* was
the tie to South Africa, not how he coddled interviewers who
wanted singular exemptions about race relations and some
ambivalence about whether or not they were fair. This was
what Malcolm X had come to in the end, a cultural, psychological link with Africa, Africa not as Black people had been
taught to see it up to that point but as a land of origin. Malcolm had put it this way in his final speech at Harvard, on
December 16, 1964: "Many people will tell you that the Black
man in this country doesn't identify with Africa. Before 1959,
many Negroes didn't. But before 1959, the image of Africa
was created by an enemy of Africa, because Africans weren't
in a position to create and project their own images." This
spoke directly to Lee. Malcolm X: "Such an image of the
Africans was so hateful to Afro-Americans that they refused
to identify with Africa. We did not realize that in hating Africa and the Africans we were hating ourselves. You cannot
hate the roots of a tree and not hate the tree itself. Negroes
certainly cannot at the same time hate Africa and love themselves. . . . We could only end up hating ourselves. Our skin
became a trap, a prison; we felt inferior, inadequate, helpless.
It was not an image created by Africans or by Afro-
Americans, but by an enemy . . ."

Spike Lee is also very clever. Sometimes he carries himself

in a way that encourages you to believe he isn't very clever. He sees the real you. You rarely see him. Lee's sense with the camera is beyond any trite criticism. Some of this was planned, some of it can't be. Prescience, hustle, and luck here and there are neither positive nor negative traits, only powerful ones which are never to be underestimated yet very often are overlooked in favor of likes, dislikes, height, weight, and other obvious ephemera. One day people might get to the real Spike Lee.

If *Malcolm X* is a great film, if there is even debate over whether it is or not, the end result is that one day it will be topped, or improved upon, and until then it will be used as a benchmark by other Black directors (or women, or whomever). The envelope of human awareness will expand. This is what defines art.

Section D, Screening Room 5. Lights up. There is an excited smattering of applause and much murmuring. Terry Semel comes over and gives Lee a we're-partners-now look. Warner's will kick in a little more money. Daly is smiling. Perhaps he wants Larry Gordon from Largo Entertainment to join further discussions in Warner exec Lucy Fisher's office, but Gordon is satisfied and out of here. His company has its good deal for the day. Dede Allen, the editor who cut *Bonnie and Clyde* and *Reds* and now is a consultant for Warner's, is smiling beatifically with editor Barry Brown. Malcolm Harding from Completion Bond Company shakes hands with Lee's co-producers, Marvin Worth, Preston Holmes, and Monty Ross. Lee says, "We're a long way from being there yet."

"Naoh Prisonawhs! Naoh Prisonawhs!" Ernest Dickerson was screaming *à la* Peter O'Toole to the January winds of the eastern Sahara as extras surrounded a re-creation of the

Ka'Ba, an Islamic shrine. The sun was barely above the horizon. The shoot would go on until after it set. A sandaled,
bespectacled Denzel Washington was off to one side, in character, wrapped in *ihram*, two white towel-cloths, twisting the
gold star and crescent ring on his finger, defying scrutiny. It
was the last week of shooting for *Malcolm X*, and he had
been working constantly since principal photography began
on September 16, 1991. It was January 19, 1992, which explained some of his brusque manner.

"Denzel was great," says Lee. "I think the fact he's handsome throws people who don't see how great an actor he is."
Washington has nothing to say about it, if you don't mind,
and even if you do. He is intent on work. Later, in a tent
near the Nile, as the *muezzin* calls for prayers, he says he
doesn't talk about work while working. He is terse but seems
to have so much to say. He begins by asking, "If I can't tease
you, who can?"

Actually, this was his way of easing up. It had been an
early call for the street bazaar scenes in Cairo. We had been
on location at the crack of dawn and had had breakfast on
the set. I spoke for a minute with Fernando Sulachin, who
had helped Spike with the locations, and with John Edgar
Wideman, who had come in to do research for a piece he was
doing for *Vogue* about Spike or Denzel or Malcolm or all
three. I took a photograph of another Black writer, Joe Wood,
and weathered more cracks from crew members about being
Denzel's stand-in, remaining unamused. Then Denzel came
silently into the billowing tent. He was stocking-capped, tac-
iturn, lovely, quite distant. The unit publicist, Anna Southall,
had told me Denzel would prefer not to interview now; later,
perhaps even back in the States. Yet here we were. So when
Denzel sat and began talking with John, an old acquaintance
of his, I sat too, and at some point I threw an innocuous two
cents into their quiet pool of conversation. Immediately Denzel flashed his annoyance. "Didn't you hear? I'm not doing

any interviews." I was about to become defensive and say I had just said something, and wasn't really asking for an interview, when he policed himself. "Aw, you can't help it," he said, cutting through to the bone. Then came, "If I can't tease you, who can?"

I thought about that. Denzel was defending his shrinking slip of privacy. He was a man who for one reason or another had learned to defend himself, and he was portraying a man who had insisted upon it. Underneath, he retained the sensitivity of the artist. He had to reveal so much of himself to be a good actor. If he wanted to keep himself hidden the rest of the time, that was understandable. His facade was the price of the ticket to his art, and the fame accompanying his position. He talked until it was time for him to go to his trailer and get into character. Later, he invited us to go back to the hotel with him in the car provided for him. It was a nice gesture I should have refused because we then proceeded to overload the car. With my usual sense of bad timing, I picked this time to announce that with all respect due to Mr. Washington and Mr. Lee, my concern was Malcolm X, because the crime had been committed against him more than it had been committed against any of us. Both of them, Denzel and Malcolm, stayed silent.

Malcolm X was born in small-town America, seventh child of Earl Little, the fourth offspring of Earl's second marriage. Earl was a part-time lay preacher and a devotee of the black nationalist Marcus Garvey. Earl Little stressed values and discipline. He died on trolley tracks in Lansing, Michigan, a death Malcolm X said was murder. Malcolm X's mother's name was Louise. She outlived Malcolm by twenty-five years. Malcolm married a woman named Betty who bore four girls and was carrying twins at the time of his death at thirty-nine. After El-Hajj Malik El-Shabazz, a.k.a. Malcolm X, was assassinated, his body was wrapped in muslin and held in state on a bier at Harlem's Faith Temple Church of God in Christ.

Denzel Washington was born in Mount Vernon, New York, in 1954, at the end of his father's second family. Denzel Sr. was a longtime Pentecostal minister in the Church of God in Christ. He stressed values and discipline. "When I finally started to do well," Washington said in Egypt, "I brought him out, showed him my new foreign car. He frowned. Said, 'Where's the G.M. car, boy?' " He divorced Denzel's mother, Lennis, when the boy was fourteen. The influence of his parents was so strong, Denzel had never heard of Malcolm X until he was twenty-three, though he'd lived in Mt. Vernon—where his mother still resides—and gone to Fordham University.

"When I read for the play *When Chickens Come Home to Roost*, I didn't know how to pronounce Elijah properly. I put the accent on the E," he says. Denzel's father was called DEN-zel, so the son is called Den-ZEL in deference. The father died in April of '91, in his eighties. "He was ready to go," says Washington, who'd married a woman named Pauletta. She's borne him four children. Washington is thirty-seven.

The gentle slap of the polluted, Stygian surface waters of the Nile seems distant even this close. Here in Egypt, everything seems so old, so distant. "Saw a photograph of Malcolm when he was on the football team at school in Michigan," Washington says. "He didn't have a number. But smiling, confident. My prayer for this film is to show how a man or woman can evolve even when the worst happens, even if you've been taught to hate."

Some months later, Denzel Washington is standing in the Paramount Theater at Madison Square Garden in New York, during an April rehearsal for the *Essence* awards show. The film is in the can. He is more agreeable about chores. There's a lot of talent in the room. Oprah Winfrey is sitting Sphinx-like amid female friends and relatives, who perk up greatly as Washington, Oprah's cohost for the evening's festivities, is sighted. He has high praise for her: "She is *good* with words, great on her feet," he says out of her earshot. Equally out of range, Oprah says, "I hear Denzel is Malcolm incarnate. The intensity, everything."

"I couldn't re-create the fact that his skin was lighter," says Washington. As for anything else he couldn't do to prepare for or execute the role of Malcolm X, he is stone silent. "You know, as I was in character, I had to give fresh speeches. The extras don't respond as well unless they want to respond. You've got to move them. And as I was giving some of those speeches, I was saying to myself, 'You know, this stuff is *true*.'

"In preparation for the role, I fasted, I studied, but by no means was I able to discipline myself to the degree Malcolm did," he says. "I didn't worry about being an imitation. Because that's what it would be. There were moments when I felt that. I'd say, 'Let's cut, Spike.' Because I found I was only imitating. Then I would try and go to the source, not to the conduit. That's what Malcolm was. The conduit. That's what I am."

Denzel is called away to run lines with Oprah. Bill Cosby camps nearby, sporting a cigar and two-day beard, deciding whether or not to tell me what he thinks. He's one of a number of major celebrities who lent Lee financial support and were thanked in public for it, whether they wanted to be publicly thanked or not. "I'm looking at the film neither positively nor negatively," Cosby says. "I'm looking at it as though Spike's an artist who should be able to interpret the material as he sees fit. Spike is an artist. Period."

One of the members of Oprah's party, a matron of perhaps fifty-five, has been eyeing Washington all along. He turns to walk up the aisle and her hand shoots out almost involuntarily, so it seems. She has grabbed his arm. "Denzel," she says. Quickly he lowers his arm away from hers and takes it away. He doesn't jerk his arm away. He takes it away. Then he flashes that daunting smile and says, "You know, you shouldn't grab people like that. I had a bad experience as a child from someone grabbing me like that. Please don't do that, all right?" The woman is smiling as though she has not heard this impromptu and apocryphal lecture. She's done what she wanted to do. She has touched Denzel Washington. Immediately Oprah is there to smooth it all over. She is great on her feet.

"As soon as I got home," Washington says a few moments later, "I was asked to do a film where I play a government guy who tracks down a fanatic Muslim. The fanatic had an A-bomb and was called the Messenger. I told the director, 'You're going to get killed doing this kind of stuff.' I wouldn't do it because the script was bad, as much as anything else. It made no sense."

Washington also turned down a script which at one time he referred to as "The Nigger They Couldn't Kill," where he was to star as a man wrongfully executed—except none of the variety of executions takes, and the character keeps surviving them. Sort of a perpetual lynching. Washington also turned down a role in *Amos 'n' Andrew*, which later went to Sam Jackson, formerly of Spike's troupe. Before that, Washington had turned down *Love Field* and a costarring role with Michelle Pfeiffer.

"They never got the script right," he says. "It was a film I passed on to begin with. I tried to work with the director and writer. It was Michelle's film, that was fine. I was just a guy who helped the story move along. I stumbled all the way to the first day of rehearsal, and I had to pass on it. It made me ill. I couldn't do it. It made me sick. I literally got sick." Before that he turned down James Cameron and the role of Miles Bennett Dyson, unwitting architect of Armageddon in *Terminator 2*.

"No offense to Jim Cameron, but when I read the script I thought, All he does is look scared and sweat," says Washington. "I had to pass. It's a burden, but at the same time, I don't see myself going back. There is stuff that I can't do, and there's never been any great conscious scheme. It's *personal*. In the past, I've done some I had to do anyway. But I've tried to patch them up while I was in them. But, yes, there is a burden now that I can't even do that. I have to feel, as an artist, that I have room to fail. I don't know if I have room to embarrass myself, or people, through my work. I may yet embarrass myself in life. You don't always control that. Sometimes you do. A script comes to you. You make a decision on it. You can, in essence, control it. If a scene says 'He showed his monkey behind, walked on one leg eating watermelon' and you shoot it, you know you're in trouble."

Who would he like to work with now? "Jonathan Demme," he says. *Voila,* within months he is cast in the role of Joe, the homophobic attorney opposite Tom Hanks in Demme's upcoming *Philadelphia*.

"Other than that, I can't say," says Washington. "Material more than people, I think. I'm not a movie star in my own perception. I'm an actor. 'Movie star' belongs to the people, not to me. Look, I've got what, $22 in my pocket. I'm of the people.

"No, it's not tough to curtail the ego once you're in my position. You don't have to get caught up in it, I don't think. You do it, and try and remain yourself." Just then, a man who is smiling too well comes and says, "Denzel, your limo has arrived." Washington pauses, then laughs deeply at himself, at his own protests. "Use that," he suggests. "If you start believing the way people treat you, you're in trouble. Movie star. I don't get off on that. I'm an actor trying to get better at his craft."

Is he finding it increasingly difficult to get better at it? Does the distance from people caused by celebrity cut off the powers of observation that made him an actor in the first place?

"Hmm. I'd say, not true. I can put on my jeans, pull down my baseball cap, go up to the Schomburg Center and do research, go out on 120th Street and study somebody, or be at home with family."

"Right now, I'm just finding it difficult to find something else to do after *Malcolm X*. What do I do? Playing this part was like winning a championship for me. Not in terms of what it is as a finished product—we don't know about that yet—but in terms of playing the role itself, the range, the challenge."

Malcolm X spent a life telling African Americans to cherish the value of their own faces and stop denying we had faces. In running the gamut of his "concentrated life," Washington appears not to perform in the role but to *become*. To an observer, this ease is fathomable, but maybe only another actor could know or recognize the arduous work behind the ease of Denzel Washington's version of Malcolm X. What does he do now? Maintain a vigilance of a kind only a very few, if any, Black actors have been able to have. He chooses his vehicles, the images of himself; chooses who can touch him as he maintains a precarious balance of tolerant intolerance, suspended between manhood, artistry, and movie stardom. It will be interesting to see how he fares.

On Thursday, April 30, as sections of L.A. burned and sirens whirred dizzyingly across national television, Spike Lee screened *Malcolm X* again at the Warner Bros. lot, telling those assembled in the screening room, "This movie is needed now more than ever." Lee screened the film July 27 in New York with Blanchard's score laid in but not mixed. Among those at TODD-AO in mid-Manhattan were Jonathan Demme, Robert DeNiro, Jim Jarmusch, Michael Moore, Chuck D, William Goldman, and Byron Lewis of Uniworld. Afterward, Goldman said, "Extraordinary. I've never seen anything like it. The performances . . ." His voice trailed off the way Haley's had.

The film's final nut was between $34 and $35 million. On

the screen, the price seems to have been higher. Spike Lee seems to have accomplished what can be the most difficult artistic feat of all: allowing the work to express itself. Unimpressed by pans for scale, *à la* Roland Joffe, the director pans wide once in a while in *Malcolm X*, like in the Joe Louis celebration scene in Harlem, but even in the desert, Lee had Dickerson keep the camera tight. The result is an intimate epic, close-up, maybe akin to what Pedro Almodovar might do with Simon Bolivar or *One Hundred Years of Solitude*. But no analogy will do for this Spike Lee joint.

Warner Bros. and Largo will make their money. And some adolescent somewhere will gaze at the full-frame special-effect shot of night riders riding into a full moon seemingly made of ice—Lee calls that shot "my homage to D. W. Griffith and *Birth of a Nation*"—or at the mass rally scenes, or at the meticulously detailed offices of Elijah Muhammad, and decide to become a filmmaker, an orator, or something else equally admirable. For him or her, I hope *Malcolm X* will be a *Birth of a New Nation*.

Denzel Washington will be hailed. He'll look for a vehicle where he can do more than look scared and sweat, where he won't compromise that suspended state between celebrity, actor, sex symbol, and man; where he can see, act, yet not be touched. And life goes on. Maybe it will get better. Maybe not. "Then I say we might as well try it this way," says Washington. "It can't get worse." He salutes you. His limo has come, and now he's gone.

By Any Means Necessary: X-ology

Welcome to the Carmichael Auditorium of the Smithsonian Institution. On the anniversary of the birth of Malcolm X, the celebration of the growth of you, and me, in honor of his own growth, I offer you his ancient greeting.

As-Salaam-Alaikum.
Malcolm X once said of the ancient greeting:

It is an expression that means "peace be unto you." So when
I say, *"As-Salaam-Alaikum"* and others reply, *"Alaikum Sa-
laam,"* why they're just returning the peace. It means we all
wish to be at peace with one another, as brothers and sisters. . . . I'm not here to discuss my religion. I'm not here to
try and change your religion. I'm not here to argue or discuss
anything we differ about, because it's time for us to submerge
our differences and realize that it is best for us to first see that
we have the same problem, a common problem, a problem
that will make you catch hell whether you are a Baptist, or a
Methodist, or a Muslim, or a nationalist. Whether you're
educated or illiterate, whether you live on the boulevard or
in the alley, you're going to catch hell just like I am. . . . So
no religion could ever make me forget. No religion can make
me forget the condition of our people in this country. No
religion will make me forget until it stops, until it's finished,
until it's eliminated. I want to make that point clear.

That was Brother Minister's crystal-clear rhetoric, and you
can understand the coinage of the icon Malcolm X when you
hear it. During this talk I will quote him further, and when I
do, I want you to realize that you have to remember what he
said in the context of the time he said it. Many things have
changed in our society. Many things appear to have changed
but have not. They have moved, but they haven't changed.
However, much of what he said is as relevant today as it was
when he said it. Some of what he said must be understood
differently. I'll begin to explain with an analogy. I hope you
will forgive my inadequacies.

Now. If you're a child at school trying to learn, trying to
better yourself and your condition and the condition of your
family, and a bully at school is bloodying your nose, knocking books out of your hand, taking your lunch money, you

might try a range of different _modus operandi_. You might try reason, humor, dissembling, avoidance. If you're brave enough you might even try to fight him back. But if that bully persists, and you're lucky enough to have a big brother, sooner or later you're going to look to him. Sooner or later, if the fire from the bully keeps getting hotter, you'll call on your big brother to bail you out—or to give you the confidence or the advice to bail yourself out. You're going to ask big brother how to get this bully off you.

I think you'll agree, if you are Black and live in this world, or if you are defined as Black, or any person of color, it's getting hotter and hotter, hotter all the time. You can see Black Haitians turned back from America's shores after having the desperate courage to brave the might of the open ocean in rickety boats—that same courage which was once the only requisite for coming to America. On the other hand, you see White Cubans (their definition, not mine) who come to America via illegally hijacked airplanes and are welcomed with open arms, admired for defecting to America. And you know it's hot. Very hot. You can see South Africa with your own eyes. You feel hot. You see the Rodney King videotape, and you know that is the law, the tacit law. Hot. The law according to some people is that we are to be no more. Hotter. Treatments for AIDS out of Kenya are being studied and praised the world over. Not here.

Rush Limbaugh is a best-selling author not because he's the second coming of George Bernard Shaw but because he says it's hot and he revels in heat. Our teenagers with unlimited access to guns and narcotics and alcohol—with our government serving as the biggest enablers since Al Capone—make it hotter than July in Washington, D.C. We know how hot that is.

Hot. Smoking. Burning up. And now here comes that bully again. So it became time for many Black people to call for big brother, who was and is Brother Minister Malcolm X, whether Carl Rowan likes it or not. Nobody's walking around wearing a baseball cap with an R on it—not yet, anyway, though that R might not be a bad idea. I'll have to see what Spike Lee can do about that.

Now, I'm not saying this to make you uncomfortable, or to make you laugh, or to rile you up. I'm telling you why Spike called me to collaborate on *By Any Means Necessary: The Trials and Tribulations of the Making of Malcolm X*. There's more to the title, but I won't go into it just yet. Spike and I are like-minded—in some ways. One of the ways we differ is I believe Spike Lee is a genius. Yes, I said genius—not as a Renaissance man or as a raconteur, but a genius at what he does, making films. It is curious, startling, that this at times nonverbal, at times mordant, contentious, rather odd brown wisp of a man with the big antelope eyes could be the repository of such genius. But, apparently, this is one way God likes to work—in a way we don't expect or understand. God knows how many Spike Lees are lost in Black ghettoes around the country, all over the world.

Back to the official title of the book: *By Any Means Necessary: The Trials and Tribulations of the Making of Malcolm X (While Ten Million Motherfuckers Are Fucking with You)*. This was Spike's idea. Wait a minute now. It was a *good* idea. I must admit I had some reservations about the title at first. But though it sounds too flip, profane, dissonant, like many of Spike's concepts do, it is well thought out. As it turns out, it is the perfect title because it reflects the unvarnished truth. The title makes you feel something—the artist raising his arms to conduct. What does it make you feel? Perhaps that people were certainly, hmm, let's call it flocking, with Spike Lee throughout the making of *Malcolm X*. You should feel it in his book. I don't know if it was ten million who were, shall we say, antagonizing him, but there were times when it seemed to be that many and more.

Let's start with the studio—Warner Bros. I'm sure there are

some executives there right now wringing their hands and talking about how they had to gross $75 million domestic in order to turn what they call a profit. Now, Warner's total outlay for *X* could not have been more than $27 million, tops, and that would include their contribution to the production budget and all the paid advertising and promotion necessary to "open the picture," as they say, plus the cost of the film prints that had to be shipped to all the theaters, just over eleven hundred. That's a figure that's "all in," as they say. Then why does it need to make three times that much to be profitable? Why isn't twice as much good enough?

We all heard about the ticket stub controversy, and people might say that was just a tempest in a teapot, a few wrong stubs here and there, stubs from *Home Alone 2* or *The Bodyguard* or *Dracula* thrown in here and there—doesn't amount to much. Well, the weekend that *Malcolm X* opened, along with *Home Alone 2*, the motion picture industry in total generated $135 million in gross sales. In one Thanksgiving weekend. I think we'd better start checking on those stubs. I clearly remember the film's star, Denzel Washington, on a cool Egyptian afternoon, long before the ticket stub controversy, talking about how he had heard of this kind of thing before, how some of his friends went to one of his movies and were issued the wrong tickets. A ticket-taker said, "S'all right, doesn't matter, go on in. Doesn't amount to much."

Yeah, go right on in, doesn't amount to much. How long have we been hearing that? So Spike Lee caught hell from the people who were doing business with him to some degree.

But then, surprise, surprise, Spike caught more hell.

In the January 9 issue of the *Washington New Observer*, television commentator Tony Brown authored a syndicated piece that called *Malcolm X* "exploitation" and chopped up Spike Lee pretty badly. Brown said the Black press was underrepresented in the paid advertising bought by Warner Bros. for the film. Brown said this was Spike's fault, where Warner's put all its money. Now, a company called Uniworld, which is owned by a Black man named Byron Lewis, was brought in and identified markets where Warner Bros. should place advertisements in the Black press. This is twenty more markets than the zero movie studios normally solicit in the Black press. But Brown questioned Spike on this.

Brown also wrote that no one who stayed out of school to see *Malcolm X* could be educated by this fellow who, in the words of Brown, "can hardly complete a sentence."

Tony Brown, who fancies himself eloquent, also referred to Spike Lee as "diminutive" and, echoing Imamu Amiri Baraka, called Spike Lee "Shorty the Hustler." Anyone who has met Brown knows this sort of teasing is not the way for him to go. It would be the pot calling the kettle . . . well, never mind.

Then Brown turned around and agreed with Hollywood and Warner Bros. stating that a movie has to gross three times its production budget to turn a profit—in other words, *Malcolm X* would have to gross just over $100 million to be successful or so Tony Brown ostensibly puts it forth. Tony Brown seemed to think the film was a failure because the film made just under $50 million at the domestic box office. This was before foreign distribution, cable, and video stores. So apparently it was "exploitation" to Tony Brown because it didn't make Warner Bros. any richer than it was already getting. But everybody made their money and some people, especially Warner Bros., will turn a tidy profit, which is what an investor should do if you want to stay in business on either end of the equation. And some people, like Uniworld and Spike and Betty Shabazz and twenty Black-owned newspapers, at the very least, made some money (but not too much money, just to keep Tony Brown happy). More important, many talented black actors, artists, technicians, and craftspeople and, yes, book writers and publishers and television producers and talk-show hosts and guests and street vendors, they all were paid to contribute to something priceless, strong and rooted in African-Americana.

Brown made no mention of the artistic content of the film—whether or not it was a "flop" as a work of art—which leads me to believe he knows absolutely nothing about film as either business or art. A flop is a movie that makes, say, $2 million, not $50 million, domestic. As I say, Brown makes no mention of the artistic content of the film, and after thinking it through I believe I may know why. It could be that he doesn't know the difference. Why do I say this? Well, Brown directed a film a few years ago. It was called *The White Girl*. If he wants to define "exploitation" and "flop," commercially or artistically, he would do better to start at home.

I paid $50 to see *The White Girl* at a special screening in New York, at Lincoln Center, I think, to help defray Brown's costs. You see, he couldn't get a distributor to touch his film with a 10-foot pole. But I paid my 50 and what did I see— amateur filmmaking looking back at me. The actors did everything but say cheese. The good ones' hearts weren't in it, because they knew they would have to explain their appearances in this stink bomb to their relatives or somebody later. I can hear them now. "Hey man, I got bills, too." The sets were threadbare; background staging was nonexistent. But I paid my $50 and sat there and winced like a good soldier because it's what we do sometimes as Black people—we bite our tongues when we should speak, and we speak when we should bite our tongues. But I felt good at least, because I'd helped Brown out of a tough spot. At no point did I write an article accusing him of raging, rapacious incompetence as a filmmaker, and, worse, of taking my fifty under false pretenses.

Spike also caught hell from the people whom much of the movie was about—the differing factions and splinter groups of the Nation of Islam. I think Spike was warned or threatened by all of them unanimously. "Better not show Malcolm doing this. Better not show the Honorable Elijah Muhammad doing that. You best be careful, Spike." And some of these people do not play. As Richard Pryor once said, you have to watch out for them double Muslims, because some of them can't wait to get to Allah.

But how and when had they been portrayed in American cinema before? Not well, if at all. That is no longer true. Now we have seen examples of Black men with straight backs and families and principles. They were not above human frailties. Lee showed that as well. The artistic record of American cinema was achieved and changed forever, simultaneously, with the film's release.

Once the film was released, here came print media and its columnists. I never saw so many editorial columns filled with such op-ed hysteria caused by one film in my life, unless it was for the film *JFK*. That's the only other film I recall that got the editorial writers so upset. The milder of the editorialists talked about how the film was "commercializing an icon." But who does Christmas commercialize, every single year? Who is kidding whom? Since when had Malcolm X become an icon of any sort to most editorial writers? They assiduously avoided writing about him, or his impact, like it would give them the plague had they done so. They'd avoided it for nearly thirty years. Why all the concern about commercialism now, especially since all the editorial writers were also getting paid to write about how Black people shouldn't get paid to tell a story about one of their own heroes or anti-heroes in the first place. And don't get me wrong when I say anti-hero. Robin Hood was an anti-hero. And Robin Hood would be a good stand-in for the symbolism of Malcolm X. Or vice versa.

One editorial writer named Colman McCarthy had me believing for years about how fair and liberal-minded he was. But when he wrote about *Malcolm X* after the film came out, I knew I had been mistaken. He was fair when he wanted to be—fair only when it suited him. McCarthy posited that Malcolm represented nothing of value, nothing worthwhile, that there was nothing to be learned from his life and death, and as I was reading I knew McCarthy knew practically nothing of Malcolm compared to what I knew. I knew Malcolm X had come up from the bottom, the dregs, the abyss, where so many of our young people languish today. He came up and assumed a position of moral, mental leader, not with the cadences of the Southern ministers, whom academics consider rather quaint once they leave the room. No. Malcolm X made the academics pay attention. He made you pay attention. He spoke their language, the way they spoke it, quick and to the point. *I'm the man you think you are,* he said. Then he spoke our language, warm and effusive. I knew the experience of Malcolm X meant anything was possible. All McCarthy knew was his own agenda. So much for liberalism. *Civil rights bill down the drain,* as Malcolm said.

This same McCarthy, a few months later, praised the release of Jean Harris from a New York prison—a woman who in a fit of pique killed her lover, Dr. Herman Tarnower, some twelve years ago. McCarthy was for clemency and understanding for a White woman who had done murder, which is fine, which is humane. But he remained intractably set against a Black man who had defended himself only with words.

Another editorial writer, Charles Krauthammer, wrote about there being no White characters with redeeming qualities in the film. The first temptation is to say, "Well, now you know how it feels," but that would be small-minded and inaccurate as well. Because he doesn't know and could never know how it feels unless he endures it for, oh, all his life, rather than three hours and twenty-one minutes. But they'd likely be one of the first ones to wax rhapsodic over D. W. Griffith and *Birth of a Nation* or *Gone with the Wind*, without a thought to the heinous characterizations of all Black people within those so-called "American classics." I felt the Whites in *Malcolm X* were well drawn. I didn't get the feeling most of them were bad people. We could see that their hands were tied. They were doing what the system made them do.

Think about it. Take the Karen Allen character. She played the social worker, Miss Dunne. She was polite. She asked to come into the Little home in Lansing. There was empathy in her eyes. But Louise Little's children were still taken away, not by any single bad-hearted White person but by a system. Then take the teacher character, Mr. Ostrowski, played by David Patrick Kelly. He was trying to help Malcolm Little, at least in his own mind, by telling him that a nigger can't become a lawyer. As far as Mr. Ostrowski knew, that was the truth. That's the way things were. His tone was kind and paternal. He was trying to be honest with Malcolm. He was trying to spare him hurt down the road, when he'd run into those racists. It wasn't that one individual White person who said he couldn't be a lawyer. It was the system. Now take the White insurance adjuster, Mr. Holway, played well by George Guidall, who told Louise Little, played by Lonette McKee, that Earl Little had committed suicide, and backed himself up with a police report. The first policeman on the scene, a White man, said that the mortally wounded Earl Little had sat up, in spite of those mortal wounds, and then made sure to tell the policeman that he had slipped trying to catch the trolley and fell onto the tracks, under the trolley wheels and therefore the insurance wouldn't pay off. Louise Little asks Mr. Holway, "You mean a man bashes the back of his own head in, then lies down on the tracks?" And you can see sympathy in the White actor's face—the empathy, the human kindness that said, "If it were up to me, I'd pay, but it's not up to me. It's the company. My hands are tied." You can see this on his face. But it wasn't up to him, his empathic look said in the film. He was accountable to the system, therefore she would get no money, therefore she would lose her children. But it was no individual's fault. Spike's White actors portrayed this nicely.

The only apparently evil White people in the whole film are portrayed under sheets, as the Klan and White Citizens Councils, and in actual sixteen-millimeter news footage spliced into the final print. We could continue talking about the ambivalent White characters Spike showed us, who were good, who knew right from wrong, whose hands were tied by the system. What about the White prison guard Barnes, played by Larry Attile? He was sympathetic. When the Baines character, played so well by Albert Hall, told this White prison guard to give the new fish called Satan a break for not saying his number, what did the White guard do? He said, "Okay, I'll give him a break," and he asked Malcolm to say his number again. Your average prison guard is not in the business of giving inmates breaks, unless it's the break of a bone. You could tell this guard had some kind of human empathy. Even later, he asked Baines and Malcolm if they were going to "take yard." The White guard didn't tell them. He asked. He's real enough.

What about the White, blond, blue-eyed Muslim in Mecca who broke bread with Malcolm? What about the White reporter who questioned Malcolm at the press conference after his return from Africa, asking if he was prepared to bring charges in the U.N.? Neither of those Whites was even slightly heinous. So is Charles Krauthammer's guilt so blinding he can't recognize the brilliance of the reenactment, the height of the cinema? Which characters is Charles Krauthammer talking about? Did he want even the people under the sheets portrayed as kindly and ambivalent? Something seems to distort his perceptions. You can tell him I said so.

Malcolm X himself put it this way, in December of 1964:

I was speaking to the American ambassador in a certain country on the African continent. First thing he told me was, "I think you're a racist," and so forth and so forth and so forth. Well, I respected him because he spoke his mind, and once I explained my position, what I believed in and so forth, he said, "You know, as long as I'm on the African continent"—he had been an ambassador in a couple other African countries and an African head of state had told me he was the best ambassador America had on the African continent, that's why I talked with him—he said, "As long as I'm in Africa I deal with people as human beings. For some strange reason color doesn't enter into it at all. I'm more aware of differences in language than differences in color; it's just a human atmosphere. But whenever I return to the United States and I'm talking to a non-White person I'm conscious of it, I'm self-conscious, I'm aware of the color difference."

I told him, "What you're telling me, whether you realize it or not, is that it's not basic in you to be racist. The society there in America, which you all have created, makes you racist."

Krauthammer and McCarthy were emblematic of many editorial writers. White film reviewers, for the most part, were able to get past feelings of guilt and see the art on film. Some Black editorial writers were worse than the White ones, from those in the Black far right, represented by Carl Rowan, to the Black far left, represented by Amiri Baraka. I suggested this to Spike: "When you make 'em all holler, you know you're on to something."

For Baraka, Spike Lee didn't paint Malcolm nationalist-Marxist-Leninist enough. Even the people who invented Marx and Lenin are having trouble carrying all that labeling around these days. There was also not enough of the Pan-Africanist, not enough "Omowale," Malcolm's given African name, in the film for Baraka—although by his tone I was beginning to suspect Lee couldn't have gotten it right in his eyes. That's a guess on my part.

Spike painted Malcolm too militant for Rowan's taste, but then raspberry Jell-O is too militant for Rowan's taste. But here's the point: Malcolm X died twenty-eight years ago, and

Lee had everybody running around sweating, writing columns—and getting paid to write them, make no mistake about that—like Malcolm is just around the corner on a soapbox. They were still in a state of belief, even though they'd left the movie theater months earlier.

Critic, university professor, and author Shelby Steele wrote that the film was "middle-brow," and many reviewers were disappointed that the film was "too conventional." People expect something different from Spike. They didn't seem to realize that in this case the conventional was highly unconventional, not only for Lee but for the subject. Think about it: A conventional film biography, a Hollywood biopic, about the once-feared spokesman of the Black Muslims' Lost-Found Nation of Islam in America.

Kenneth Turan, the film critic of the *Los Angeles Times*, called this convention "subversive."

Lloyd Rose of the *Washington Post* called it "an act of immense political imagination." Rose pointed out that Lee had made many small films within the larger film—only he filled the all-White roles he grew up watching with the Black people of his life. Musical. Gangster movie. Prison flick. Biopic. Epic.

Then Dick Gregory checked in with complaints. Cathy Hughes said that Spike showed Malcolm kissing the blonde White woman, the character Sophia, played by Kate Vernon, but he didn't show him kissing Betty Shabazz, played by Angela Bassett. But this was the inverse of all those portrayals of the Black woman as vacuum-headed, vain, whorish, loose, or altogether asexual, and the White woman as on a pedestal, pure. It's about time we had a portrayal of a real Black woman, and not a lusty wench or a fat maid. Intimacy between Malcolm and Betty was portrayed, but not lust. I admired Spike's rectitude, and Dr. Betty Shabazz didn't seem to have much of a problem with that either, a minor upset.

Other women suggested that Ella Collins, Malcolm's half-sister, should have been portrayed in a central role in the early part of the film, instead of Shorty. I myself might have had Muhammad Ali as a character. But then all those would have been personal choices we would have made had we made a film.

What I think people have to understand is that a film comes from a concept, and in this case the concept was the autobiography, by Malcolm X and Alex Haley, informed by a script by James Baldwin. So you're not only taking on Lee, you're taking on Malcolm X, who told the story, and Alex Haley, who wrote the story, and James Baldwin, who crafted the script with Arnold Perl, and Spike Lee. Spike is the only one left alive now, so he is the one catching all the hell. But no matter how you cut it, that is a lot of African-American talent on the case. Spike took the heat because he's the artist in the medium that is in question, film. Again, some of the reactions are unfortunate, but in the end, if one is an artist, it is the reaction that informs you if the art works, starting with your own. If the art grabs you by your shoulders and shakes you until you have to holler and protest, you might be on the right track. If you can't ignore it, it's halfway there. Art makes you protest, think: This is what art does. I was beginning to get the suspicion that this film was art. All the people I have named told me by their reactions. I explain to them: The vehemence of your reaction is correlated to the power of the art. I myself would have done some things differently had it been my film. I would have added more of Malcolm's speeches within the narrative, speeches that spoke directly to the people, of which Malcolm made many:

Now, if there are White people who are genuinely and sincerely fed up with the conditions Black people are stuck in here in America, they have to take a stand, not a compromising stand, not a tongue-in-cheek stand, not a nonviolent stand, but a committed stand. . . . Now, in speaking like this, it doesn't mean that we're anti-White, but it does mean we're anti-exploitation, we're anti-degradation, we're anti-oppression, and if the White man doesn't want us to be anti-him, let him stop oppressing and exploiting and degrading us. . . .

This is our investment. This is our contribution—our blood. Not only did we give of our free labor, we gave of our blood. Every time America had a call to arms, we were the first ones in uniform. We died on every battlefield the White man had. We have made a greater sacrifice than anybody who's standing up in America today. We have made a great contribution and collected less. Civil rights means, "Give it to us now. Don't wait for next year. Give it to us yesterday, and that's not fast enough!"

. . . . The white man wants you to remain a boy, he wants you to remain a lackey, he wants you to remain dependent on him, and come looking to him for some kind of advice, some kind of teaching. No. You teach yourself, and stand up for yourself, and respect yourself, and know yourself, and defend yourself, and be yourself, and you will be recognized as an intelligent person.

Now, I might have included speech excerpts like that and let Denzel Washington deliver them. But I also know that even the speeches in a film must help drive the film's narrative, help tell the story we're watching. It is not as simple as letting a man make a speech you want to hear. And besides this film wasn't my vision. It wasn't Dick Gregory's vision. It wasn't Cathy Hughes's vision. This was Spike Lee's vision. I have every right to go make an X movie of my own. But having seen Spike's version, I'd rather not suffer greatly by any comparisons. Maybe I'll just stick to writing an occasional book. The nature of truth depends on the teller of truth and the listener. Even Malcolm told his own story for dramatic effect, the better to master its imagery.

The art of film begins with what is called the suspension

of disbelief. The filmmaker tries to leave nothing false within the frame for the eye to take in and cry, "bogus." For example, if the frame is depicting the year 1942, and you put a McDonald's cup or a Los Angeles Dodgers baseball cap in the frame, then you are going to lose your audience because they will stop believing they're in 1942. It sounds simple, but when you stop and think about all the details there are in most films, you see it's not. I tell people Spike must have made a great picture because a lot of you are still in a state of belief.

But how does this genius manifest itself further than merely the suspension of disbelief, which is just the backdrop? It becomes manifest in the first frames—the Rodney King videotape, the burning flag, the introduction and voice of Malcolm X making a speech. Then we CUT TO: Boston, The War Years. What is it we first see? We see a huge billboard towering over Roxbury, Massachusetts. And what is depicted? A lovely blonde lass, surrounded by four White sailors. The advertising is for a cola. The words on the billboard: "The Coke's In." There's a lot of symbolism in that shot. We get it subliminally because we then PAN DOWN TO: Shorty, played by Spike. The artist will have his indulgences. It is the price we pay for the art. Small enough. Soon we meet young Malcolm, who is getting his hair "conked" so it resembles the hair of the sailors, really. Soon he will meet Sophia, who is just as blonde as that lassie in the billboard.

The dance scene of Lionel Hampton's "Flying Home" speaks for itself. In his autobiography Malcolm X had taken particular note of that song and of the free-fall lindy-hopping he'd once loved. But let's examine the background staging during these scenes. Did you notice, after the production number, when Laura, played by Theresa Randle, excuses herself and goes to the powder room, when Malcolm sees Sophia? I'd say we all remember this. But how many noticed, as Sophia and Malcolm move onto the dance floor, *Laura is there in the background,* moving along with them, looking over the couples, tentatively peering around them, through them, full of anxiety, as she sees this man she cares about being transfixed by Sophia? And no matter how close Sophia's and Malcolm's faces come to each other, Laura's remains between them, to haunting effect. Extraordinary background staging. Malcolm later becomes Malcolm X and recruits numbers so high the Nation of Islam needs huge halls to hold its rallies. In front of a large mural of Elijah Muhammad, Malcolm is giving a speech on racial separation. His head is framed directly between the eyes of Elijah in the mural. Symbolism: Malcolm is saying what Elijah would have a good soldier say. Malcolm, of course, of his volition, later said this: "We have to keep in mind at all times that we are not fighting for integration, nor are we fighting for separation. We are fighting for recognition, as free humans in this society."

A film like this is that kind of recognition—if we can see it for what it is and get past all our unleashed emotions. It's not often you get to see Black men controlling their images, being good and bad, strong and weak, capturing the gamut on film.

Malcolm X, verbatim:

They master this imagery, this image-making. They give you an image of extremist, and from then on, everything you do is seen as extreme. They can paint an image of you as someone irresponsible. The press is powerful in its image-making role. It can make a criminal look like he's the victim and make the victim look likes he's the criminal. If you aren't careful, media will have you hating the people who are being oppressed and loving the people who are doing the oppressing.

Why is it we have difficulty standing on our own two feet? The Negro has no self-confidence. He has no self-confidence in his own race, because the white man has destroyed your and my past. He has destroyed, shrewdly, our knowledge of our own culture and achievements, and by destroying it, now we are convinced we've never done anything. As long as you are convinced you have never done anything, you can never do anything. . . . This is why the white man shrewdly teaches his children about George Washington, and all our children ever hear about is picking cotton. Well, cotton-picking don't move me!

I wanted to capture some of this in the book about the film, without being too obvious. The structure of the book was my idea. That was my contribution. I gave Spike the blueprint, the floor plan, the four walls and the frame and the roof. He filled it in with the building materials he chose, what he chose to tell me. He also added a window seat here, a sunken tub and Jacuzzi there, a deck here, a skylight there, an archway here, a glass door there. I wanted his book—hear me clearly on this—I wanted his book to read as the story of *one mind thinking*.

So this was Spike's mind thinking, as he was making this one film. It was not haphazard, this structure.

This reminds me of a nice woman over at National Public Radio who got me on her show and then said, "Well, this just seems like you turned the tape recorder on—what do you want people to get out of this book?"

I knew right away she hadn't read the book, which is okay, but she sounded as though she believed it wasn't worth reading, which was not okay. I wanted to say to her, "Really, ma'am? Do you think it's simple? Why do you think it's simple? Because I did it? Because it reads as though it was simple? My dear, that is the art of it. To make it look easy. If you think it's easy, maybe we should give you a tape recorder and point you toward a movie set and see what you can do." I restrained myself. I was taught rhetorical self-defense by a master, Malcolm X. Except I am not him, because he was a rhetorical genius. Myself, I usually think of what I should've told rude people an hour after I've left their company: "Aw, I shoulda told her that." I was there to talk about the book. It was hard to turn the other cheek.

The voice of the book was to be *one mind thinking*. I knew that Spike was filming Malcolm's mind thinking, which, to the best of our knowledge, had been captured by Haley in *The Autobiography of Malcolm X*. That, as far as we know, is the story Malcolm told. And Alex Haley constructed that story as the story of one mind thinking, Malcolm's mind. It was told in cold, clear, almost telegraphic sentences, not dialectic unless he was quoting people—cold and sober American English-language rhetoric.

Of course this was reflective of Malcolm X, because it was rhetoric that he had mastered, coming from the abyss to do so, coming from the dregs, from prison, to debate at Harvard, at the Oxford Union, the Audubon Ballroom, 125th Street and Seventh Avenue, Selma, Alabama, the capital cities of Africa and the West. *The Autobiography* is the story of his mind thinking.

I, on the other hand, had Spike's mind to translate. It doesn't think the same way. I wanted to compose *The Autobiography of the Malcolm X Film*. Spike's mind thinking. He thought the film should be made this way at least in part. As an example, you recall Malcolm as a railroad porter hawking food on the train and the sailor stopping him and buying a sandwich and saying, "You're awfully pleased with yourself, aren't you . . . boy?" In Malcolm's mind, he pasted the sailor's face with a wedge of lemon meringue pie—just as all of us, Black and White and tan, have done in our minds. Spike was smart enough to film it, then cut back to "reality," as it was evoked in the film, where you could see that Malcolm had not really done it, he'd only *thought* about doing it.

People have mentioned the profanity in this book. I can't speak for Terry McMillan, who wrote the introduction, but I *had* to speak for Spike. Spike uses profanity the way a black kettle uses a whistle vent. When the profanity appears, it is usually a venting. Sometimes it can be an accent mark to his dry humor, his humor *noir*, but usually it is a venting of anger, a way to rid this particular artist of nettlesome rage that at times can be harnessed in the creative process but often becomes a hindrance to be disposed of, vented in some way—like profanity—before the artist can move on to the higher level of creation, reenactment. The profanity is what keeps Spike Lee from having an aneurysm before he gets a film made, I think. Particularly this one.

Even here, the one mind is thinking and must confront the use of profanity. As Lee has told Malcolm X's brothers and sister, he tries to put some meaning behind the "motherfuckers" he uses in films, but he is guilty as charged of using them. In this film, Baines tells Malcolm, "a man uses profanity when he cannot find the words to express himself." Lee finds himself in that dilemma regularly, I think. The book would be an inaccurate portrait without the profanity. I've had people—White people, usually—ask me if Spike is a racist. I usually don't answer them. I'll say this to you now: I've never seen, read, or watched the work of a truly great artist who was unaware that the universality of human experience was transcendent over particulars of race or gender or religion. So when people ask me if Spike Lee is a racist, I usually say to them, "I don't know. Are you?"

Also, within the book, I decided to use other voices—I almost said a Greek chorus, oh hell, I will say a Greek chorus; we've got to give them credit for something—of the people, the artists and craftspersons who worked with Spike not only on this project but on others through the years leading up to this project. The chorus was made up of Monty Ross, Jon

Kilik, Preston Holmes, Ruth Carter, Barry Brown, Wynn Thomas, Denzel Washington. I wanted to capture their minds as well, their minds thinking as they met and joined up with Spike, how they "cut into him," as we used to say. Their own version, their mind's eye of this meeting, what they thought of Spike when they first met him. How they came to see him after working with him over a number of years and projects. I wanted them to respond in a fresh new way that maybe they hadn't thought about before. The trick, if it can be properly called that, was to get everyone to be completely honest, or as honest as possible. To come up with something new.

In doing this, I noticed that Lisa Jones had collaborated on three of the earlier Spike Lee film books. By the way, Lisa Jones is Amiri Baraka's daughter. Yes, she is. This is why writing fiction is so hard—because it would be impossible to make this sort of stuff up. I also wanted to keep the narrative tight, not have so many voices that the soloist—Spike—was drowned out, so I decided not to have casting director Robi Reed's voice. That was a mistake, because I believe if anybody deserves recognition for his or her work in this film, it is certainly the casting director. I console myself with an old Asiatic proverb which states that the artist should build a flaw into any work—not a deadly flaw, but one to remind you that only God is perfect and we can never be. Sorry, Robi. All praises are due you. Only the mistakes have been mine.

The greatness of a person, place, or thing is related to its most simple qualities. The greatness of the story of Malcolm X has nothing to do with the Nation of Islam, Pan-Africanism, films, or books that might be flawed. The greatness of his story is that he came from nothing, from the bottom, to triumph and endure.

I hope I've shed some light on this portion of our mad little dash through a part of recent American film and media history. I hope you'll find your own fascination with the film. I hope you'll use it as a springboard to learn more about Malcolm Little, Malcolm X, El-Hajj Malik El-Shabazz, a man to whom all of us should be able to point with understanding and say, I know of him. I know of his effect. I respect him. I respect you. Let's move on from there. I leave you now with his ancient greeting:

As-Salaam-Alaikum.

How Black People Regard
a Certain Movie Star

SONNY STORM: But if I pray for other peo-
ple, how am I supposed to get what I want?
MASON STORM: Well, that's kind of why
God invented work.

God didn't invent Steven Sea-
gal, movie star. Not unless Michael Ovitz *is* God, after all.
Seagal is a sleek cigarette boat plowing through the Action-
Adventure Triangle, where American film patrons (including
some 35 percent who happen to be Black) vacation to the
tune of a half-billion dollars a year, domestic. Warner Bros.'
Hard to Kill and Twentieth Century Fox's *Marked for Death*
took in $87 million combined in 1990, and Seagal's end of
the Schwarzenegger-Eastwood-Stallone (or Lundgren-Norris-
Van Damme, depending on view) universe increased, starting
with the release of Warner's *Out for Justice*, followed by *Under Siege* in October '92. Naturally we recognize the above
dialogue from the doting-father-to-cute-son scene between
bloodlettings in *Hard to Kill*.

What? You don't recognize the repartee as flowing from Seagal's mind, pen, and lips? You say you have not yet found occasion to confuse him with Orson Welles, or even Kevin Costner? You say dialogue is all but superfluous to a film genre in which "Make my day," "I'll be back," and "If it bleeds, we can kill it," play like Paddy Chayefsky or August Wilson? You think an action-adventure film is where a great soliloquy is knitted eyebrows? Who does Seagal think he is, and what does he want? Aren't those the questions?

Or is it the other way around? Who do *we* think Seagal is? What do we want him to be? Michael Ovitz is said to be the most powerful man in Hollywood from his station as the head of the Creative Artists Agency. Is Seagal the monster of Ovitz's grandiose visions? Is Seagal the flav-of-the-year ocean liner every Hollywood barnacle wants to attach itself to while it's iceberg-proof? Or is Seagal the genuine article? It depends on whom you ask and who you are.

If you are Steven Seagal, you are convinced you're the genuine article, the McCoy, and that would be putting it quite mildly. Either Ovitz has convinced you, or you have convinced yourself. You are convinced either way.

It is early afternoon on the East L.A. warehouse set of *Out for Justice*, which at the time was titled *The Price of Our Blood*. The film is being directed by John Flynn, who also directed *Best Seller*. *Out for Justice* is Seagal formula all the way: Brooklyn lawman is disenchanted by those around him. Loved ones are offed by bad guy—big mistake by bad guy. Lawman exacts a gory and well-choreographed revenge, replete with guns, kicks, and signature limb-breaking. Seagal is never far out of character. He's in his bus, attended by an assistant named Raeanne. He holds an apothecary jar filled with tablets of concentrated papaya, which he is eating like popcorn. The names of the characters may change—Nico

Tosceri in *Above the Law*, Mason Storm in *Hard to Kill*, John Hatcher in *Marked for Death*, and Gino Felino in *Out for Justice*—but we know it is Seagal. He is wearing a charcoal gray shoulder-padded shirt, his six-foot-five frame folded into small sections behind a table. He's comfortable where it appears impossible for him to be really comfortable. The meandering nose; the delicate ears; the close, recessed eyes under unwavering brows; the ponytail; the faint buzz of a voice—everything is in place. If he is an illusion, he is consistent. He is made up for the day's shooting and slightly pissed off, or ready to be. But he thinks he *will* get his writer's credit this time.

"And from now on," he says. "I am a filmmaker, and one day somebody will write it," he says. He studies you with those hooded eyes as if to add, you could be the one to do it. "The studios know it or they wouldn't have given me the clout. C.A.A. knows it. I know how to make films. I think people will see it with this picture. I am not a thespian. I am not somebody who loves acting so fucking much that I'll delve into a character and live there the rest of my fucking life. Frankly, most of the actors I meet I don't even like. I think some of them are emotionally shallow individuals.

"Michael Ovitz always said to me that this is the only business where people root for everyone else. They root for your defeat. Yeah, Michael Ovitz gets credit for me. He's the one who gave me a shot, and that's worth everything in this town. But I know how some people in the studios feel. One day an executive pulled me aside and said, 'We did not want to make this fucking movie, okay? We were forced to make it because of this and this. But we want you to know as far as we are concerned, you ain't nothing but a fucking karate teacher for some guy. You don't know shit. And we are going to teach you that you don't know shit.'

"The only thing I could appreciate was his honesty, his directness. See, people hate an honest man. Some of the most powerful people in the world and in this business"—wonder who, I think—"keep saying to me I've got to learn how to lie. Look into their faces and lie. And I can't do it."

If you work at a Hollywood studio, it's possible you are going to have a problem with some of this. To you it may seem Seagal is all but the antichrist's archangel, a symbol of what has gone wrong, the harbinger of doom—or at least the harbinger of downsizing, mergers, foreign takeover, and loss of creative control—the Big Wrap. To you, Ovitz's C.A.A., with its packaging and blinding client list, makes business difficult. He can make a star out of nobody if he likes, and to you, Seagal is a no-talent nobody.

"Steven started at the top," admits Paul Bloch of Rogers & Cowan, publicist for Seagal as well as Sylvester Stallone, among many others. "It was just there, in those eyes. You can't fool the camera. It looks inside. In five minutes, you're figured."

Then why can't most people do the same?

Is it because he's a Japanophile? For years, off and on, Seagal lived in Japan, starting with a stretch of four beginning in 1971. He was nineteen. He spent four years without seeing his homeland, at a time when many teenagers are worrying about Econ 101 and frat rushes, or whether to pull an overtime shift with a delivery or food service company. Seagal, a *gaijin*, a foreigner, became a student of aikido, one of the gentler of the martial arts. He studied at the feet of Deguschi Naohi, the spiritual connection to the founder of the discipline, Morihei Uyeshiba. He came back to L.A. eventually, married a Japanese aikido teacher, Miyako Fujitani, and fathered two children—a son, Kentaro, sixteen, and a daughter, Ayako, who is twelve. He even met his current wife, Kelly LeBrock, in Japan, though in the classic Hollywood fashion: Her publicist called in 1984.

Seagal returned to America to open a dojo in L.A. called Ten Shin and eventually became aikido's Spiritual Connection to the Stars, showing the likes of James Mason, Sean Connery, Ovitz, and others how to fend off imaginary attackers, sweat a little, and listen for a change. They liked him. It was as simple as that. Now Seagal is a star with a deep background in the CIA—a deadly martial artist who depicts the worst nightmare about governmental covert operations, while his ears look like they've never been hit. If you're a well-known martial artist with puffy ears for trophies, you look at Seagal's delicate, unhit ears and wonder if he's legit. Then, on top of that, he gets to rewrite his scripts and pick his personnel and call himself a filmmaker. As a mid-level studio exec, you doubt whether a relative novice can pull all this off. But what's to doubt? It's Hollywood. You mean Marilyn Monroe wasn't actually blonde? You mean Rock Hudson didn't want Doris Day in quite that way? You mean things aren't always what press releases say they are? Yet it makes no sense to identify you because your suspicions are uttered off the record, in that same Pan's whisper Seagal uses:

JOHN HATCHER: *Father, I've slept with informants. I've falsified evidence. I've taken drugs. All to catch the bad guys. I realized I had become that which I most despised.*

It's a winter night in Hollywood, and you've joined a few C.A.A. account executives and movers and shakers gathered at the Coronet Theater to cluck over the innards of a one-act play that might have future uses. You are a director of creative affairs at either Universal, Tri-Star, or Disney. Sometimes even you can't remember. Your escort for the evening is a female vice-president of production at the same studio. You're both a little weary of the guerrilla fighting with agents and talent that you have to engage in just to get a movie made, much less to get it made the way you'd like to see it made. You watch the C.A.A. people. If any deals are going to be cut, they are the ones who will cut them. Are they swaggering? If they work for C.A.A., they seem to swagger whether they do or not. You are a director of creative affairs at a movie studio, and you are out in the cold.

"Look at them, swaggering around like they own the town," you say.

"They do," says your escort.

"Now here comes your friend, writing about Seagal, making it worse, making one of their creations legitimate."

"But Seagal's selling tickets," your escort says. "Isn't that good for the whole business in the long run?"

You don't want to hear that. "Yeah, yeah, yeah," you say. "We're all looking for good material, but pay attention to what's happening to the guy's head. I mean, in the first place, he can't act. We all know that he can't act. And now he thinks he's a filmmaker? But more important, look what's happening to the guy! He's becoming like Bruce Willis! He's becoming like . . . Eddie Murphy! He's out of control!"

"But isn't this the Last Great American Business? Aren't people going to get out of control sometimes?"

You sigh at this ill-informed babble from the wrong coast. You know the end must be near if Seagal can get away with being called a filmmaker. You try to drown your mood in cabernet and continue to dis Seagal—until you get lucky and hook into a package. Then your tune becomes different.

"We are happy—no, we're thrilled with Steven. And not just as an actor but as a filmmaker," says Rob Friedman, standing in for Terry Semel, CEO of Warner's. So there is no doubt Seagal will get a new agreement with Warner's then.

"No comment," says Friedman.

"I only know one studio that's run by a filmmaker," Seagal says. (Does he mean the rest are run by bankers, agents, and lawyers?) "They're run by people who know how to count really well," he says. "They know the laws. How to distribute really well. Distribution and marketing have nothing to do with making films. You don't have to know a hell of a lot about filmmaking and you can still make money.

"Talk to some of the people here on the set and they'll tell you. I cast everybody on this picture. The technicians are all people who waited and didn't work so they could work with me. Every word in the script, either I wrote it or left it in because it was right. The confessional scene from *Marked for Death*? Those are my lines. And that confession pissed a lot of people off because I was saying a lot of shit that nobody wanted to hear. Did Warner Bros. or Fox or anybody else want to hear me say I've taken drugs? No."

"Steven is sort of a dichotomy," said Jerry Orbach, who co-stars in *Out for Justice*. "He does action-adventure maybe better than anybody. But he wants to be an intellectual at heart concerning producing and writing. I don't know if he's going to be able to do it. He's still gonna have to kill two dozen people per picture or his fans aren't gonna be happy."

Marked for Death was Seagal's most interesting film to date, partially because it was made for $12 million and grossed $42 million, domestic. His initial effort, 1988's *Above the Law*, was murky at best. Siskel & Ebert can tell you the specifics of all that if you're interested. But somehow Steven Seagal sailed through this seaweed-infested Sargasso Sea, the cigarette boat cleaving still water.

Associate producer Peter MacGregor-Scott is chain-smoking Salem Lights and remembering *Above the Law* from a back office at the Lacy Street studio. "I saw this film and I said, 'This guy is a movie star.' No doubt in my mind. When you've got it, you've got it. It's not something you can buy. This is my seventy-fifth film, and I'll tell you, it's a pleasure. I did *Marked for Death* as a negative pickup because I was absolutely interested in working with Steven." A negative pickup—which refers to rights to a film that is already made, and not to balance sheets—is not unusual in Hollywood. MacGregor-Scott was testing the writer's frame of reference.

Veteran art director Gene Rudolph came aboard *Out for Justice* after seeing *Marked for Death* and saying, "I would have been proud to have my name on that picture." "I come up with the big referral lists," says MacGregor Scott, belching smoke. "Steven makes the call. He saw *Trading Places* on tape and said, 'Get me that guy for art director.' He wanted [editor] Bob Feretti, who cut *Die Hard*. We got him. It doesn't hurt that people know with Steven, the movie's going to get made."

"Is it easy to work with him?" says director Flynn. "It never is easy. I've worked with James Woods, Brian Dennehy, and Stallone, and it's never easy. No question Steven has an underlying sense of morality beneath his toughness. There is a lot of Yojimbo, the bodyguard from Kurosawa's *Seven-Year Storm*, in his character. He suggests attitudes, points of view. Again, a lot of Kurosawa. He knew all the man's work. *Stray Dog. High-Low.* He knew the titles—in Japanese."

Seagal is sensitive to any lack of faith in his skill as a cinematic quick study. "They almost broke me on *Hard to Kill*. Could have been a great picture, but I ended up with a director who didn't know the first thing about directing. I was lucky to live through it. I was not allowed to get involved in the cutting, and even after I rewrote it, I was shut out. That will never happen again. Everything that goes on with this picture, I'm the boss.

"Real soon," he says, "this town will know what I can do as a writer. I've gone along, and I've gotten burned. Now they'll see what I can do."

So now you are a Hollywood screenwriter and you have your suspicions about Seagal as well. You know concept *is* more important than dialogue. And dialogue isn't easy.

"On *Marked for Death*, I did research and paid close attention to detail, from casting to wardrobe," says Seagal. "I did it all because when I got the script, it was babbling shit. It was unreadable, and the whole town knew it. It was the worst screenplay I ever read," he says. One then wonders, if it was so bad, why was it shot?

"I mean unfuckingreadable. I learned to speak the Jamaican patois. I made it my business to understand. And then the Writers Guild says they always go with the first writer. They say, okay, you have to change the story over 50 percent, because dialogue is easy. In the first screenplay [by Michael Victor and Mark Grais], a man goes to Chicago, kills a bunch of Black people, and becomes a hero. Now the story hasn't changed much, so see you later. No credit for you, because you ain't the original writer. I don't want to talk about it because I don't want to tear up this table. I was promised if I fixed it, I would get credit for it. It didn't happen, because I was in bed with lying scumbags."

As a screenwriter, you don't appreciate being called a scumbag. So now everybody in Hollywood who is a screenwriter and not currently working with him—does that make it nearly unanimous, or what?—suspects Seagal.

"We're not looking to get into a confrontation with Steven Seagal," Grais told the *Los Angeles Times*. "The record in the Writers Guild speaks for itself."

JAMAICAN POSSE MEMBER: *Don't know who ya-arr, but I promise yousa dead mon walkn'!*
JOHN HATCHER: *So what else is new?*

Steven Seagal was born on April 10, 1952, in Lansing, Michigan, to parents of Italian and Russian-Irish blood. They lived on the outskirts of Detroit, in an area he describes as "verging on ghetto." At the time, the 1950s, Detroit was a different sort of town from how it is perceived today. But it has always been a town of great fighters.

"I grew up around some Black people and mostly hillbillies," he says. I briefly wondered: If he were being interviewed by a hillbilly instead of a Black man, would the racial proportions he recalled have been reversed, as well as the particulars of this story he went on to tell?

"I fought as a matter of course. I got my butt kicked plenty of times. It was like a ritual. When the hillbillies weren't cleaning their guns, they played horseshoes. Was a hell of a horseshoe player myself. Then one day there was some violence across the street over a game. It sounded like murder. So my mother called the cops."

Thus was formed a scene:

HILLBILLY'S SHOTGUN *pointed at* PATRICIA'S *throat.*
SEAGAL *(voiceover)*: "He pointed that gun at her and said, 'Where we come from, we don't do that. Ah'll kill yewe!' "
PATRICIA: "Then kill me."

No wonder Seagal was less than enthralled by the humdrum at Buena Park High in Fullerton, California. After a desultory year at Fullerton College, he pursued what he says had been his father's great interest: Japan and things Japanese. "My father, *he* was the Japanophile," Seagal says. Seagal believes a martial-arts demonstration in Michigan convinced him to set his sights for the Rising Sun. Near end of January 1991, while wrapping up the interiors for *Out for Justice*, Seagal came to accept that his father, Steven Sr., was dying and might not live to see the movie open. Earlier that month, the shooting schedule had been broken so Seagal could go to Ayabe, in the mountains above Kyoto, for the funeral of ninety-four-year-old Deguschi Naohi. She was in her seventies when Seagal met her. He believed she was a holy woman. He believes Steven Sr. is a great man. He believes he is the product of both. He lives on.

"One of the edicts of being a great warrior is always to throw your life away—to have already died," says Seagal. "And I have met my maker a handful of times. I've been in those situations where I've said, 'This is it. I'm dead. Good-bye.' And if I think I'm going to die now, you aren't going to see me panic. You'll just see me saying, 'It's my time. Let's go. I'm not afraid.' Do I know Kurosawa's work? Have I seen *The Seven Samurai*? I don't want to offend you, but that's like me asking if you ever saw a typewriter."

RICHIE (playing Russian roulette): What are you gonna do, Gino? Arrest me? I'm outta bullets!

GINO FELINO: That's a shame, because those bullets could have saved you a lot of pain.

If you are a movie-ticket buyer in Bensonhurst, Brooklyn, you think you're oblivious to such Hollywood ephemera as what is real and what is not. You want your four bucks' worth, when you can catch the matinee, because the $7.50 feature is ridickalus. Unless it's Steve-O. You don't mind being quoted on the record about Steven Seagal. Nobody knows you anyway.

From two Black ticket buyers, the first in Albuquerque, New Mexico, the second in Harlem, New York City:

"When Steven Seagal does them up in a movie, they deserve to get done. I like him. I would like to know him."

"I admire him. I'd like to get to know him. He's *down*. Kind of man who will look you in the eye and not look away."

Their quotes came after showings of *Marked for Death*. Since at least 35 percent of the ticket-buying audience in America is Black, you become this Black ticket buyer, and Seagal is intriguing to you because the hardware he's using looks real, the cinematic situations he's in seem, to you, authentic. He does in fact seem like he could kick a little ass. And two times out of three so far, you have been his celluloid sidekick, and one of his better villains—Screwface (Basil Wallace) in *Marked for Death*.

"I have a piece I want to do on AIDS called *Pandora*. You know, AIDS started in a lab," Seagal says.

You are Black, and this could easily be construed as blow-ing smoke. But it's easy to test. You're accustomed to finding out things about people around you without them knowing it. "Green monkey meat," you say, innocuously pushing at the breadth of Seagal's frame of reference.

"Fuck you," he says, not missing a beat. "Give me a break. A disease that's political? That only goes for homosexuals and Black people?"

So if it is an act, then he is a better actor than people give him credit for being. If he is that smart, to pull off sincerity on such volatile issues, then you, as this Black ticket buyer, give him credit for such convincing bravura. If it isn't an act, then he's *down*.

"I'm no more different, no more special than you," he says. His eyes are unwavering. The hair on the back of your neck stays flat. "We are the same. You're a lot better than I am at a lot of things, and maybe I'm better than you at other things. It doesn't change a thing. I know we are all one family. That's the way I am. That won't change.

"I was shooting once with a Black actor. It was cold. One of the brothers had been trying to shake his hand for days. His bodyguards would say, 'Get the fuck out of here, man.' I watched this. Then one day the brother comes in and says to the bodyguard. 'Hey man, you know the martial arts?' The bodyguard says, 'Yeah, I know martial arts.' The guy opens his coat and says. 'Are you faster than this, motherfucker?' The Black actor is saying, 'Hey, brother, take it easy, brother.' That's what it took for the guy to be a brother." You are Black, and this sounds like it could easily be the worst kind of con. The hair on the back of your neck rises, then quickly goes flat again. So you trust that, for the time being.

So where does the cigarette boat go from here, you ask?

"I'd like to be able to work with [Sydney] Pollack, Dick

Donner, or Jim Cameron," Seagal says of these famous directors. "I could really trust myself in those kinds of hands." It is true; who was Schwarzenegger but a guy with muscles instead of aikido technique until Cameron got hold of him in *The Terminator*? What about that comparison with Schwarzenegger? "I find that comparison difficult to fathom," Seagal says. "We are very different individuals, to say the least."

Stallone? "Room for all. We're all different."

Van Damme? "We're talking different universe."

Eastwood? "Complex individual. Intelligent. He's a filmmaker. There is sort of an enigma attached where people are fascinated with him. He's one of the few who have lasted with dignity. Even though everybody's saying he's finished now after his last two things. (Within two years, Eastwood would make *Unforgiven*.) Just the same, he lasted a long time. Clint's a friend. He's a gentleman and a good guy, and I think he's a good director."

So if we're still not sure who Seagal is, we can at least speculate about what he wants. He wants to last, to be enigmatic, a gentleman, a good guy, and someone to be taken very seriously as a filmmaker, all at the same time. This is at minimum time-consuming work, which is a reason why Seagal says he gets by with only three hours of sleep a night. What happens now, as the design grows grander around him? What happens to this sleek cigarette boat in open water?

"Never trust a coward," says Seagal. "Never. Swim? I can swim. I'm scuba certified. I just don't like the water."

I screened *Out for Justice* a few weeks after the film premiered. Steven Seagal has not gotten any writer's credit, nor should he have wanted any for this hopeless dreck. The opening scene of the film contained one of the crudest, most stereotypical, ridiculous versions of a Black pimp I have ever seen—a Black pimp so unabashedly stupid he was cursing his whore (who was White, naturally) and slapping her around right in the middle of this fictional Italian Bensonhurst 'hood. Seagal busted the pimp up and went on to deal with a crack-smoking White former neighborhood friend. It was really painful to watch. The swells were rising around the cigarette boat. The film didn't do that well at the domestic box office, but well enough, I suppose—$39,673,161 in all. I heard nothing about it from Albuquerque and Harlem, New York City. Fool me once, shame on you. Fool me twice . . .

Under Siege opened the second week of October 1992, with Seagal as a career SEAL who has been demoted to the chief cook and bottlewasher of a motley bilgewater crew of cooks and Negroes in the officers' mess of the battleship *Missouri*. The battleship is then taken over by a renegade officer and former governmental operatives and mercenaries gone haywire. *Under Siege*, with its proliferation of Black characters in the periphery—not particularly well done but there and not immediately insulting—showed in advertising on inner-city billboards and on the Black Entertainment Television network. And *Under Siege* did $51.4 million in one month at domestic box office, and $81,652,508 after four months, a record by far for a film starring Steven Seagal.

Magic

May 18, 1980

In the realm of Los Angeles, as well as nearly all others, there is a game called hoop. Los Angeles, or El Lay, is different from other places in that in those environs, the highest level of hoop is practiced in a place called the Forum, by a team called the Lakers. And long, long ago, and for many years, the king of these Los Angeles Lakers, within this Forum, was the great and glowering Abdul-Jabbar.

Abdul-Jabbar is a giant among men, a giant even among giants. He stands half a hand over seven feet and was chosen to lead his chosen subjects, the Lakers of Los Angeles, on a successful quest for the Grail, called the NBA championship, in the far-back years of 1979 and 1980. The team that wins this NBA championship is the finest hoop team in the world. Hoop is the true believer's term for the game of basketball.

Now hoop is not as easy as the seekers of the Grail make it look, nor as difficult as the true believers who only talk about it make it sound. It is in the end a simple game: The bigger they are, the harder they are to stop. Abdul-Jabbar ruled over the Forum and the Lakers, though with far from an iron hand. He once won the Grail while in the land of Milwaukee, where a soothsaying hooper and post-feeder named Oscar Robertson said, "The king don't care what they throw up there." Oscar was right in more ways than one.

But for years on end, the trouble with the Lakers was that they didn't get the ball to the king very often, and when they did, they just stood around and watched him. The respect for Abdul-Jabbar waned throughout hoopdom. The Forum became a place for the uncaring, the aloof, the well-heeled with the price of a ticket and nothing else to do. Then a wealthy land baron named Jerry Buss purchased the Lakers and hired a youth expressly to get the ball to Abdul-Jabbar by hook or crook, as Robertson had done in Milwaukee. Obviously such a man would have to be Magic to be able to get the ball past the quick hands of the other NBA warriors, who were always sloughing off their own men and back on Abdul-Jabbar and double-teaming him. This frustrated him to no end.

To make this fresh youth with the quick hands less conspicuous, since he was already six feet and nine inches, it was decided his last name should be Johnson. Young Magic Johnson to King Abdul-Jabbar became the ultimate weapon, the kingdom's salvation, and the hottest ticket in smoggy El Lay.

The Lakers would have gained the Grail easily enough and Abdul-Jabbar would have been hailed, just as he insisted that he be, but from the other side of the country came the Brobdingnags, also known as the Philadelphia 76ers. They had been molded for the purpose of gaining the Grail for their own and for their benefactor, a financial wizard of sorts named Fitz Dixon. And the 76ers were well molded. There was Caldwell Jones, seven feet of him, created with river mud, powdered bear teeth, and beard hair clipped from Bill Russell. There was Chocolate Thunder, the huge Darryl Dawkins, who could tilt the world with one stomp of his foot. Then there was the quiet, ghostly Bobby Jones, the stealthy one, who could jump out of the gym, murder the backboards, and steal lightning if it wasn't careful.

But that was not all. The leader of the Brobdingnags was also a king, but he preferred to be called the Doctor. His name was Julius Erving, and the gods had given him a way of playing that was devastating. But the gods didn't want anarchy, so they made the Doctor only six feet six inches.

With the Grail at stake, with glory as the background, the Brobdingnags and the Lakers clashed in a best-of-seven-game match. Even with their might, the Brobs found Abdul-Jabbar above them. The Lakers won three of the first five battles, the Sixers two. The winner of four battles would find the path to the Grail clear, except for a few cameras.

Ah, but here the tale turns left. While winning the fifth game, Abdul-Jabbar was injured. The Brobs jumped with glee. Abdul-Jabbar looked at Magic and said, "Here, take my scepter—the sky hook—and play center. Try not to let the Brobs make you suffer too badly as they kill you in game six at Philly. I'll be back Sunday for game seven in El Lay. I hope."

Young Magic laughed and started the sixth game at center and promptly sank the sky hook. Then he laughed some more. "This is not my game, I need to be free," he said. "I can play guard and forward *and* center. I can score too."

Though it seems a dream, he did it all. And as he did, those who were not blind could see he was no hireling but of royal lineage himself. His scepter was not his height, nor a particular shot. It was the ball—the ball was subject to his mildest whims. He shot it into the basket and into the other Lakers' hands when they had good looks at the basket, especially the dexterous hands of Jamaal Wilkes the Eager, who dropped in a cool 37 points. The 76ers were game, talented, but helpless in the end. They put the Doctor on Magic in the first half. Magic scored 20 points. "Well," they reasoned, "the Doctor doesn't play great D. We'll put Bobby Jones on Magic in the second half. Then watch Youth die."

Magic scored 22 points in the second half. It was then the Lakers realized they had their choice of kings. Magic, though he was but twenty years old, had transformed himself—it seemed insane—into a basketball itself. In Los Angeles, Abdul-Jabbar sank his frame onto a couch, flexed his bad ankle and rested his weary bones. He'd reigned for ten years, and it was nice watching somebody else in the same uniform do it. He must have smiled a long and contented smile.

But Magic's smile was brighter.

May 18, 1992

When I first saw Mister Master Earvin Earv Buck Magic Johnson do up hoop back in '77, he was fresh out of Everett High in Lansing, Michigan. Even now he makes me pause and wonder. He'd won a state high school basketball championship back then. Two springs later he would win an NCAA college basketball championship for Michigan State University. The spring after that, he would win the first of five National Basketball Association world championships with the Lakers. What the vast majority of even the finest hoopers cannot do in twenty-five years, Earv would do in four. When I say he won these titles I mean he had the largest hand in winning them. He didn't just happen to be on the court when it happened, like some ballplayers are. He *won* them. And nobody gives them away, especially all three heroic feats in four years' time. He didn't seem in that much of a hurry when I first saw him.

Back in 1977, in Oakland, California, there was this fellow who loved high school basketball so much he helped organize the Sunshine summer basketball tournament. He had called around the United States and invited many top high school hoopers to come on out to Oakland to participate in the small, dusty gymnasium at Laney College downtown. He offered to pay the expenses of the top five of them, which he would recoup from ticket sales. I can't remember the rest of the hoopers because the one who stood out was Earv. He was tall, thin, with a halo of an Afro on his head and that old man's smile of his, looking as though he were holding the secret of eternal life in the gums below his front teeth.

I went to a couple of the exhibitions and it sure did seem odd, watching him play. At first Earv played down low, as a forward, near the basket, because that was what people expected of tall, thin young players with halos of Afros. But near the ends of these games, he'd ease into the backcourt and call for the ball and bring it up himself and make all the instantaneous decisions and make them all properly. His teams never failed to score when he switched to point guard. But it looked odd because he was so tall—odd somehow seeing him bent over the ball, handling it as though it were his own thumb. The other guards, smaller men, licked their chops, figuring they would swipe the ball from this tall man, but that was not to be. He smiled at them and evaded their attempted steals and drove in because now the defense was out of balance; burned them for getting out of position hoping to pick his dribble. He laid the ball up time after time—whenever he wanted, it seemed. He was very impressive, especially when he made the winning basket after feinting a blind wraparound pass. Every defender jumped one way. Earv laid the ball into the basket from the other way, looked over at me, winked and smiled and laughed this completely engaging and musical laughter. I laughed too, and remember him thus.

Two springs later, in 1979, Earv was playing for Michigan State University in the NCAA championship game against Indiana State University and its star, Larry Bird. Earv's team happened to win the game and the championship, and I believed this was a function of Earv being able to go get the ball, either by rebounding it or stealing it in a passing lane or off a dribble, and then bring it up the court himself to make those lightning-fast decisions that nobody seems to notice when Black men make them. Black men don't make good decisions. They get lucky. On offense Bird had to wait for someone to get him the ball after he rebounded it and passed it to a guard. But Earv got to implement his ball sense as soon as it struck him, both on and off the ball. Other than that, I saw precious little difference between them as players, but this was the beginning (no, the continuation) of a racial dynamic that was the fault of neither man but in the future of both.

The irony of course is that in many ways, they were exactly the same player, only Bird was three years older. Neither one of them was a powerful jumper, but they both could jam down a hard dunk from a variety of positions in those days, lest you forget that, and jumping is relative. Compared to you or me, they were leaping fools, but compared to their contemporaries they seemed earthbound. Both had superior hand-eye coordination and a strong will. Both had an overwhelming, innate sense of the instantaneous right thing to do on the court to advance the ball to the basket on offense and cut down good looks at the basket on defense. They were geniuses at this.

Hoop is a game, and also a function in which genius can certainly show itself. Hoop is mathematic and intuitive, both science and art. There are certain constants—there are five players on each side, the hoop is 10 feet high, the court 94 feet long, a shot must be taken within 24 seconds of possessing the ball, 6 fouls will disqualify you from the game, etc.

Then there are ever-changing variables: the height and skills and weaknesses of the four other players on your team who are on the court with you, the same traits among your five opponents, the score, time remaining, number of fouls a player has left to give, the tendencies of the players, their rough percentages of success and skill at each separate ball function—handling the ball (with which hand best), shooting the ball (from what distance), rebounding the ball (with or without much authority). There must be a constant calculation of this data, a continuous re-evaluation, a total orchestration of humanity if one is to achieve ball genius. And no one will ever ask the galleries to be quiet as you play through. Oh yes, hoop is a great game, all right, and Magic was a genius at it—and so was the White man, Bird. I have no problem with it at all because it is what's there, and ball is ball.

Bird was a forward-forward—he could play either the "power" forward or "small" forward with equal efficiency. In fact, he turned out to be, perhaps, the finest forward ever to play the game. A hypothesis was often advanced in the mainstream (read White) media that Bird was not only the best forward but the best player who ever walked on court.

Earv was a center-guard—could play center and point guard to great effect. Eventually a good case could be made that he was the best point guard ever to play the game. But to say anyone at that point in time was the best player who ever walked on court was still problematic at best.

Soon both were in the NBA, the highest level of hoop in the world. Before their arrival, the NBA had not exactly fallen on hard times. It had never known anything but hard times. It had always been seen as something less than major league baseball and the National Football League as a marketable entity. This might have led to a greater, faster evolution of the game of basketball. The NBA was encouraged to change, speed up, get better, because its image was said to be bad.

Hard work is rarely fun, and playing world-class hoop eighty-two nights a year is hard work on the body and mind. Some great basketball players were forged in that fire. Many of them, in fact. But with Earv and Larry Bird, the NBA took off as a marketable entity, because Earvin made hard work look like fun again, and because Larry Bird, his foil, was White. Americans are always much more fascinated by their precious racial dynamic—more fascinated even than by the brilliant dynamics of high production in the field of hoop. Without the racial dynamic, we all seemed to be so terminally bored.

As I've described, Earv won the NBA championship in his rookie season, and he was named the Most Valuable Player of the playoffs. Bird was named Rookie of the Year for the season. The next year, Earv missed a short shot in the play-offs and the Lakers didn't advance to the finals. The Boston Celtics, Larry Bird's team, did advance and won the title. Immediately, many White people in the media began to say that Larry Bird was superior to Earv, a better player all-around than Earv. I still thought God had made the same player in both of them just for this purpose—to flush out the idiots and the bigoted (inadvertently bigoted or not) among all these bored and disaffected Americans. A young man who was my co-worker at *Sports Illustrated* told me that Earv smiled too much, that he didn't take the game seriously enough, that sometimes the game wasn't fun. Between the lines this was highly insulting. He was saying that Earv was just a clown and that he could not muster production under adverse circumstances. He seemed to be having too much fun, and this wasn't the Globetrotters. Personally, I thought that in the first place, nobody could—or should—win them all. And then, all there was in the end to appreciate about ballplayers, beyond how many they won, was how they looked doing it. Did they somehow make you watch? All that was left to appreciate about any ballplayer was how the observer felt he would have played in relation to that player, should the observer have been lucky enough and disciplined enough to have been a hooper instead of a bond trader or a draftsman.

I call this Personal Transposition to the Distant Subject. In my case, the transposition would have been to a player named Keith Wilkes, later Jamaal Wilkes, a thin hooper known as Silk, who played at U.C.L.A. and then with the Golden State Warriors and the Lakers. I like to believe I could have played like him and fit in with the hoopers who could fit in with him. So I believe he's one of the best players I ever saw. I'm not talking about the player. I'm talking about myself. I used to be thin, and I like to think of myself as smooth, a winner everywhere I go. White people need to admit this to themselves, admit that they think like this, admit that it's personal, their likes and dislikes, and not some provable and final theory of evolution. They should stop this incessant nattering about them being the best at every single thing they ever saw done, not in theory but in fact. I pointed out to my young associate that in the next breath, he and some of his fellows would be whining about Georgetown's team under John Thompson. The "thugs" never smiled, the White associates of mine complained, and they played too hard and took themselves too seriously. So according to these rules of merit, Black ballplayers could never win. They had to win with the proper disposition to these unprejudiced Whites. Winning is hard enough as it is—but to win with the proper demeanor? What kind of flexible rule of merit was that? A very American rule of merit. Very '80s.

Earv and Bird dominated these '80s, and the NBA fell upon unprecedented good times. Magic vs. Bird. Lakers vs. Celtics. Earv came to be known as "Buck" to his teammates and grateful members of the Lakers' organization. Eventually Earv's Lakers won those five NBA titles and Bird's Celtics won three. Since they were pretty much the same ballplayer (unless you had your own agenda), I found it symmetrical because of assumptions upheld in the nineteenth-century legal system of America, as in the Dred Scott case—that a Black man was a fraction of a human being, amounting to three-fifths of a White man. So those five NBA championships won by the Black player and the three won by the White player (who was the same player) strike me not as random numbers but rather as a historical flourish by God. Nothing against Bird. He reminded me of Jack Johnson in his own country way. His people put such pressures on him, and all he wanted to do really was play and win and let his playing and winning do the talking for him. But White people tried to put him too high. And Black people didn't want to hear it anymore. Had heard it quite enough, thank you. So keep it off the court where your flexible rules of merit are not translatable.

I felt I understood Bird. Once I even told a small gathering of Black people that at times I felt like the Larry Bird of *Sports Illustrated*. Now, imagine Black people insisting, with authority, that I was not only one of the best writers at *Sports Illustrated* but inarguably the *best* writer in all the history of *Sports Illustrated*. I wonder how White people would take that. Not very well, I would guess. My feelings on being similar to Bird could be held in abeyance at any time. For instance, when the writer David Halberstam wrote that Bird would have made a great Laker, but Earv wouldn't have made a good Celtic, there were even illustrations in *Sports Illustrated* of Bird in a Laker uniform and Earv in a Celtic uniform to accompany the piece. This was after the Lakers had won the title one year. Had the Boston Celtics won the title that year, the article would have been about how Bird was the greatest ballplayer that ever lived. If Bird's Celtics had won five NBA titles and Earv's Lakers three, you can bet White people would be insisting until today that Bird was a better hooper than Magic. Magic had to win five to Bird's three for White people to begin to mutter that, yes, they might be the same.

As this was happening, though, history was whipping up

more dust, in the form of Michael Jordan, who plays for the Chicago Bulls. Michael plays well, don't you think? You can say Earv (or Bird) is the best you ever saw right up until the time you see Michael play. After you've seen Michael, the question of which player is the best who ever walked on court no longer seems so problematic.

By the middle of 1992, the center of the hoop universe had become Chicago Stadium on the near west side of Chicago. The exploding supernova inside was caused by the emerging Michael Jeffrey Jordan, and the Chicago Bulls won consecutive NBA titles behind him in '91 and '92. He'd worked without a net—with much less talent around him than either Earv or Bird had luxuriated in during their heydays. The Bulls have a game-opening ceremony that is out of this world. The drafty old bowl is first darkened, and twenty thousand people begin a low guttural roar, like a hurricane or the rumble of a great train. The sound seems to occupy space. A rock song with a zooming zing of a bass line thunders from huge speakers, making the air seem even more dense. Spotlights search the stands and further disorient you in this world. You'd think that the Dipper, the Big O, Jerry West, Dr. J, Thor, Zeus, and Isis herself were about to be introduced. But it is usually only Grant, Pippen, Cartwright, Paxson, one by one, the music thundering behind them. The sound continues and grows—it seems to move under the skin and dapple across the spine. The anticipation grows to a fever pitch with each introduction. The roar of the crowd turns into a wall of sound that shuts out the rest of the world and makes time hang there, waiting to move. Finally, Jordan is introduced. The sound washes over you then, and makes you understand what it is like to be human, movable. At that line of demarcation, Michael Jeffrey Jordan is the finest athlete in the world.

You can still say Earv (or Bird) is the best you ever saw and be right as can be measured in terms of statistics, winning percentages, testimonials, most tangible data and real numbers. Put Michael in the equation and it changes. The numbers stop adding up. That is how well Michael plays. Michael can do all that Earv and Bird did plus some things they could have only considered—shoot the ball from deep, drive it to the hole and cram it over your best defender, dish it off, rebound it, pick your point guard's dribble at the top of the key, block your center's shot on the low block, keep your top scorer quiet, shut him down completely, come off the ball and intimidate your best frontcourt scorer, even a seven-footer, with blocked shots; see everything with a magnificent vision that sweeps from behind one ear to behind the other, and do all this with a pharaonic majesty that defies belief and leveling by mere numbers. Michael Jordan so confidently escaped the bonds of gravity and flew into the imagination of hoop fans. Michael added a new dimension to the science of hoop being played as well as it can be played. He added art.

It was this visual aesthetic that separated Michael from the other two, and it flowed naturally from his superior athletic ability. Earv and Bird were highly athletic and aesthetically pleasing as well. People don't win eight NBA titles without being highly athletic. It's that Jordan was so much more athletic, not only more athletic than the other two, but more than any of his contemporaries. There are panthers that are not as athletic as Michael Jordan. But if you had to win one basketball game, any good coach would take any one of the three men. The wisest coach would let you pick one and then take the two you didn't pick and beat you because those two were mad that you didn't choose them first.

Bird could go and hit seven three-pointers, yet grab 20 rebounds and end up with a 60—30 points, 20 rebounds, 10 assists. Earv could go get 30 points on drives and hooks and a couple of threes, and add 20 assists and 10 rebounds. In the grave '80s, during the final game of the 1987 NBA championship series against Detroit's Pistons and their star, Isiah Thomas (who is the best six-foot-even player I have ever seen), Earv had 13 points, 13 rebounds and 13 assists. His numbers that game were precisely what was needed by the Lakers, and they won. Either man, Earv or Bird in their primes, would give you an equal chance to win the game— probably as much a chance to win as you would have with Michael Jordan, although your eye would doubt this. But you have to understand hoop to know not to always believe your eyes. If your eye was untrained, then you would pick Jordan every time. Even with a well-trained eye, you might still prefer Jordan because he was in another league from Earv and Bird as a defender. Jordan was the next stage of genius after Bird and Earv. He took their horizontal brilliance and stretched it out further, wider, and then made it vertical; he cubed them, placed ball into another dimension. He was a defensive genius as well. Not all people like it when you change ball on them. It doesn't always go down easy.

Michael Jordan became a singular performer, the nonpareil of his era, a near-perfect melding of opportunity, grim resiliency, and epic mental acumen. Jordan became an artist of the first rank, the avant-garde, an innovator for whom conventional rules were there only to be improved upon. Jordan became Picasso in satin shorts, Ellington with ungodly lift, Nijinsky under control. And he knew it.

I recently asked Jordan about some other players of the NBA. No matter the name, Jordan was accurate in his assessment—brutally, refreshingly, pinpointedly accurate, technically and aesthetically. In the end he was firm in his ability to look down upon them all from his throne. He knew his place, and he didn't get there by deferring attendant responsibilities. He would define himself. He would know what was humanly possible. And then he would go on to expand the envelope of that possibility. As for us, we could catch up to him later if we kept our eyes open and our mouths shut and paid attention. He was twenty-nine years old at the time, February of 1992. He felt immortal.

But it took until 1991 for Michael's team, the Chicago Bulls, to win the world title, and he had come into the NBA in 1984. That's how good Earv and Bird were, a testimony to how well snooty Isiah (two NBA titles) could play the game. The summer before that fateful season of 1990–91, Earv held his usual summer fete, an all-star game to which he invited other NBA players to come out and play at the Forum. The proceeds of this game go to the United Negro College Fund. I have always found this to be endearing, although it is bittersweet. I know, deep down, that as long as there is a United Negro College Fund, there still stand the twin towers of despair and hope for Black people. But better to have both than none of the latter. Earv's game brought in funds, people were helped, and that is the bottom line.

Bird came out for the first couple of these summertime affairs, and Michael never failed to show up. It was Michael, after all, whom people wanted to see. Again, if you had to pick one man to help you win a basketball game, you could not go wrong picking Earv, Bird, or even the likes of Isiah at the tops of their games. But if you wanted to see elegance and élan, the aesthetic cutting edge of human endeavor, if you wanted to see someone play ball if you would never see ball again after that, undoubtedly you'd have to pick Michael Jordan. One year the score of Magic's game was 203–202. It was fun watching these artists improvise for a good cause. No one ever got hurt. Earv, Bird, and Michael all overcame serious injuries during their careers, to show you how hard it really is to hoop—no matter how easy they make it look.

After the summer game in '90, Earv threw a party at a downtown L.A. nightclub. It was attended by a large number of handsome and appropriately famous people, the overwhelming majority of whom were disappointing in one way or another up close. But Earv was cool. Earv was Earv. And there were two or three attractive and determined ladies laying well-planned ambushes for him in the room. He didn't seem to mind, but then it always seemed Earv had time for everybody. I saw him once up on the Strip getting a hot dog in the company of a woman who seemed to have been made by a particularly gifted sculptor. I had merely told him, "Good luck," and I hadn't meant anything about her at all. I was talking about ball.

In the club, I said to him, "Yo, Earv, I went to one of those charity schools once upon a time. So I think you are doing a good thing with that. Most great ballplayers live insulated lives. You get out. You help out." His smile was a perfect V, as usual. He bent over so not to tower over me and said something like, "Awww, nah. Wasn't all that much, what I did. People have done things for me all my life."

So I was walking in a mall in Dallas, Texas, on Nov. 7, 1991. I was killing time. A Black man came out of an upscale store with a vacant look on his face. He stared blankly and turned his head toward me mechanically. He stared at me. He just stared at me. I was somewhat put off by his staring because he seemed to want time or sympathy and I had little of either to spare. Then he said, "Hey, man, don't you follow basketball?" He seemed to be almost begging me. I answered brusquely, bordering on rude: "Whadya think? Sure I hoop."

"Have you heard Magic's got AIDS?"

I sneered. "Yeah, right. C'mon, where do you get that?" I was walking away, but then I looked back and I could tell by the way the man stood there staring at me that this was what he'd just heard, and he could not believe it himself, and perhaps my reaction comforted him for only a second.

"They say there's a press conference at six o'clock."

I stopped. We talked from some distance away.

"Magic?" I said, to no one in particular, as if it were a question to whatever God might be listening.

"Magic, man," he said. It was he who walked away.

Just like that? Explain this. How can it be? I watched the news with dread and revulsion. In the press conference Earv seemed much too calm for a man who had just been given a death sentence. He advocated safe sex. "It's not sex that's killing us," I thought. "It's a virus. Where did it come from?" Later the vice president, Dan Quayle, came out and said Earv should have advocated abstinence. I thought, "Fuck you, White man. Even your priests do not abstain from sex with young boys, and all you can say is 'abstain'?"

Earv was HIV-positive. Earv was a good man. Earv was a Black man. Rage, fear, hatred all rose up in me because the rest of us could go at any time, but not Earv. Earv stood for something. Another part of me was not enraged or fearful or hateful. Another part of me admired the tactics even as they were killing me. The virus was doing what I believed it was made to do—destroy the Black people, the Black men, and intravenous drug users, and gays, and anyone who is among the undesirables, but most especially the Black men.

This was supposed to be about Earv, not about how Earv received his death warrant. I like to think about how I first saw him, when we were much younger and he was smiling, and we all became immortal together. Not everybody in this life is as accommodating as Earv. Michael might have been a better hooper, but I knew no better man. Earv smiled a V through it all, and I knew he was a better man than me, not only at hoop but at living, because when I receive my death sentence, I already know I will be bitter about it. Through it all, as this inexplicable virus clung to him waiting to work its unholy purpose, I felt deep down Earv was good and didn't deserve it. I still feel that. I knew this would not go away and must be dealt with soon, somehow, by our people. I thought about Magic, and the beautiful vagaries of hoop, and how they helped keep my mind off larger matters.

ABOUT PERCEPTIONS

Why Black People
Sing the Blues

In the autumn of 1989, a student at Brown University in Rhode Island, Douglas Hann, presented himself outside of his dormitory on his twenty-first birthday. Being free, White, and twenty-one, he could do and say what he damn well pleased. So he pleased to shout what a number of people who are free, White, and twenty-one have shouted for what appears to be eternity but is actually only a few hundred years. Something to the effect that his parents owned Black people, especially any students who had the temerity to be at Brown and within earshot.

It was said he was drunk. With what, they don't say.

Hann also threw curses at Jews and homosexuals and pretty much everybody who wasn't free, White, and twenty-one—and even some who were. He made particular note of his antipathy to thick-headed, inferior Black people in close proximity to him who hadn't figured out who owned them yet.

So what? you ask, and you are correct in asking. In a way, Hann had done all Black people who weren't free, White, and twenty-one a favor. He rattled before he struck. He could be avoided altogether in the future. But here in the United States of America such conduct comes under the defense of free speech, so you were liable to run into somebody else talking like this if you weren't careful. In fact, if you didn't talk like this at the top of your lungs, especially if you happened to be on the campus of a university, then you were considered "politically correct" and distasteful.

Hann's incorrigibility was turned into another round in this debate over political correctness by an array of people who should have better matters to discuss: critics, writers, politicians, ombudsmen, and even the faculty at places like Harvard (and, one assumes, Hampton, though it likely was a shorter debate there and never got past the coffee machine).

During this brouhaha, a free, White, twenty-one-year-old named Brigit Kerrigan hung a Confederate flag outside her window on the fourth floor of Kirkland House, a Harvard dormitory, and dared anyone to say anything to her about it, much less suggest she take it down. Anybody, especially a student at Harvard, should know the significance of the Confederate flag. The White female student pressed down her petticoats under her hoop skirt, shook her ring curls, and said something to the effect that at Tara, er, Harvard, "if they talk about diversity they're gonna get it. If they talk about tolerance they better be ready to have it."

She was soon prevailed upon to take down her flag, and the faculty responsible for the conduct of Kirkland House wrote a nice note putting some air between them and Ms. Kerrigan. But she didn't take her flag down until she was ready to do so. Free speech and all that, you know. As for the rationale that groups like the Ku Klux Klan also fly the Confederate flag, she noted they flew the American flag too, and nobody was taking that one down. "If they talk about tolerance, they better be ready to have it," Kerrigan said.

Rightly assuming she was probably lumped in with this amorphous "they" of which Ms. Kerrigan spoke, a nineteen-year-old Black female student at Harvard named not Mammy but Jacinda Townsend, from Kentucky, then hung a make-shift Nazi swastika outside her dorm window. Jacinda was also prevailed upon to take down her makeshift flag/debating point. No doubt she was told something like: "Just because one person is acting childishly doesn't mean you should. Just because you have the right to fly a flag and debate doesn't mean you should do it all the time. It makes you look quite idiotic and, in some minds, a real threat." The Black Student Union at Harvard even asked Jacinda Townsend to desist, for her actions might damage Black-Jewish relations on campus. No one supported Jacinda's right to hang a symbol out of her window, but a goodly percentage of people—25 percent, 35 percent, 55 percent, 75 percent?—supported Brigit's right to hang a symbol out of her window. Townsend found that as far as any rights she might have were considered, she was in this alone . . .

Jacinda Townsend was forced to take down her debating point: Kerrigan was not. So Jacinda found out how much freedom she had . . . compared to twenty-one-year-old Brigit Kerrigan. After removing her makeshift debating point in order to stay in good standing at Harvard, no doubt in my mind, Jacinda ground her teeth until the muscles in her face and neck bulged and receded like bubbles in a boiling pot. So this was the education for which she had come to Harvard. Jacinda Townsend had learned her classmate Brigit was free, White, and twenty-one and that she, Jacinda, could stay Black and die. She will get over it and do well. The blues are in her now. Blueswoman Koko Taylor sings Jacinda's anthem, from "I Got What It Takes":

> They call me the voodoo woman
> And I know the reason why
> Lord if I raise my hand
> You know the sky begin to cry
> They call me the voodoo woman
> I can look through water and spy dry land . . .
> I got a rabbit's foot in my pocket
> Toad frog in my shoe
> A crawfish on my shoulder
> Looking dead at you . . .
> I got dust from a rattlesnake
> Got a black spider bone
> If that don't do it
> You better leave it alone . . .
> They call me the voodoo woman
> And I know the reason why
> Lord if I raise my hand
> You know the sky begin to cry.

Meanwhile the debate swirled on. Why, White people could say anything they wanted about Black people in public because of this hot news bulletin: They had freedom of speech! They had the right!

From Jonathan Yardley, the estimable book critic of the *Washington Post*:

> Of course it's offensive—repugnant, contemptible, loathsome, whatever you want to call it—for a college student or anyone else to go into a public place and shout words such as those used by [Hann] in his little scene last fall. But displays . . . are among the prices we pay for being not merely a free country but one of unexampled heterogeneity. One of the lamentable but inescapable truths about human beings—

Even American human beings! Even college students!—is that not all of them love everybody else and that some of them are given to saying so in public. It's a truth about which the universities would do well to instruct their students, in the hope that they learn to observe standards of civility, tolerance; but telling them to keep their mouths shut is scarcely the way to teach them anything except blind obedience . . . strictly a lesson for fascists.

On the face of it there is certainly no hole in Yardley's logic. But, then, this was America long before 1989 and remains so until today. They taught you in places like junior high school civics or American history that Americans had certain inalienable rights, and one of the very first rights was the freedom of speech. So no one was doubting that Douglas Hann, being American—free, White, twenty-one, and male to boot—had that right before anyone did. The question beclouds the issue. The issue was: *what he said*.

Brown University expelled Douglas Hann for *what he said*. This was Brown University's action, and it too, run by other people who are free, White, and over twenty-one who have plenty of rights, must be accounted for in this instance. The president of the university, Vartan Gregorian, had said earlier in 1989: "I issue a solemn warning that it is the policy of my administration to take action against those who incite hatred. It is my intention to prosecute vigorously, and to expel immediately, such individual or individuals for any attempt to inject and promote racism and thus insult the dignity of our students as citizens of Brown." There was no hole in that, either—and fair warning besides. Black people know above all that fair warning is the best right. That is why we sing the blues, to tell the story or give a warning.

So Mr. Hann shouted, and Mr. Gregorian responded. Mr. Hann was expelled posthaste. The people running Brown agreed that Mr. Hann had a right to say what he said—as long as he said it somewhere off the Brown campus. There were plenty of other universities where Mr. Hann could go and shout these things at the top of his lungs and be patted on the back for the boldness of his creativity. Like Harvard, for instance.

I will admit I have a soft spot in my heart for Brown University. I go a long way back with it even though I've never so much as seen a photograph of the place and have never come close to setting foot on its campus, or even in the city of Providence, Rhode Island, for that matter. I've known of Brown since I was seventeen, a senior in decent enough standing at Melrose High School, in Memphis, near the spigot of the Delta, in the school year 1969–70. These were the late days of broken segregation. I had begun to have some White teachers and administrators at school, but few fellow White students, at most one or two or three—certainly there were none who ran around hurling insults at Black folks. People would've noticed and not taken kindly to it.

In the fall of 1969 I was approached by one of my guidance counselors. I had three competent and committed Black adults who filled this role and were at my disposal, whether I liked it or not—usually not, as I recall it. They were Mrs. Dean, Mr. Lindsay, and Mrs. Ruth Strong. Mrs. Strong matter-of-factly approached me one day and told me Brown University was interested in giving me an academic scholarship. At that time I had never heard of Brown, didn't know where it was. I had heard of some of the traditionally Black universities and colleges, like LeMoyne-Owen right there in Memphis, and Tennessee State, Lane, Fisk, Kentucky State, and Morehouse in Atlanta, moving concentrically outward to the likes of Howard and Florida A&M and Lincoln of Pennsylvania. I knew states like North Carolina and Mississippi had plenty of these colleges; and I assumed each state had a traditionally

White university named after it, e.g., the University of Tennessee; and I knew of local traditionally White colleges, like Christian Brothers and Southwestern at Memphis and Tennessee at Martin; and I knew of some others mostly from their athletic teams on television, like Notre Dame, Oklahoma, Southern Cal, and Ole Miss. Some schools had somehow made an impression on my mind through the sheer weight of their academic reputations—Yale, Princeton, Harvard, Northwestern, Stanford. Even young Black people in the Delta in the last days of segregation had heard of them. But Brown was quite beyond me. My mother had married a man named Brown, but that didn't really help matters any.

I told Mrs. Strong that I might pass on any more Brown just then, but she changed her tone from matter-of-fact to firm. She said I had to take a meeting with this one recruiter who was coming to town. Having no choice, judging from Mrs. Strong's behavior, I took the meeting.

I remember talking to a quiet White man in wire-rimmed glasses. He asked me if I knew what I scored on the SAT. I told him, oh, not quite 700. I waited for a frown. He didn't. On the verbal half, that is, I said, thinking this would impress him. Only then would I jilt him, after I'd impressed him. I had no intention of going to Brown and being some sort of Black guinea pig, some sort of target for testing the rights of the White people who up until that time had segregated themselves from me, saying this was for the best.

You understand this was the same Memphis where people sang the blues, and not merely at the intersection of Beale Street and Third, or at places like the Club Paradise, where White people and Black people from out of town and mind might venture in search of the blues and find them and label them "official." The gospel of the blues was heard all over Memphis, in the Hollywood subdivision, or in Binghampton, Klondike, Douglass, Bearwater, Orange Mound, Buntyn, Castalia, the Beltline, the Walker and Foote Homes, and always on the AM radio stations, WLOK and WDIA and God knows how many churches. The blues were heard in other places not far away where Whites lived—along the parkways, Overton Park, in the low outlying subdivisions of White Station, Whitehaven, and Germantown—where many people felt the blues as much as heard them. The blues were born in places where the poverty was intrinsic, a collective millstone that hung even around the necks of the well-off. The poverty was an ineradicable birthmark and only real birthright, correct or otherwise; this was where the sharecroppers were not a generation away—this was where people, Black and even some White, still sharecropped, and never thought of colleges unless they were places where one, if fortunate and within walking or bus distance, might find custodial or landscaping work, or perhaps be buried if one lived righteously; where Martin Luther King, Jr., had been killed only one year before, shot in the neck, where we would surely take the hint. This was where the schools were by largest measure still "segregated." There was a feeling of some kind of change in the air, but this change was not to be trusted, not yet fact—only something in the air, like a scent that might swiftly fade away. Even the smell of rotting bodies fades, except to those who've been close enough to smell them.

This was the place where dusty, hardened feet of the impossible survivors trudged out of the Delta into Memphis singing the hardcore, real blues, blues born of the gospel used as the most effective means of communication between people enslaved, entrapped in their imposed wretchedness and kept uneducated and beaten down and crushed, stripped of everything that once had meaning to them except the power of their hearts and their own uplifted voices. They sang what? Of this odyssey of which a Homer could not have dreamed, an experience that you or I could not have survived, much less survived singing. Albert Murray writes about the Hero and the Blues, about the relation of those who must face this harrowing world with only the powers of their senses, only and all that. This is what produced the link of human commonality in the blues, an art form so powerful that it has permeated Western culture. When the blues are sung by the non-White Western culture of artists, they are plunged into their past, and then we must wonder if we could have survived the horror of worse than murder, of miscreation, of turning men and women into something less, or attempting to, for all these years on end, and then finding, through the gospel blues, of course, that all men and women here in the West would be defined by the fate of those denied.

It's difficult for me to see the blues in the context of anything else, in the writing of Malraux or Hemingway, as Albert Murray has pointed out, or Mark Twain, as obvious, or Homer, or anywhere else. Not one of them could have dreamed this particular story or quite imagined a denouement for it, or, if so, would not have made the denouement be music.

It has been asked: "Millions of people were enslaved, so why was there only one Bessie Smith?" I believed there were many more than Bessie Smith. I'd heard Mavis Staples. And Al Green singing "How Can You Mend a Broken Heart?" And Roberta Martin. Clara Ward. I'd heard recordings of Dinah Washington, and Billie Holiday, singing of how the blues were nothing but a pain in your heart. In Memphis you can hear Ruby Wilson and Joyce Cobb and Etta James, and more. . . .

An acquaintance of mine likes blues and insists that Robert Johnson was their finest practitioner. My friend is White. I pointed out to him that in this case he was talking about what he'd read. I was talking about what I'd felt. This is why I heard the blues before I knew of Ernest Hemingway, or Albert Murray, or Twain, or Malraux, or even Homer; I had heard these blues and felt them played. Felt them pouring from my unhardened foot. Heard and was them.

Robert Johnson, yes. John Lee Hooker and Z. Z. Hill

singing "I'm a Man". . . . Sunhouse, Blind Lemon Jefferson, T-Bone Walker, Rosetta Tharpe, Muddy Waters, and Bobby Bland. W. C. Handy and Louis Armstrong. Yes. And thousands of lesser lights but just as good bluesmen and women who found acceptance because the people in Memphis knew without being told that they sang their lives, and sang for their lives.

You would've heard tiny Ann Peebles, no bigger than a large Raggedy Ann doll, singing, "I can't stand the rain on my window, bringing back sweet memories. . . . Hey windowpane, do you remember?—" and known it was the blues as well as the blues was surely Aretha Franklin singing "I Never Loved a Man (The Way I Love You)" while playing cascading gospel piano chords. This was the apotheosis of the blues.

It did not take much translation, or much transposition of characters, to make this lyric epic, not the way Aretha Franklin rendered it. It was inspiring. Soon a White woman, Carole King, helped Aretha proclaim "(You Make Me Feel Like) A Natural Woman." The individual seen as collective without being detrimental to either—the blues is that quintessential rarity among American performing art forms.

No one taught me this. I learned it in the laboratory. Later, blues became known as rhythm-and-blues, and sometimes jazz. Record labels made stunning points of profit off them. The rhythm-and-blues division of the gospel blues became known as the Memphis Sound, which had purveyors too numerous to mention here, because they were within the Motown Sound, the Philadelphia Sound, on Columbia and Atlantic Records and the Stax and Volt labels, and, as I say, too numerous to mention here. I grew up hearing all this the way one heard, say, the snarling traffic in New York, or madrigals in seventeenth Century Europe or the pounding surf on the Hawaiian archipelago shore. It was simply there. People can tell me what they've read about or seen. I'm telling of what I've heard and felt.

I know where I heard Aretha sing the gospel and feel down-home blue. There was a junior college called S. A. Owen College nearby to downtown Memphis once. I was there from 1954 until 1964. It was a college predominantly for Black students. It had a snug, bucolic campus where I spent many of the first eleven years of my life. My mother was an instructor there. She'd gained a master's degree in English curriculum and supervision at Northwestern University, up the pipeline in Evanston, Illinois, while I was in her belly. She had lived on the near South Side of Chicago and caught the el to school. At Owen, we lived in a wing of Roger Williams Hall. By then I had my own separate body and fed myself.

Samuel Augustus Owen was the pastor of the Metropolitan Baptist Church. Everyone knows the Baptists are frugal with both money and souls. Reverend Owen was also an official with the Tennessee Baptist Missionary and Educational Convention. He persuaded all these earnest Baptists he knew to buy the grounds of what once was Siena College and St. Agnes Academy, situated on an eleven-acre lot at a corner of Vance Avenue and South Orleans Street near downtown Memphis, and move the Memphis Baptist Bible and Normal Institute there. They felt they had means to do so, and in 1954, down among the poverty-stricken and held-ignorant in the Delta, they did it.

By 1958, when I became cognizant, I found I was comfortably ensconced in the late fall and winter on a campus lined by shrubbery which thinned enough for me to see through into the larger outside world. The main entrance was just off Vance Avenue, nothing fancy, not even to a boy. There was a narrow gravel driveway that pierced into the campus like a flat broadsword and then split into a circle around flagstones at the base of the flagpole, where flew only the American flag, in front of old Roger Williams Hall.

Roger Williams Hall was the centerpiece of five buildings, all the rest of them downslope and to its right as you faced it. RWH was struck in a pose of permanence behind the circular driveway. The office of the registrar, Mr. Leotis Peterman, was on the first floor, as was the college cafeteria, run by Mrs. Elizabeth Applewhite, with the assistance of the dietician and home economics professor, Miss Dorothy McKinnie. The chapel was on the second floor. It was presided over by the dean of men and minister, Rev. Fred Lofton. Separated by a partition and adjacent to the chapel were the faculty quarters. Across the hall from our suite was one occupied by Professor Donzaleigh Patterson, a lively woman who became my true Aunt Donza and who took me for rides in her neat yellow Ford, and still later became the business department head at Tennessee State University, far, far away, in another country called Nashville.

My mother and Donza were friends with Ernestine V. Guy, the administrative secretary to the college president. Mrs. Guy, a proud and efficient woman, had three comely daughters, Beverly, Carmella, and Francine, who were older than I and unapproachable, though I distinctly recall thoughts of approaching them somehow.

To the right of Roger Williams Hall, a walkway with a canopy covered with green shingles led down to a rose-red brick administration building of three stories with a white multifoil facade facing South Orleans Street. It held the classrooms and the offices of the president, Dr. Levi Watkins, who looked like Joe E. Brown, the comedian—except he was a Black man. And that was a whole lot of difference according to the rules of the game I would learn later. The gymnasium was on the second floor of the ad building. I remember keeping the score of the games between the Owen College Hornets and all opposition on a black chalkboard, which was nearly as tall as I was. Meanwhile two hundred or so fans screamed their hearts out for the Hornets—"We love the Horr-nets"—and checked my math, which for this duty was adequate. The Hornets wore shiny green satin trunks with buckles, high-topped Converse Chuck Taylor sneakers, and faded green singlets. We won as much as we lost, or vice versa. I remember a bowlegged, almond-eyed young man named Cazzie Russell came to the gym to shoot around. He never seemed to miss. It was said he was going to the University of Michigan. I watched, thinking, "We could use him."

On the ground floor of the ad building was the indoor six-lane swimming pool, where I nearly drowned once when a group of sophomores with nothing better to do threw me into the deep end to see if I would float. Luckily for me, one of them pulled me out. I think I remember him from my mother's humanities classes, so he was no fool. Drown me and he could forget about humanities. From time to time, I would go right into mother's classes and make faces at those few coeds I considered my type, the ones who were like Beverly, Carmella, or Francine. It seemed they were not all that plentiful.

Across from the ad building was Howe Hall, a musty, cavernous old building with a great spiral staircase screwed into its walls, and chandeliers dangling from its eaves like giant salty tears. I ambivalently took piano there from Mrs. Mildred D. Green: Bach, Mozart, Beethoven, Tchaikovsky, Grieg, Schubert, Schumann, Liszt—their simpler work, scaled down by ghostwriters and other elementary piano instructors, and then only such as I could handle. It is beautiful, difficult music. I often heard my mother direct the college choir in Howe. She said the acoustics were special there. This hall made me think of ghosts, and gray movies about Frankenstein's monster made up of dead limbs. These thoughts never took away my appetite. I always stopped by the tiny college grill located between Howe and the ad building for a burger on my way back to RWH. Singing and playing the piano can make you hungry.

I remember many frosty November mornings when I would push my feet through the fallen leaves of the tree-choked campus, watching my breath burst in front of me through a woolly scarf, gliding at a gauged diagonal across the front of the home campus, on the way to catch the city bus to elementary school. I remember the wind rushing through the trees and the leaves giving up, dozens at a time, then in patches, then one by one, and as each left the tree, the sound the wind made rushing through trees lessened until full winter came, when the sound became only the wind again and not the same music at all. It seemed to me such a great distance to cover on that diagonal. Looking back now I can see it was not that far. I remember having no feelings about Owen College but marveling at how swell my mother was.

From the Owen College Bulletin, 1957–58:

"Owen College is a distinctive two-year Christian institution. Concern is given to the development, as far as possible, of character through knowledge and training that give emphasis to spiritual values. The faculty is able. Classes are small. Association between student and teacher is close. Dormitory life is regulated for good study habits. Social life is well-planned and wisely guided."

Now, thirty-three years later, I could not have done a better job of describing it myself. Notice how honest the people were at Owen College. Notice the leanness of their descriptive writing. Owen said it would develop, as far as possible. No false claims about changing sand into marble. I appreciated my mother and her associates being called "able." At least somebody recognized it. They didn't mention the tuition, which was a whopping eighty dollars per semester.

They did mention spiritual values, always the yellow light to me, but I don't recall being hit over the head with religion. There was chapel, of course, but I don't remember it as a torture chamber or solitary. In fact, we lived directly above it. Aretha Franklin came and sang in the chapel once. I remember her, and then Carla Thomas, and they sang "Oh Mary Don't You Weep (Tell Martha Not to Mourn)." Mary and Martha were the sisters of Lazarus, the man Jesus raised from the dead. Aretha and then Carla were brought there by the Tennessee Baptist and Educational Convention—and my mother and her friends Aunt Donza and Mrs. Ernestine Guy. I have an old photograph where such a group of women, including the contralto Marian Anderson and my mother and Madame Florence Cole Talbert McCleave, the soprano, is seated at a table taking tea. Mother said Miss Anderson was at her most expressive when singing "Sometimes I Feel Like a Motherless Child." I wondered why that was.

It was only recently that I found out these people were sponsored by the Baptists. I had to look it up. That's how subtle they were. It was a suitable environment for a child, and I feel I was made somewhat better by it, even though I was nothing more than a young mascot and did not understand reality, that it was a tiny school, a Black school, hardly worth noting in a larger world. It was doomed from the start.

Dr. Watkins was the first to go. The teachers received eighty dollars a month, and then one month came when the Tennessee Baptist Convention said they would have to wait a while because the Baptists were indeed frugal with money and souls, at times to the point of ridiculousness. Two years after we left, in 1965, Owen was melded into LeMoyne, a small four-year school some twelve blocks away, and became

LeMoyne-Owen College—smaller than Owen had been in the first place. But at least it's still there. Now the campus of Owen College, once laden with so many personal anchors for me, has long been torn down. On that memorable lot stands an ominous brick junior high with no facade, no mature trees, no windows that can be seen from the street.

In late 1969, they gave us this mysterious rite of passage called the Scholastic Aptitude Test. I made passing marks, especially on the verbal half, I believe merely because of my environment when I was a child. To this day my mother says I made a point of choosing *Lady Chatterley's Lover* from the vast collection of books in her studio in the teacher's dormitory at Owen College when I was but ten, having run through what I could handle and might enjoy from the other books, and having never had a prayer with Beverly, Carmella, or Francine. So when I scored relatively high on the verbal half of the SAT in 1969 in spite of not knowing its import, or attending any Holiday Inn seminars on how to beat the blasted thing, this made eyebrows go up.

Which brings us back to Brown University. This unusual test score was how I had come to the attention of Brown. Not because it was all that stunning as a test score—the top score on the verbal half is 800, as I learned when I was nearly thirty—but because my score was attained by a Black boy in a "segregated" high school down in the Mississippi River Delta who might be familiar with the blues, but with nothing but the blues—not books, not in the slightest. No sane anthropologist would accept it, much less normal folk.

By the time I was in my senior year in high school, I knew my grade-point average very well, and knew what I had to do to keep it at a steady click of 3.0. I could slide by with a C in trigonometry because I was all but assured of acing English. But I wasn't a member of the National Honor Society.

I didn't deserve or want it. Young Black boys in the Delta who feel the blues, and who play on the football team because they are obligated to try to play the game to become men quick before they die, aren't supposed to care about honor societies and SATs. This was the surely sullen methodology of the sons of preachers and sharecroppers who went to school with me and populated the corners I passed on my way to what version of manhood I could manage. They had never heard of Owen College, and I kept silent.

But Brown sought to brand me a scholar. This made me uncomfortable for a variety of reasons. First, they removed one disguise and tried to replace it with another. I've been around some scholars, and for the most part they are more boring than penguins, much less boys who hang on corners. I usually give scholars a hard time. I keep promising myself I'll stop, even though they tell me I'm not "qualified" to make decisions, although they are forever doing it for me. But they say they have the right. They're intellectuals, and they have papers to prove it. They have researched. They know it not because they have lived it, but because they have read what someone else thought. I'd better leave thinking to those qualified. The difficulty is in knowing whom to trust.

Now I must admit no one I've ever met from Brown was ever anything like this, and some of the people I have met from there were surely intellectuals. So not all scholars are haughty toad frogs. The recruiter/alumnus from Brown had been a quiet man who smiled on seeing me, with my flawed Afro and my slumping blue jeans containing in one rear pocket a dog-eared paperback copy of, I don't remember, it could have been Twain, whom I loved, or perhaps Wright, or Dickens.

Later I told Mrs. Strong that in spite of this quiet man's good intentions, I couldn't bring myself to say yes to Brown. She sighed and looked at me and saw I was serious, and merely admonished me to do well wherever I went. The Air Force Academy was very much interested, she said . . .

Instead I went to a small, historically Black school, Knoxville College. No, of course you never heard of it, and there were times I wished I never had. I almost left after one year on account of homesickness for the Delta. You can imagine how this immaturity would have been multiplied at Brown. There are Black intellectuals who will tell you what a bad decision I made. And maybe for my son, that will be true. But then, judging from the conduct of certain coeds at Harvard, maybe not. My son did not live through those times and see all these leaders who were only talking sense be shot in the head for their troubles. Whoever White people were (beyond the merchants in all the stores who smiled because they were getting your money), I surely was not going to give them a chance to kill me. Given this state of mind, however subconscious, for me to be delivered to the hands of the kindly Presbyterians in Knoxville was what I needed. I'd forgotten what I knew from Owen, sublimated it, because I was only supposed to be educated in the blues, and death.

I made it through college, had several interesting misadventures along the way that don't go well here. When people ask me what did I learn there, I usually say, "It's not so much what I learned, it's what I didn't learn. I didn't learn to begin to hate myself." And to this day, whenever I commit some rare act of competence, some person, either Black or White, will look at me and ask, "Where did you go to school?" as if the school will explain me and this competence to them. I usually tell these people, "You never heard of it." Invariably, the White people haven't. They are better off than some Black people in this regard, for some Black people have heard of the school and still can't bring themselves to understand a link between it and competence.

I left Knoxville College with its paltry intellectual papers in hand, tried to use them to enroll in the graduate school for journalism at the University of California at Berkeley. I had begun to ease myself into an integrated setting in life by moving into California and journalism. I found both to be not half-bad, but that might have been because no one had yet shouted that they owned my parents.

Two of my friends were Jaime Diaz, who had gone to the University of San Francisco, and Hugh Delahanty, who had gone to Brown, of all places. We were copyboys at a local newspaper, the *Oakland Tribune*, and did plenty of shouting. It comes with the job of copyboy. But we never did this Hannian style of incorrect unshouting, and we represented three distinct ethnic groups (although we never had to make a point of it). We were, I suppose now, judging ourselves against each other's example. Later we all worked at *Sports Illustrated* together, which either says something for us or less than something about depth in American journalism.

I digress. I performed the necessary preliminaries to enrollment at the University of California at Berkeley, such as taking another test, this one called the Graduate Record Examination, I believe. Tests of this kind have never been a bar to me. Again, I did reasonably well on this test. But we all find our bars sooner or later. I went to the building housing the journalism department on the Berkeley campus of the university. There was a young White female at the desk of the office I entered. I told her of my plans to enroll and said that I wished to speak to the department head about the other requirements. She looked at me and began laughing a derisive, howling laugh ending with a supercilious snort and a dismissal. She turned her back to me and went on with her work. I stood there, speechless, senseless, except I faintly heard Mahalia Jackson singing "The Upper Room." At the time, the B. B. King blues standard, "The Thrill Is Gone," had become popular nationwide. It was supposed to be some kind of brand-new thing. I heard the song over and over again during this time, even when it was not on the radio.

Believing I had no other option, I left the building, and enrolling at the University of California at Berkeley never came up in my mind again, except in a wistful, might-have-been sort of way. I had been raised to believe that if people don't want you around, then don't stand around, unless what you need is there and only there. Then accommodations have to be made. But if there are acceptable options, use them. There are easier ways to get heartburn. So I do not intend to cast blame at the girl whose derisiveness sparked my reaction. This is America. She can laugh at whatever she wants. I must blame myself for hoping not to be rejected.

I was also turned down, more formally, for the Summer Program for Minority Journalists, held at the same Berkeley campus, and this program was run by Black people, including Robert C. Maynard, a Black man from Barbados who would eventually become the publisher of the *Tribune*. You have to have the heart to work through this, and maybe schools do not give it to you. Eventually I got my graduate papers in journalism, but not from scholars. I got them from doing the actual work of journalism itself. It can be hard work. In fact, it can make going to any school seem like a summer vacation. Eventually, by dint of showing up, I became a reporter, and in time Mr. Maynard, the Bajan, offered me a job as a sports columnist, saying, "I'm going to give you a chance to fail." I wish he'd said, "I'm giving you a chance to produce," but that is small potatoes. The chance itself was the important thing. Mr. Maynard was the first Black publisher of a major daily newspaper in America outside of the traditional Black press. That was where I got my chance. Was this coincidence? Perhaps. Perhaps not.

Here my blues became superannuated; they transformed, turned sharper, more urban, but no less mine. Here the blues became jazz and I began to play them now on my keyboard of the alphabet, my own musical scale, my combination guitar mouth harp drum, where Aretha and Koko and B. B. and Z. Z. helped me see, and made me be, and helped me endure, and overcome, and run, and trudge, and fall in love with the broken heart that was now both my inspiration and legacy.

For me, jazz stems from blues. I don't know all that much about the former—you'd need to read Nelson George or Greg Tate to get the 411 on Ornette Coleman, Lester Young (whose sound impressed me most), or John Coltrane, everybody from David Murray to the Marsalis Brothers to the new culture of hip-hop. I have also been told about the likes of Bix Beiderbecke of Davenport, Iowa, how you never would have known he was a White boy just listening to him blow. I've never heard him. There is so much I don't and can't know and will never know. But I know Miles Davis got together with the rest of his Sextet—Julian Cannonball Adderly, John Coltrane, Bill Evans, Paul Chambers, James Cobb—for the 1959 recording *Kind of Blue*. I know that is the music that defines jazz to me. I wonder if my reaction to it stems from the track "All Blues." As I say, I am not a jazz critic or in any sense a professional musician or music critic so I cannot specify bars, key, be-bop's relationship to cool jazz, the struggles of group improv. I only know what gets me—a rhythmic bass line of the like I've walked all my life. Onomatopoeia will not do, but it's all I have available to use. The rails were the walking bass of Chambers, there, then up, then down, then up, then down: *dooom-Dup-DOOOM-Dup-dooom-Dup-DOOOM*. . . . I remember counting per bar in music theory, counting Bach, counting ONE-two-three-FOUR-three-two-ONE.

The shimmering bass line rode over a track of the trilling piano of Evans, a sure, steady hand, the track on which the locomotives would ride. Cobb whisked drums as the sound of sights, sighs whizzed past. Cannonball and Trane, twin locomotives, joined this movement with soft horns. And then, above the track and rails and behind the locomotives and Cobb's whisper, riding on and over and behind them all so smoothly, came this clear, pure sonic expression of Miles Davis's trumpet, with a mute: *ta-dahhhhhhhh*. Davis soon removed his mute and put on a moving, blues lyric that told a story you must decipher for yourself— some of the most brilliant, beautiful, difficult music I've heard.

I also know it relates to me. I can do something more with it. I use it still. At the same time, I can see it in others. In his book *Another Good Lovin' Blues*, Black writer Arthur Flowers makes the blues sound right there on the page, and you can hear them: "I am hoodoo, I am griot, I am a man of power. My story is a true story, my lie is a true lie—a fine old Delta tale about a mad blues piano player and an Arkansas conjure woman on a hoodoo mission. Lucas Bodeen and Melvira Dupree. Plan to show you how they found the good thing. True love." In his book of essays entitled *Broken Vessels*, White writer Andre Dubus included a piece called "Railway Sketches": "Perhaps this comes from knowing the train so well, from the camaraderie of work, from the skillful legs and hands that don't stumble or spill, from feeling finally that it's *their* train, and it occurs to me that this is good work for the dispossessed of the land: seeing the country's landscapes from a clean mobile home and place of work, a place they know and command, as if The Man Without A Country had been given command of a ship to cruise America's coasts and rivers." While reading these passages, I could hear "All Blues" by the Miles Davis Sextet. Listen to the track and read the passages and you might understand. Listen to the art form of the New World: Listen to everybody. We are all invited to solo, like it or not.

Occasionally I like to go by the elementary school in suburban Maryland where my own son navigates the fifth grade, and quite skillfully enough in my book. He knows his parents expect A's and a sprinkling of B's, and this is what he brings away. I tell him they're not really for his parents and he looks at me as if to say, "Really, Dad? I think I could get by without them." I like that look. It means he'll be resilient.

I like to go by his school and wait for him because it is a good public school, one of those called "magnet" schools now. It is the most well-integrated school I have ever seen. There are the fairest White children with blue eyes and blond hair, and brunettes. Then there are redheads with green eyes, Mediterraneans, children whose parents are from India and Nigeria, Austria and Ghana, even Australia. There are Hispanic children and Asian children and there are Black American children of various hues whose ancestors have been here for hundreds of years, and their various hues show it. Their hair is black and brown and red and amber, and their eyes are black and brown and gray and green and hazel, and you cannot count the different shades of their skins.

The school is very good. It has won awards in spite of it. Even the principal's name is Miss Brooks. It is idyllic, as some times in a child's life should be. Sometimes when I go and watch the children released from school, hearing their yips and whoops, their collective hum, watching them huddling into their confabs and laughing at each other's ways and lining up for buses, I wonder what they will mean to each other when they grow up. I am happy for them now, just so, but I know sooner or later my son will be made to feel blue. I want him to understand, not take it personally.

As an aside, to show you how some things do not change,

I noticed a reticence on his part to ride with me after school and miss the yellow bus. This disappointed me until one day when an attractive young girl just beginning to bud into young womanhood asked me, "Will Cole be riding the bus today?" She's the safety patrol officer of the bus. I said, "No, he'll be riding with me, all right?" She nodded primly and began to count her other charges.

Later I said to my son, "Hmm, I see where missing the school bus might have its disadvantages." He took it well, saying, "Aw, Dad. She's sixth grade." Unapproachable. I was reminded of Beverly, Carmella, and Francine and the old days, and I had to smile. Later I found out that this girl hadn't been his type, but he'd known what I meant. I sometimes wonder, had I gone to a school like this, perhaps I would not have left that office at the University of California at Berkeley those long years ago. Perhaps I would have laughed, too, and asked the young female, "Are you tickled, or do you have gas?" and stayed until I was awarded my place among the scholars in the graduate school of journalism.

Perhaps.

But elementary school is not like college, I do know that much of it. Children are known to say strange and cruel things and be right back playing with each other two minutes later in elementary schools. They have not yet learned the lessons of hatred. As you get older you take things more personally. Such lessons take more time than children have available. In college people are free to insult me (or my son), and we are supposed to say they have the right.

Well, don't ask for my permission to insult me. If you want to insult me, go ahead, do it, revel in it, you are doing me a favor because I will recognize your face now, but don't insult me and tell me it's for my own good I've been insulted, that my rights are protected by these insults.

• • •

I am now miles from the Delta, but the blues stay with me like a second skin. At one point during the year 1991, I was called by a representative of "Larry King Live," which airs on the Cable News Network, CNN. She asked if I would care to come and talk about the situation at Georgetown University, where one Timothy McGuire, a senior student at the law school, had caused a minor tempest by revealing the confidential LSAT scores of the Black students at the law school. What is an LSAT? It is some test any aspiring law student must take. Life is full of them.

McGuire's point, apparently, was that even though he'd not scored very high on this test himself, they'd let him into Georgetown Law School anyway, and he'd in fact scored higher than many of the Black law student attendees. If you compared his entering test scores to theirs, it made him look all the better. He didn't position it this way in the media, but however he positioned it, it caused a tempest, so I suppose he's to be commended for gaining attention.

I said I'd come on "Larry King Live," not because of Mr. McGuire in any fashion but because I know King to be a good conversationalist. I would put up with Mr. McGuire for the chance to talk to Larry King and, of course, to promote a book. I showed up on time and was taken into the control room for the show at the CNN Building near Union Station in downtown Washington by a woman who smiled but gave me no other preparation. Upon entering the control room, I saw Patrick Buchanan sitting in for Larry King.

"Oh, did I mention Patrick Buchanan would be sitting in for Larry King?" the smiling woman said. Apparently, Larry King was on vacation.

Patrick Buchanan is a member of the conservative school of thought and media, a former White House administrator and veteran wraith of several media television shows. He soon would announce his candidacy for President of the United States. He is pretty much known as a bulldog who chews on words like *quota*. "Nice," I thought. "Nice indeed." I could hear Miles and the fellows throwing down on "So What?"

Buchanan was busy strategizing with T. McGuire, a wee lad whose posture reminded me of a bantam rooster about to be spurred and pitted. No doubt he and Buchanan discussed the tactics they would employ to somehow enrage or expose me, hoping to reflect on my entire kith and kin. In the meantime, I was led up to the podium, where I noticed that my adjustable chair had been ratcheted down so that my chest was even with the table. It made me look a little bit as though I were back in elementary school. This was so I would not appear to be given a superior position to Mr. McGuire, who was seated to my left, with his chair appropriately ratcheted up. Although his chest was higher than the table, the tops of our heads were on plane for the camera, which in spite of its claims to reality can only show people, places, and things in two dimensions. It can be limited.

I smiled at McGuire and told him not to worry, it was just television. He gave me a double take. Why was I calm? I think it surprised him that I didn't appear thrown, but, really, nothing White people do surprises me anymore.

The show started. Patrick said, predictably, "Quota!" I suggested he'd always been a brawler. I thought to myself how White people loved to press the fullest advantages they could. To them, there was nothing unfair about advantages. Just as there was nothing unfair about this TV show, not to Buchanan and McGuire. Patrick Buchanan seemed to assume that if a Black person showed up, that meant a quota, and that quality suffered for the sake of racial quotas.

Say you have a section of a newspaper with ten editors. There are five White males, three White females, and one Black male, and a Black Woman is hired for the tenth job. One of the White males complains thusly: "Quotas have become more important than merit. White men have rights, too, even though the bleeding hearts don't believe it." Now, this kind of White person *needs for that Black hiree to be mediocre*. White people like this are always more comfortable with mediocre Black people than with Black excellence. Black excellence ruins their whole point, frightens them out of their wits.

Mr. McGuire talked about releasing the scores and how angry the Black students and other people had been. He couldn't understand why we weren't supposed to talk about it. Why were Black students so defensive? They weren't on Georgetown's prestigious Law Review. They this. They that. I suggested that McGuire wasn't doing this for the good of humanity but for self-interest. Maybe these Black people wanted a chance to prove themselves and be judged on how they left Georgetown, not on how they'd entered it.

We went back and forth, and they expected me to be angry, because, likely, they knew they would have been angry had they been me. I gave McGuire the Martinique I.Q. test. I asked him if he were sleeping in a room in Martinique and noticed a small lizard race across the room, what would be the proper action? (a) Leave the room, (b) light a scented candle, (c) ignore it, (d) open a window. Buchanan, under instruction, went to commercial. During the commercial break a female technician yelled, "Light a scented candle!" I sat there and raised my eyebrows a bit and said, "Good answer," never really dreaming that Mr. McGuire would take the bait.

We came back on the air and Patrick asked the question, and sure enough, Mr. McGuire said, "Light a scented candle," and sat there looking pompous, as though he would never, ever crib. Had it not been impolite, I would have fallen out of my ratcheted-down chair laughing. As it was, I said he got the answer wrong; of course you ignore the reptile. But I told him not to feel bad. Very few Americans get that right. I told him he might make a good litigator one day. At the end of the show Pat shook my hand to make sure I was real.

On my way off the set, Mr. McGuire stopped me and said it was interesting that I was older and more experienced in televised debates than he. He believed that was the only way I could have outquicked him, through a bad set of circumstances, or a set of advantages I had—age and experience—that he had not. He said that he hoped we would cross verbal swords again one day. I told him I doubted it, that if he crossed verbal swords with anybody it would be with my lawyer, who was also a White Georgetown lawyer. Later McGuire wrote me a letter and wanted to have lunch with me, but from my point of view there was nothing to be gained by it, so I never replied. I had already been polite.

I hope my son goes to some college one day, although I would not push him to do that or anything. I'd suggest and suggest strongly, but I would not demand. I want him to be flexible and to be resilient. I want him to understand his rules and live by them. I know that soon he'll feel blue. I want him to know he can be an impossible survivor too, even though the odds are stacked against him. He has plenty of time to feel the blues, and only a very short time to sing.

Why Black People
Shoot the Jump Shot
for Nothing

Anfernee Hardaway may
have been the best high school basketball player in America
when he graduated from Treadwell High in Memphis in
1990. But he sat out the 1990–91 season at Memphis State
because he was admitted under the guidelines of NCAA By-
law 5–1–(j), the controversial measure better known as Proposition 48, which states an athlete cannot participate without
both a minimum score of 700 on the SAT and a 2.0 high
school grade-point average. According to the 1990 Knight
Foundation Report, 86.5 percent of the football and basketball players who have been affected by Prop. 48 during the
last three years are Black. These athletes have been unfairly

*labeled as intellectually inferior. Yet behind every Prop. 48
athlete, there is a story . . .*

Anfernee Hardaway comes to the field house alone, while his
schoolmates rest on a Sunday. Diffused winter-afternoon sun-
light seems to transmute this old wooden court into a golden
floor. Hardaway moves lightly over it. He retrieves a single
stray basketball. His expression resembles that of a paleon-
tologist investigating a fossil find. His large hands move over
the leather surface of the ball, checking the pebble grain and
the depth of the seams. He estimates the circumference to be
true, pronounces the ball authentic, and bounces it, the report echoing in the empty gym on the campus of Memphis
State University. The night before, the Memphis State Tigers
played not far away, at the Mid-South Coliseum. Hardaway
sat in the crowd. The reason he's on the court now is to go
one-on-one with his shadow. He appears to be confident.
Most teenagers do.

"To ten," his shadow says. "By one. Make it take it."

"Not to fifteen? Okay. Any way you want," Hardaway
says.

"My ball?"

"Show me what you got," Hardaway says.

SWISH.

"Good shot," Hardaway says.

"You're just rusty."

"Not really," he answers.

"You are and you don't even know it."

"Short."

CLANG.

"You saw that was short pretty quick for a rusty guy."

"Saw it short right off your hand," Hardaway says. "Maybe
not as rusty as you?"

"I am rust. Mister Rust, to you."

Hardaway laughs, bouncing the ball lightly and high.

"High dribbles get picked in the big leagues."

Hardaway lolls his head to the side, then ladles a dribble behind his back, wraps it around, goes between his legs, back and forth—*WHAPWHAPWHAPWHAP*—reverses, spins, crosses over, changes pace. His dexterity is noteworthy because Hardaway is 6 feet $7^{1}/_{2}$. No one so tall this side of Magic Johnson ever handled the ball this effortlessly under duress. But without resolve, what is it? Hardaway explodes into a whirlybird reverse jam, hanging like a banner from the rafters.

The shadow hand-checks and hip-checks, pushing Hardaway's body farther out, away from the basket.

Hardaway says, "Is this NBA three-point range?"

"No. This is farther."

Hardaway hoists a shot as the shadow lunges to block it. No harm, no . . .

Hardaway says, "And one," as the ball lands in the net.

"Memphis State is in desperate need . . ."

Rip.

"The clock is winding down . . ."

Rip.

"Left hand . . ."

Rip.

Rip.

"Maybe I'll stay out here . . ."

Rip.

Rip.

Rip.

"*Jesus* . . ."

Rip.

"Ten-one," says Hardaway. "Shouldn't have let you get one, should I?"

•   •   •

Anfernee Hardaway's nickname is Penny. "To me, Penny is great. Dribble. Rebound. Shoot. Especially pass. Like Magic. You see him in warm-ups, he doesn't look like much. Then he lays his head over to the side, the game starts, and pow!"

This testimonial comes from ten-year-old James Finch, son of Memphis State's varsity basketball coach, Larry Finch. James was describing his reaction to Hardaway's play at Treadwell High, where from 1988 to 1990 he was the finest prep basketball player Memphis has produced since, well, 1988, when Todd Day emerged from high school to become a star at mighty Arkansas.

There are forty-three high schools in greater Memphis, Tennessee. Each of them has a varsity basketball team running twelve to fifteen deep, in turn fed by twice as many junior high schools. The high schools in turn feed many universities with talented basketball players. Some teams, like the nearby University of Arkansas, go five-deep with these players.

"In Memphis, the kids never stop playing," says Nolan Richardson, the coach at the University of Arkansas. "By ninth grade, the good ones play one hundred organized games a year."

Memphis State's roster barely has room for any out-of-towners. Hardaway was the cream of a bumper crop, perhaps the most talented high school player in America, surely the best freshman basketball player since, well, you name him.

Yet, in 1990–91, he was much more a teenager than he was a fantastic ballplayer with a kaleidoscopic game who entrances savants who watch him play. Some adult observers of Hardaway's skills make James Finch sound like a cynic:

"Anfernee can do it all—drive, post up, handle the fast break," say Craig Esherick, the assistant coach at Georgetown who scouted Hardaway for the university. "Going one-on-one with him is no way to stay healthy."

"We almost got him," says Arkansas's Richardson. "Oh, if we had."

"I love him," says Larry Finch while standing on the construction site of the Great American Pyramid, which will house the game and the paying customers of the Memphis State Tigers, on the fallow banks of the great river. Finch looks out over it. "See that river? That Mississippi is nothing to play with."

Finch has slight epicanthic folds over his eyes, adding a sleepy look to his drawl and thickening middle. These attributes belie a basic truth about the forty-year-old coach who at fourteen played in cheap, soggy sneakers held together by safety pins. By age twenty-one, he was an all-America player at Memphis State. A fire burns smartly behind those eyes.

"The picture that's been painted—of being stupid, of being idiots, really—isn't fair, but understandable, for him, Anthony Douglas, and Billy Smith, who sat out last year. The pressure was great to keep Penny in Memphis. We need the attraction, no question about that. But he needs us more."

Anfernee Hardaway is a Proposition 48 student.

Hardaway sits with his shadow after educating it, 10–1. He hears the shadow whisper. "See the zipper on this knee? That's why. Tomorrow, this joint will be nearly useless from this kind of hard workout." Hardaway appears puzzled. At the time, concepts like age and infirmity are difficult for a teenager who doesn't have a major scar on his body and who has just won, 10–1, while hardly breaking a sweat.

A few months later he began to face his own mortality, lying face down on wet pavement outside the home of a cousin at 77 North Merton, with a robber pointing a small-caliber pistol at his neck. Hardaway was shot in the right foot, the bullet breaking three metatarsal bones—some of the fragments remain in his foot to this day. "I kept thinking,

'He's going to shoot me in my back. He's going to shoot me in my head,'" Hardaway said. "I'm lucky to be alive." The shooter, who remains unidentified, escaped.

But back in the field house last winter, in January of 1991, Hardaway had been more cavalier. "I can hoop with anybody you name," he said quietly. "But I could not pass that SAT test. I took it four times. I think I did better each time. But not good enough. Now, I can't even practice with the team. I'm taking seventeen credits this semester. But."

But, seventeen credits are not why in the 1991–92 season he's expected to fill the 20,000 seat Pyramid. The Mid-South Coliseum, the Tigers' old lair, holds 11,200. Hardaway makes it obsolete. And twenty large don't show up for any study hall, baby. You don't star in sneaker commercials for going to study hall. The NBA doesn't award million-dollar contracts to All-Study Halls. The logic has a kind of rhythm but is shortsighted when universally applied—the kind of logic in which teenagers often find themselves inextricably immersed.

"We won the gold medal for the South at the Olympic Festival last summer. I gave Shaquille O'Neal a no-looker on the break. He tore down the rim. They all said, 'Ooo!' The passing, I do best. I see things. But people think I'm dumb, and that's just the way that is. I get it from both sides. Some people here, but some brothers from the 'hood do, too. I went over to this girl's house once. A guy came in and said, 'Oh, yeah, you that dumb ballplayer.' He's known for selling cocaine. But I'm the dumb one, right?

"I can hoop with anybody they have. Alonzo Mourning, I would love it. Give him a ball fake in the lane. He's going to go for it. You know he's going to go for it. But I can't do that. Not right now."

Is that bad, Penny?

"I don't know yet."

• • •

Memphis State opened its doors in 1912 as the Western Tennessee State Normal School. The athletic teams' first nickname was the Teachers. In 1957, that nickname was changed to the Tigers. The school's name had been changed to Memphis State College in 1927, but in the years after 1957, it eventually became a house of educational ill repute for the student-athletes on its basketball teams. Barely six out of sixty—10 percent—of the players graduated during the tenure of coach Dana Kirk, from 1979 to 1986.

Kirk had a .718 winning percentage. His most notorious stars, Keith Lee and William Bedford, supposed wunderkinds, had little if any impact in the NBA—although Bedford was employed for some time by the two-time world champion Detroit Pistons. He rarely played. Baskerville Holmes managed to eventually make a club team in Finland, so at least he saw some of the world. Andre Turner, the Little General, got a whiff with eight CBA and NBA teams. Vincent Askew stuck around a while with the Golden State Warriors. He'll need a day job soon. None of them has to this point received an undergraduate degree. Dana Kirk was fired in 1986, the year after the Tigers went to the Final Four, the championship round of major college basketball, where they lost to Villanova University. Only two of twelve players on that Memphis State roster won degrees from the university.

"The biggest ripoff was rationalizing that they had gotten the chance to go to college," said Charles Cavagnaro, a former newspaperman and the athletic director at Memphis State since 1982. "Boy, that was a crock. We came to the conclusion that we had to spend money and try and graduate 'em. Race is usually seen as a factor in most things in American life, and basketball isn't an island. But if we hadn't changed, we were exactly what people said we were."

Gina Pickens came to Memphis State as an academic counselor for football and basketball athletes on Nov. 1, 1987, after a ten-year teaching career at Central High. To start, she was given a small room and a desk. "I would tell the kids we were getting a new facility where they could get together and do the work. They said, 'Sure, Miss Pickens. Right.' These kids can smell hypocrisy a mile away.

"But now we've graduated nine seniors in a row and ten or twelve overall in basketball including our only Prop. 48, Cheyenne Gibson, since committing educational resources," she says, now speaking from the Center for Athletic Academic Services beneath the field house—a set of offices costing $400,000.

Sophomores Billy Smith and Anthony Douglas went to East High. Smith is a 6–4 guard of superb physical skill. He plays off a trampoline, as if desperate to prove something. Douglas, 6–7, 260 pounds, is much more controlled. "I never thought we were dumb," he laughs. "Slow, maybe, in my case."

One out of two people you meet along the Delta has some discernible African heritage, so to deny race as a factor in this educational equation is hopelessly naive, or tactical, although similar dilemmas within American higher education are neither new nor restricted by any means to African-Americans. "Our Illiterate Collegians," a Richard Hovey essay bemoaning the slacking of entire enrollments, was published in the *American Association of University Professors Bulletin* in the summer of 1958. "College Athletics: Their Pressure on the High Schools" by Eugene Youngert ran in the *Atlantic Monthly* in October of the same year. These portentous essays came long before a $1 billion, seven-year television contract was signed by the CBS network and the NCAA institutions for the rights to televise the high drama of the NCAA Tournament, which ends with the Final Four. The essays came before widespread integration patterns appeared in the country.

Lester High School was reduced to the status of a junior

high school in 1972 and eventually became an elementary school. Before that it had been a segregated Black high school that Hardaway, Smith, and Douglas would have attended had they come along fifteen years earlier. It stands in the center-city neighborhood of Binghampton. It was 1969 before Memphis State recruited its first local Black high school star. His name was Larry Finch, from Melrose High in the neighborhood of Orange Mound, adjacent to Binghampton. Finch was booed by some of his own neighbors as he announced his decision, standing next to Memphis State's head coach, Moe Iba. Some people screamed, "Uncle Tom!" Not a year had passed since the murder of Martin Luther King, Jr., at the Lorraine Motel—just off the bluff over the beautiful river.

Four years later, in 1973, Finch led the Tigers to the Final Four and the NCAA championship game in St. Louis, an unheard-of and profitable extracurricular activity for a commuter school in the capital of the Upper Delta. Then the Tigers, coached by Gene Bartow, lost the championship game to John Wooden and UCLA. Finch, a senior, scored 29 points. He then received a bachelor of science degree in education that same spring. So, eventually, did twelve of his thirteen teammates. The three seniors on Finch's 1990–91 team won degrees in the spring of '91. Most of the credit goes to them, but some must also go to Memphis State.

"I'll be proud to graduate from here," says guard Tony Madlock, a senior on the 1991–92 team.

"They all have lives of their own to live, decisions of their own to make," says Finch. "I can't set priorities for them. I tell them what we expect. They are humans with human emotions. Penny and Anthony will make it. I hope Billy will."

Later, the visage of a bearded man comes over the Delta via prime-time television. "What happened is our own fault," says Professor Harry Edwards of the University of California. "Parents and teachers have set these kids up, encouraging them to place a higher priority on playbooks than textbooks. We Blacks have allowed ourselves to be moved from the cotton fields to the playing fields."

The sun went orange as it began to dip into the flat horizon. The oppressive air was finally cooling as Louise Hardaway walked with her sons, Lester and John, on the rich, black earth beside state Highway 18. It was a late summer day in 1943, just below the Missouri bootheel, four miles east of Blytheville, Arkansas. She'd left the fields with her boys not far from a bend in the sweet river, where they'd stooped their way through row after row of cotton since dawn and had come up owed $2.50. With her conscript, she might be able to buy a small bar of scented soap for her face and neck, in addition to the sorghum, flour, and coffee. She'd scrubbed the walls of the shack in the dark morning hour, before she took the boys up and went to work. She was bone tired now, but her wash was clean and out to dry.

She stopped occasionally to pick sunflowers and violets to put in the glass Mason jars she'd boiled. After canning peaches, apples, pears, okra, and figs, she'd had a few jars left over. The flowers would add life to the porch of the shack, which wasn't as ramshackle as many farther south along the Delta. She wasn't a complete sharecropper. At some things— the care of her surroundings—she worked free and clear. A chicken clucked somewhere. Its neck would be wrung soon. The tomatoes she grew in the back of the "tenant house" on the farm of the Moore brothers were ripe and sweet. Soon dinner would be simmering in her iron pot and skillet while she bathed in a galvanized tub and massaged her feet. Then she'd wait for Sylvester. She was walking now to the fine accompaniment of a symphony of crickets. Her back ached. She was five months pregnant with her third child. She'd had the second boy, John, in 1935, and assumed she'd have no more. But, after all, she was only twenty-seven. She wasn't old yet. She'd buried the little brother she raised; he was killed in Chicago, but her own children were healthy and she kept them close.

"Right then, a car come by," says Louise Hardaway, now seventy-five, mother of four, grandmother of nine, great-grandmother of fifteen, sitting in an easy chair at her home. Her eyes are failing now, but not that badly by her own calculations. She stands erect, her stomach is as flat as a washboard, and she figures she can still walk with the best of them.

"There was three men in it. White fellers. One of them chunked a brick and hit me in the stomach. Felt I was gonna die. Just knew Gloria—that's who I was carrying—was gone. I said, 'Naw, hell naw.' I wasn't gon' die like no dog on the road." Sylvester came home later and found Louise in agony. He ran back out. He came back in later with bloody fists. He had pounded them raw against a tree. Gloria was born healthy in January. Sylvester was never quite the same.

From then on, Louise suffered in the fields. The heat made her sick. "The doctor told me to go to the city," she says, "but the city was more than just a notion."

In 1949, after six more years of sharecropping, the Hardaways worked ten acres free and clear. They brought home the entire crop of cotton by themselves, and Louise took the money, the whole 365 dollars in mostly ones and fives, to Memphis and paid down on a house. With the boys and Gloria in tow, Louise and Sylvester crossed the deep river to Memphis, arriving on New Year's Day, 1950.

They found a place at 2977. They made it a home. She sits in the parlor of the same three-room shotgun house that seemed like such a godsend then, a stone's throw from the intersection of Broad and Tillman, a nondescript corner. Take the turn there accompanied by the thundering blues of Etta

James singing "Shaky Ground" and there it is, a few steps away, a tiny street, an alleyway, really, with no signs or sidewalks.

Across from 2977 squat two houses in such disrepair the wonder is they can stand on their own. Such poverty in the rural Delta is not uncommon, but in 1992, in the central city of Memphis, it seems absolutely stunning.

"See them houses over there?" she asks. "This house was just like that when we first came. You could look down here and see the ground. Tar paper for walls. Bathroom was a hole. But I decided I was gon' get it in living condition for me. Not for the King of England, but for me and mine."

Louise began to do day work in private homes, cooking and cleaning, and one of her better employers was a Father Carrier, who was sympathetic and generous to her up to a point. One day, Louise overhead him talking to someone. "He said, 'Poor Louise. What she wants out of that house, she'll never get.' Don't blame him for saying it. But he didn't really know me. I made a promise to myself. I said, 'If I live, one day you won't know it's the same house.' "

Fae Hardaway was born on Nov. 18, 1951, at John Gaston Hospital. As a baby she slept in the beds of those who were the beneficiaries of Louise's day work. Sylvester and Louise parted ways in 1956. He died in 1975 in Lakeland, Florida.

Louise found work in the school system, in the cafeterias of elementary schools, where she made meals. In 1970, Fae came up pregnant. "Penny was brought here from the hospital on 18 July, 1971," says Louise. "Fae was a child herself. She wanted to name him Golden, after his daddy, Eddie. I said, 'Naw, hell naw.' I gave him my name, Hardaway. Anfernee was so pretty. He's mine, I know, I shouldn't say, but he's so handsome. I can't deny it. Won't even try."

"When he was born, his hands were so big it looked like he was wearing gloves," says Fae Hardaway Patterson, sitting across from her mother in the parlor at 2977. "When I was in school at Lester, there had been a boy named Anfernee. I always thought it was a beautiful name. People think I don't know how to spell. People can have things so backwards. His nickname, Penny? Now, that came from Mama. She called him Pretty, but in the country, when you're talking to a baby, in baby talk, that comes out 'Pweddy.' People just took it from there."

Fae Hardaway was a member of the final graduating class from Lester High in 1972. A couple of years later she struck out for a new life in Oakland, California, with a young man named Zack Patterson. "She wanted to leave Penny with her sister, Gloria," says Louise. "But Gloria was on the way to having six of her own. I told Fae to leave him with me."

Louise never used a day of sick leave from the cafeterias of the Memphis city school system, from 1964 through 1978. "We slept in there, him on a rollaway bed, from the time they brought him home 'til his feet hung off the mattress," Louise says. "Penny was six before he saw his daddy. It was that long before I ever saw him myself. He said, 'Lemme have him.' I said, 'Naw, hell naw.' Hadn't bought him a diaper and now you want to be a daddy? Why now? If he walked in here right now I wouldn't know who he was, unless he was with Calvin." Calvin is Eddie's brother. "He's a nice man," Louise says. "Sometimes he calls me mama."

Louise kept what little she had immaculate. Across from the squalid row of shanties on the dead-end street, 2977 sticks up proudly, the well finger on a sore hand, with bars on the windows now. But it also has a cozy paneled parlor, window dressings, a gorgeous spread on the bed, a complete bathroom, including a shower, and a relatively large and well-furnished kitchen worthy of its experienced cook. The gas jets on the stove still burn all night during the winter for heat, but other than that, it's not the same house. She tried to keep the boy immaculate, too. For years they went to Early Grove

Baptist Church around the corner together. When she was in her late sixties and could no longer always muster herself, Penny went by himself.

"I hope the best for Penny," she says. "Every boy he was raised up with on this street seem like they been in jail, or the workhouse, for robbing and stealing. One of them boys end up getting life. Another one got double life. For a long time I didn't let Penny out of my sight. 'Course I couldn't pick his friends, but I could tell him where he could and could not go."

On Sundays that was easy, and during the school year not that hard. But there was always summer. The house was too small and the weather too hot for him to stay in and be a growing boy. Yet there was nothing on the streets but trouble. He found a welcome place among the rusting outdoor goals on the asphalt playground of the obsolete Lester school.

"I played on those goals eight hours a day since I was eight years old," Hardaway says. "It got to where boys came, played, went home, ate, came back, and I'd still be there, playing. Mostly, I played by myself."

For years they went along like this, with the Bible usually the only book in the house. Their world was piped in via drama and sitcom through the small television set they fell asleep by in the tiny bedroom. In 1986, when Penny was fourteen, Fae came back from divorce and bad times in California. He remained at his grandmother's house. He walked the two miles to Treadwell High every day, passing the Black lawn jockeys on some of the estates in between. The faculty and student body were awed by and conversant about his basketball skills. It wasn't until his senior year that his performance in the classroom was equally scrutinized.

"You can't blame the high schools completely," says Gina Pickens. "We can fine-tune what's already been started, but it always starts in the home."

And who can blame Mrs. Hardaway—and others like her—whose test had been survival, getting 2977 in the shape of a home where a boy might grow healthy and be *able* to learn? Can she be blamed for not having a library?

Her phone began to ring like never before. "Forty or fifty times a day," she recalls, still marveling. Recruiters descended like locusts. "They came in smiling at me where they wouldn't have before," says Louise. "Well, I'm one that color don't excite, 'cause I know we all Black, and we all White." For a time, Hardaway considered attending Arkansas. "I heard 'Arkansas' I said, 'Naw, hell naw,'" Louise says. "I told Penny, 'I got you this far, don't you fail me now.'"

Hardaway thinks of this and says, "I don't want what happened to Anthony Douglas to happen to me." Douglas's mother, Christine, died three days before last season started. She never saw her son play college ball, much less graduate.

"Just let him be who he is," says Louise. "I just heard 'bout one of these eleven-year-old boys shot hisself 'cause he didn't score but so much on a test. Ain't but one test that count. Ain't that right? The longer you live, the more you learn. I have *slaved*. But it *paid*. I made this home. I'm thankful to God. As for Penny, I ain't got to be here for him no more. But I plan on being here. That's the way you've got to look at life. Got to make your own. Happy? Child, I wouldn't tell a mule to get up if he was sitting in my lap!"

Anfernee Hardaway received seventeen credits in largely remedial courses, with a grade-point average closer to 3.0 than 2.0 in his first academic semester at Memphis State. He received fifteen more credits the following spring, this time in more difficult classes, and nine more in the summer session before the 1991–92 school year. It takes twenty-four credits to qualify for participation in sports under Proposition 48 guidelines, and 132 credits to graduate from Memphis State. In the fall semester of 1992–93, Anfernee Hardaway emerged with a 3.2 GPA. He then declared hardship and entered the NBA draft.

Hardaway is still sensitive about his recent past, about the deprivation around 2977, about his grandmother's dialect, about knowing his mother as Fae, about not knowing his father, about being labeled dumb. He thinks the labels are a hindrance, something he wants to forget now that he has performed on AAU and Olympic Festival teams, stayed in the nice hotels, seen his name in big-print type, and been wooed by the clipped speech patterns of recruiters, coaches, and alumni old enough to be Ed Golden.

But Hardaway never wants to forget where he came from. That is what made him. The basketball is how, but 2977 is why. The hotter the fire, the tougher the steel.

In fact, he has had many riches—a grandmother, height, a face more than just his mother could love, a good head on his shoulders. Even the squalor of the neighborhood led to a rich practice regimen, dropping the odds of athletic success from 25,000 to 1, to even money. It's 50–50 that Hardaway will be not only an NBA player but an NBA star someday. "He has a real chance to get them out of there," says Finch.

Any gambler will tell you the house can make a good living off 50–50 odds. The American Society of Orthopedic Surgeons makes a good living repairing the damaged joints of many an Anfernee Hardaway. And even the lucky ones have to be able to learn to conceptualize, read, count, and mature.

Hardaway's roommate, senior student manager Steve Miller, comes to lock the gym, ending Hardaway's reverie.

"C'mon, full court," Hardaway says to Miller and the shadow. "That's how I keep in shape. I get tired sometimes. But then I get a second wind."

He wins again, but only by 16–14. Hardaway will get the lesson that there's much more to life than hoop, how and where and when it occurs to him. That lesson will have been inspired by Louise, who once walked a dirt road and found strength in a boy who was as pretty as a penny. So 2977 is home, no matter how far from it Anfernee hopes to travel.

"Three wishes?" he says. "I never want to do anything to embarrass my grandmother. I want her to see me . . . do something. I want her to live."

Anfernee Hardaway goes down into bright rooms marked Tiger Academics beneath the field house. Billy Smith bops in, followed by the more deliberate Anthony Douglas. There is no ball here. No cheering. Hardaway opens a book of stories. It is, by far, his best move of the day. No one is around to cheer it. But somewhere nearby, an old woman is laughing.

It's a Black Thing
That Nobody Understands

It's a Black thing: You wouldn't understand.

This slogan confuses me. Has there been a codebook passed out lately that I didn't get? Is everybody in on something I missed during a nap? I've seen the slogan on T-shirts, along with others like *Black by popular demand*. Some of these slogans are supposed to represent the sensibility of My People, who want other people (probably White ones) to know what hardball exclusionary practices feel like. This slogan is used when some of us don't want to be bothered.

Just what qualifies as "a Black thing you wouldn't understand"? Unfortunately, plenty. Here are some Black things I don't understand. See if you can help me out on:

1. *Al Sharpton's hair and Don King's hair:* I know you can't tell My People anything about hair. But seriously, Rev.

Sharpton, my man, needs a wash-n-set every week. People kept unfairly fettered by a double standard of applied law need justice. Rev. Sharpton needs an appointment. If his salon is open, that's justice to Rev. Al. He can talk about poverty until he sets the sky on fire, but he can't be taken all that seriously because there's a table for six at the Four Seasons spent on Rev. Al's hair every month. Madame C. J. Walker herself was not as fastidious. The *New York Post* gives Rev. Sharpton raves: "I'LL SHUT THE CITY DOWN (if I don't make my five o'clock shampoo and chemmy rinse)!"

As for Don King, who knows what he's got going on upstairs anyway? Somebody once told me Don's hair is like that because it knows what he's thinking. Black people have not seen anything like it since the salad days of Buckwheat when he saw something scary. Don seems to enjoy the look.

It's a Black thing. You wouldn't understand.

Right. Save it for Al's hairdresser. While you're at it, ask him to loan me five dollars out of all that money he's making so Al can resemble his idol, James Brown.

Speaking of James . . .

2. *"Real down" rappers cracking foul on Hammer:* Rap definitely started off as a Black thing, the singsong diary of the streets and life—what Chuck D of Public Enemy calls "Black people's CNN." Many older people disparaged it, but if they would only compare it to what they listened to when they were young, they might shut up. Rap turned into an art form, a collective vehicle for expression among people who wanted to be creative musically and couldn't afford trumpet lessons. Some rappers, like some academics, started taking themselves much too seriously eventually, as both good and bad artists will do. One rapper named Too Short took on a much more famous rapper named Hammer, claiming Hammer wasn't a real, legitimate rapper, he wasn't *down*, wasn't "dropping knowledge" with his lyrics, as many rappers did. But then, most of the conscientious rappers didn't complain

about Hammer, because Hammer was getting people to listen to him—the bottom line, even for the greatest artists. Too Short, for his part, gave live shows and invited, "Bitches! Come up to the stage!" That's how deep Too Short was.

Strictly speaking, Hammer isn't really a rapper. He is an entertainer. He is kind of like James Brown, at least to me. People used to disparage James too. They said he couldn't sing. Well, they weren't far wrong there, but James wasn't selling singing. He was selling a tight rhythm band and dancing and an exceptionally good time so you could forget about your troubles—the same things Hammer's selling now. Michael Jackson disparaged Hammer, too, said he wasn't a proper entertainer. Hammer can outdance Michael, at least to me, and Michael, creatively, is no Prince. Period. So who said anything about singing—or, for that matter, rapping? I too didn't agree with Hammer's endorsing a chicken product that was nothing but grease and no meat, but as far as his general showmanship was concerned, I had no complaints about him at all. After all, I knew from whence he came.

I knew Hammer when he was a kid named Stanley Burrell, working for the Oakland A's owner, Charles O. Finley, as sort of a living lawn jockey and unofficial mascot. He must have been around thirteen at the time, and he was always a cheery young fellow, the kind you'd like to have around. Charles Finley liked having him around, in case he wanted to rub his head for luck or needed to tap his foot to a buck-and-wing. I do not think I am really being unfair to Charles O. Finley. I once sat with the man and watched a ball game and listened to him joke about watermelons. I told him I'd take mine and him with a grain of salt, and that my day would come. Well, it's here. It was Charles O. Finley who named little Stanley Burrell "Hammer," a sort of homage to Henry Aaron, whom Finley never had the pleasure of underpaying. I liked it when Hammer found a way to make a profit off a backhanded homage to a legend. Hammer worked with what he had, and he worked hard. So Hammer's not down with the rappers, the ones who say, "It's a Black thing—you wouldn't understand."

Right. Try and take that to Hammer's bank.

3. *Trying to "act White":* Since when did learning at school become "acting White"? Why isn't robbing, stealing, drinking, carousing, and spreading illnesses considered "acting White"? Who makes up the rules on what is Black and what is White? Now that's something I don't understand. I'd rather have learning at school called "acting Black." I wonder if anybody would understand that Black Thing?

4. *Black neoconservatives:* I'm thinking about Alan Keyes, Republican candidate for senator from Maryland in 1992, who went to the Republican convention demanding time to speak, then wagged his finger at the backs of the Republicans who left the hall when he was finally allowed to speak.

5. *Nouveau X:* This is that Black thing where people wear the X symbol on caps and T-shirts, then call each other niggers and run to do all their business with White people.

6. *Clarence Thomas.*

7. *"Crabs in a barrel":* This is when you try and do something positive and around fifty Black people reach up and offer you everything from a punch in the nose to cheap thrills, anything they can come up with on the spur of the moment to take your mind off whatever that positive action was that you were about to start up before they came around. As soon as you regain your lethargy, they leave you alone.

8, 9, and 10. *Overaccessorizing:* This one I understand best—and least. Some Black people will take a basic car, say a Chevrolet Corvette, a Ford Thunderbird, a Cadillac El Dorado, or a Mercedes-Benz, and drape it with everything but earrings and a tablecloth. Chain-link license-plate holders with purple night-lights, skirts all the way around the car, rims and hubcaps deep enough to swim in, or pillows and pine trees and bobblehead dolls in the rear window.

"How do you like the car?"

I'd probably like it fine, if I could just see it.

Some Black people don't overaccessorize their cars, because they've already put all that stuff on themselves or their children. Then they try and tell me it's a Black thing I should understand. And I should understand, too, because when I was fifteen, I had my front tooth knocked out playing varsity high school football. I didn't consider this bad fortune because there was a dentist close by. He proceeded to file down two of my good teeth and cap them with gold open-faced crowns to support the one false tooth he inserted into my mouth. I don't recall asking for any gold open-faced crowns, but I guess it was a Black thing I should have understood.

When I got out of the chair I resembled nothing so much as a young golden open-faced idiot, and I am ashamed to say I didn't mind looking like one all that much. I didn't have anybody brave enough around me to tell me otherwise until my Aunt Barbara, in perhaps the single most sagacious moment of her life, said, "There's nothing nicer than a mouthful of pretty white teeth." Didn't she know a Black thing when she saw one? And that it was a little late for her unwelcome analysis? I also knew right away she was right, eventually, and within a few years, more suitable arrangements were implanted. Gold teeth are another way of overaccessorizing. The people who sell overpriced accessories love to see Black people coming. We accessorize the facsimiles we have, after we are sold yet another bill of false goods. The Black thing I don't understand is why we don't object to any of this.

ABOUT TRAVEL

On the A-Train
to Venus with Isis

There are six narrow categories under the broad rubric of *For Black Women Who Are in Close Relationships with Black Men (When the Shower Is Not Enuf)*:

1. Lovely Black
2. Angry Willa
3. Honey Child
4. Black Pearl
5. Down Twala
6. Licorice Chick

Before you start the bonfire, let me explain:

"A nice man will win out over a bowwow-
wowyippeyoyippeyay."

Lovely Black

Like New York City, love is not for everybody. Many people
find they feel, act, and do better outside of it. They tell themselves this after they find they can't deal with it day to day.
They can't get work done when they are in love. It flays their
nerves. They can't hear themselves think. And it's always so
crowded in love, there are so many people on line. Those
that aren't on line in love are in line on love. It's hopeless—
or it makes them feel that way. It's too big, too busy, dangerous, dirty, overwhelming, so leave me out, I'm better off
where I am now, thanks anyway.

One thing that always amazes me about love is how you
find it when you're not fishing for it at all and can never locate
it when you've got out all the maps looking. There we were
waiting to be inhaled by New York City with the rest of its
daily breath of flotsam and jetsam, standing on a train platform minding our own business. Like everything else within
two hundred miles, we were resigned to our fates.

You know how you laugh to yourself when you meet couples and the man (or the woman these days) says, "I met her
(his) fine butt walking down the street!" You know how ridiculous that sounds when somebody like Sir Mix-A-Lot or
Bobby Womack or one of your old friends says it. We all
know they walked up on a problem walking down the street.
Those people who are not properly introduced, who attract
each other purely on looks, will never get along. We know
this. And when it happens to you, bang-bang, you wonder
what took so long as your brain bows to the body of life.
People tell me the brain is the key to attraction, and age has
proven them to be right. But when you're young, it's hard for
your human brain to convince your human body who's boss.

It may be true in the end, but the body has a hell of a lobby and can put up a good filibuster, and if you're caught weak or missing, if you are caught being human, there you are, all in lust, hoping it's not love but maybe wanting it to be because we've all seen the same movies, heard the same fairy tales. We've all been asked to dream the same blessed dream.

But that very interior sizer-upper that caused you to be stopped in your tracks by Lovely Black once, eventually may cause you to notice others as well, especially when you are young and your eyes are still good. Just to look, as one looks at the works of art hanging in a good gallery, or an exceptionally long mural. Just to look at their soft, good countenances, upright characters. Their trim constitutions and luscious smiles. But those very people whose qualities stopped you in the past and caused you to compliment and pet them end up becoming upset if you notice the same qualities in others. It's said you get only one true love in life. The hard part is knowing which one. The subway can be confusing if you don't know where you're going in the first place.

> "I hate men. And I don't care why anymore."
> *Angry Willa*

Why does your woman ask you if you think some beautiful actress like Halle Berry is fine, and when you say, "Maybe, a little bit," she gets mad? She won't ask, "Do you think Aunt Esther is fine?" Heaven forbid a gimme like that. She won't even ask, "Do you think Halle Berry is smart?" Instead she'll ask, "Do you think Halle Berry is fine?" You hold your hand over your nose so this woman won't see it growing like Pinocchio's, but she sees it anyway and then gets mad and asks, "What you mean, 'a little bit' fine? Oh, you think she's 'a little bit' fine, huh? My friends said if I asked you, you'd tell on yourself. Let's see you go try and get Halle Berry to make you 'a little bit' of dinner."

"Er, sweetheart, you didn't make *any* dinner. And since you brought it up, you haven't made dinner in three months. I'm the cook around here. You said so yourself."

"That's right. Now you know why. And I'm sure not going to make dinner now. So Halle Berry is fine? Well, there's people around town who think *I'm* fine, you know."

"I know, dear. I used to think you were fine myself."

Every time I see a fine sister now, I pause and think to myself, "Somebody, somewhere, is tired of that woman." That can't be my line. But whoever thought of it was a man.

"Thank you."
Honey Child

At least I know it can be done. People can get along. We just shouldn't try to put any time frame around it. Honey Chile and I put up with each other for ten years. I never thought I'd do anything for ten years. I always thought that whatever it was, I'd get it done in less time than that.

Honey Child had youth, energy, anger, a sense of humor, good looks, a serviceable brain, and a dead throwing aim on her side. I suppose I take the role of general and supreme commander of my life a little too seriously at times, but this was a good campaign we'd mounted, and Honey Child ended up a general herself, battle decorated. I thought I might get a thank-you for encouraging instead of discouraging her in going back to school for a bachelor's degree or taking classes to get anything from a real estate license to a better understanding of Zen or Mary Kay—you know, things people do and then later wonder how and why they did them, if they are successful. I suppose it could cause resentment when you constantly remind somebody how much you've helped them be successful, and sort of gloss over how they might have helped you. People make their own decisions about what they do in life. Husbands, wives, friends, and lovers only suggest. Honey Child was not beyond saying, "Thank you." Never said it loudly, unless it was much too loudly and slathered with sarcasm, but after ten years, you can tell.

"Nooo, thank you."
Black Pearl

Sometimes a woman can help you most by saying no. This happened to me on one occasion before I decided to come and face New York and work there among all my good White folks. "Nooo, thank you," said a fine, talented, experienced friend. "I've been there. I've put up with it before. You'll never be seen for what you are, only for what they'd like for you to be. Which, by the way, isn't very much." When she said it, it intrigued me. I soon learned what she meant.

I'd heard "no" before, when I was young. Young men often hear "no" because they ask questions impossible to answer in the affirmative. Young or old, sometimes men overstep themselves. We want what we can't have, we want to hear what we want to hear. If more women knew this they'd have an easier time keeping us in check. No means no.

It wasn't until later I began to hear a different, more strident and angry kind of no. It was coming from sisters who had been hurt, and it resonated in *For Colored Girls Who Have Considered Suicide (When the Rainbow Is Enuf)* and *The Color Purple*, and other works that cut deeply into the scar tissue of pain. Time passes and heals, but only if you let it. If you stop picking at the wounds of the heart, they have a better chance of healing. A physically abusive man is not a wound but a cancer. But a man who steps on a woman's feelings doesn't always know what he's doing. Sometimes he might be rather clumsily protecting his own feelings.

So what happened was this: I went to a Black-owned television station to be interviewed. The person who was going to interview me was a sister with a lovely hairstyle and a bad disposition. Her smile was not sincere.

"I can't *wait* to hear why you have titled this book *Why Black People Tend to Shout*," she dripped.

"Irony," I begged. "Lady, please, it's irony."

"Yessss," she said. I thought of the serpent god Set.

She was a "senior producer," she said. The show began, and she said, "We had Marita Golden and Terry McMillan and several other Black women authors on our show yesterday, and we all were commenting on how we're *tired* of men *whining*."

"It's going to be hard for me to love this woman as a fellow human being when she's hardly giving me a chance," I thought to myself, but I couldn't show that on my face because the cameras were rolling and the show was live and at the time neither one of us could afford to be completely honest. So I just said, "Well, Miss, we will whine. We are Black men, after all." That tossed her off her high horse for a while, and by then a couple of people had called in to the show who had actually read the book she talked about so very knowingly for someone who had read maybe two pages.

Maybe we'll get along next time, though.

I got along okay with Terry McMillan. You all know Terry. She's the author of books—*Mama*, *Disappearing Acts*, and, most notably, *Waiting to Exhale*—and she does a good job of examining relationships from her perspective. Once we had a brief conversation—again, the conversation took place in televisionstudioland. I was at what is called a "remote" location. I thought it was unfair that Terry and I didn't first get to know each other, or at least get to know each other's delivery, before being asked to be on television together. However, I enjoyed talking to her, and Terry, for her part, allowed I was "better than average" as a man, on sight (I'm not asking for Womanist Papal Dispensation from Terry or anybody—to *hell* with Womanist Papal Dispensation). If women only knew, all any man wants to hear, honestly, is that he is better than average, especially coming from a total stranger. I gave Terry my disarming line about the way many men feel: To far too many of us, commitment is to love what Twain once said golf was to a good walk: "The perfect way to ruin it." Terry laughed like she didn't want to, but had to, and that is a good laugh to pull from somebody. I also mentioned that I'd never heard of "masculine wiles," and Terry seemed to get that one too.

I came upon Terry at yet another made-for-television event, a forum of writers who got together in Washington, D.C., at the behest of the group called Black Issues in Higher Education. On the panel were Marita Golden, the novelist Charles Johnson, Terry, and poet Nikki Giovanni. They discussed some of the few joys and many pitfalls of writing. I admired all of them, for I know what it is, to try and write. I know what it can do to you. Nikki Giovanni was born in Tennessee, but insisted she'd grown up in Ohio, outside Cincinnati, and felt a kinship with her fellow Ohioan Toni Morrison. She wore a rhinestone pin that said JAZZ, a recent Morrison fiction title. I sat in the audience ruminating on all this. Well, I was from Tennessee, and so were Alex Haley and Ishmael Reed and Vernon Jarrett and Carl Rowan. (Maybe I can see Nikki's problem.) And what about Mary Church Terrell and Beverly Guy-Sheftall and the melodic Gloria Wade-Gayles? Ida Wells and Richard Wright were from Mississippi, but found inspiration in the long state. So what could be Nikki's problem with being a writer and coming from Tennessee at the same time? She then hummed a few bars from an old television show that I'd forgotten. "Davy, Davy Crockett,"

Nikki sang. I found myself completing the chorus under my breath. "King of the wild frontier." I told you, being a writer can make you crazy. The host of the show, Renee Poussaint, mentioned it was odd for Nikki to sing this song when they were supposed to be talking about literature, but Nikki, not one to be cornered, had already put her faux pas behind her without mentioning she had suffered one, which was the way to do it.

Then a Black female student called in to the show and read a portion of a paragraph from Terry's *Waiting to Exhale*, something about a group of women sitting around talking about how most Black men either had no job, were married, or gay, or in jail, or on drugs, or just plain can't fuck (Terry is a good writer who can get raw—and it seems to work for her, too). The female student asked if Terry thought this was advancing a cruel stereotype. Terry didn't have to say a word because the other artists, especially Nikki Giovanni (I have some of her albums, by the way, and *damn* Womanist Papal Dispensation), leaped to her defense, as they certainly should have done as artists. Terry recreates that which is in her to recreate. What else can she do?

Nikki's defense was particularly strident: "Well if you don't like it, change the reality," she said. Not five minutes later, Spike Lee's *Malcolm X* came up. Nikki again piped in. She was beginning to resemble a hungry baby robin in a nest of them, demanding to be fed first. "I hated it, *hated* it," she said. "It was horrible, horrible, this guy acting like he was coming on to Malcolm in prison, and Malcolm looking like some kind of doofus in the barbershop, getting his hair conked, and then kissing this blonde White woman and never kissing his own wife! I hated it. *Hated* it!"

Unfortunately, Nikki had just mounted a tirade about the very images she had defended when coming from Terry. *No job, on drugs, in prison, gay, married, won't fuck.* That was what she had described as hating, although I'm not sure where she saw all this. I'm not sure if she hated the film, or if she hated Spike Lee, or if she hated me. And I was beginning to feel I didn't have a hell of a lot of time left to find out.

After the show I asked Terry why she didn't defend Spike. Terry looked at me. The last time I saw Terry, she was laughing and had a chicken bone in her mouth. And I love her for being her own artist, and *fuck* Male Papal Dispensation.

Professor Derrick Bell left the Harvard Law School faculty in the spring of 1990, on leave until "a woman of color" was granted tenure on the faculty. Two years later he was still on leave, and his job was revoked. I didn't see his kind of male character in sitcoms or popular novels. Just a point.

"Kill the head and the body will die."
Down Twala

There was one outstanding occurrence around the publication of Shahrazad Ali's controversial *The Blackman's Guide to Understanding the Blackwoman*. Sister Ali sold a lot of books. I met her, you guessed it, at a television station. This is getting ridiculous, I thought. They used to say if you wanted to meet a nice woman, go to church. Now if you want to meet any kind of woman, you have to go to a television station. Sister Ali was getting eyes cut at her from the sisters, whom she had pissed off in her book, but I have to say, she didn't let this stop her. So I asked her the real question: "I've heard your book sold 200,000 units. Is that so?" Sister Ali said, "Honey, 200,000 units is low." I immediately became mentally aroused. I wanted to know how to practice that particular kind of togetherness. But Sister Ali wasn't telling me any specifics.

A while later, she came out with *The Blackwoman's Guide to Understanding the Blackman*, which didn't do nearly as well. Black women thought she was just coming down hard on them. Sister doesn't discriminate. If she makes you mad, she figures, you're going to buy her product, or at least talk about it, whereupon someone else might buy it. Later Sister Shahrazad said she had never been invited to speak at the Smithsonian like Terry McMillan or "Roger Wiley." Hmmm. Here's one way to understand the Black man—get his name right. I think the sisters have to get past Sister Ali's book and get to the sensitive spot she rubbed in Black men. We all want to be made to feel special. Some women know this about men and feed that part of the male ego in order to be fed in return, or not, depending on the I.Q. of the man.

"Ragglely."

Licorice Chick

I am more likely to fall in love with great talent from afar than with good looks up close. Show me a woman with skill who lives out of state and I'll show you a woman with sex appeal. I also like a woman who can speak a form of dialect that can make me relate and laugh. I'm from the country, no matter what airs I put on, and I like people who can understand my sense of humor. So let's get right to it. When White men and Black women, and Black men and White women, get together, some sisters have been known to point out, somebody's stuff can get "ragglely". But I really have no comment on it either way anymore. It seems as if a large percentage of talented Black people, men and women, end up marrying people other than Black people after they get pseudo-rich and semifamous. I hate to see the talent and the wealth dispersed, but on the other hand, what fool would try to legislate against the power of love? It would be like trying to legislate against a straightening comb.

When people are in love, there's no reasoning with them

anyway. We all know this happens, so we might as well applaud when two human beings, whatever color, can get along. We should say, "Great job! Wonderful choice! *Voila!* Bravo! Woof-woof-woof-woof!"

That should make them question what they're doing quick enough. That's what we *should* say, all right. But you know and I know that we are going to listen to the gossip, section off in groups, make a noise and that face like you smell something fishy, and say, "No he/she didn't, girl!"

"I love you."

Dear Jesus

I must confess here that there is a seventh category of woman, just as there's supposed to be a seventh heaven, a seventh sign, a lucky seven. This Seventh Woman of the Hidden Heart is not so aptly named, though, because meeting any more than two in one lifetime might kill you. The Seventh Woman is that woman who, when you see her, you say, "Damn!" even if you're in church or with your mother. Or she kind of sneaks up on you like a normal everyday woman, and then she smiles at you one day and you see her as you never saw her before and your cold heart feels as though it's been transplanted to Negril. She is the woman you cannot help but love. She warms her way into your soul.

The Seventh Woman is the woman who fits you in all ways, who is your match, whom you love, the one you hit your knees to thank God for sending you—all those things you'd scoff about if you weren't under her influence. All those things you have to convince yourself to do in order to be with other people, you think you already are with her, the operative word here being *think*. Clear thinking seems to go out the window when you are confronted by the Seventh Woman, and then if she tells you she loves you too, well, that's the ball game right there—unless she decides to change her mind, which, after all, is a woman's right.

It's a man's right too, come to think of it, but the Dear Jesus Seventh Woman is not a woman you can leave. You never do leave her, even if she leaves you, or even if you walk away out of abject fear of the power and vulnerability of true intimacy, which scares most men worse than death itself. The Seventh Woman of Life is the woman you meet who then makes you say, "tra-la, tra-la, maybe all that moaning and groaning about real love is true. Maybe I can be happy." Maybe this. Maybe that. It is the "maybe" that makes life worthwhile. You ask me how I know this. I've met the Seventh Woman. Ducking her did no good.

It's up to Black men to provide more than love at this point in history. It's up to Black men to provide a presence, a buttress. We have to get busy working business plans. Love has to wait, not according to me, but according to the way American society has treated Black men and women so far, which is to say to try and get rid of us. Sometimes work comes before love. We do love you sisters, we love you because you brought us here, every walking one of us.

Hang in, hold on, and do what Patti LaBelle says in "Love Never Dies": "You've got to fluff up, baby, I mean fluff up. Beat your face into place, get back in the race . . ." For as Sterling Brown once revealed, "Strong men keep on coming."

"Need some help?"
Dare Have a Dream

Did I say seven categories? Make that eight. No, make that nine . . . no . . .

ABOUT LIFE

The Death of Cool

I don't know. Maybe I'm getting too old to know anything. When Miles Davis died in 1991, it was almost like he took cool with him. Shortly after his death I was told cool had become something that escaped me. I'd hit forty, the Big Four-Oh. I was now beyond the boundary of cool. People who wouldn't know cool from the Fourth of July said so. The same people who tried to tell me Steve Martin was a comic genius, or that Kenny G could blow with David Sanborn, were telling me I wasn't cool anymore. I have to understand these people, or try, for the sake of the work. I remember back when I laughed at people who were too old and out of it to be cool. I never thought I could be forty. I could *know* people who were forty, but I myself could not be forty.

I can remember going to a photography studio in downtown Manhattan one sunny day, seemingly only a few years ago, when I was not forty, when my shades and my dark, Italian-cut double-breasted suit and my disarming, dissembling smile were irresistibly intact. I was clean, sweet-smelling, razor-sharp. I was cool, as I saw cool then. The photography studio belonged to a White man who was civil to me at least in part because he was under contract to take my picture, and not because of the completeness of my toilette or the lines of my apparel. His wife, however, having no such pretext as money to make off me, made no attempt to hide her revulsion (though she did not know me), which no amount of cloth or scents could hide. But I was cool, which meant I didn't give her anything back at all. She was no more than a tick to me. A fly. Uncool. I ignored her.

But I knew I was out of there when the photographer showed me a photograph he had recently taken of, yes, the man, the cold one, Miles Davis. This accommodating White photographer took great pains to show me the weave pattern on Miles Davis's scalp, where the roots of his receding hairline were intertwined with the stems of that monstrous inky wig that he wore near the end of his life. I looked at the photo, looked at the photographer, looked at the wife, winked at them all, and eased out of there so cool they still may not know I'm gone. He didn't take good pictures.

Somewhat later, I read *Cool Pose: The Dilemmas of Black Manhood in America* by Richard Majors and Janet Mancini Billson and assumed, "This is one of those grim publish-or-perish efforts professors must compile in order to have something to brandish while eyeing the department head at the faculty retreat." I suspect there is some sincerity at the heart of some of these efforts. But often, these books are designed to make the authors seem academically "cool." So who is to say what cool is, what it means? Ah, there's the heavy weight.

The preface stated that *Cool Pose* was a book for Black males in America—as well as their parents, wives and lovers, teachers, neighbors, friends, and, one assumes, photographers—in short, all of us. But as presented, the book is not likely to hold any of us in thrall. It should be labeled "one of five required books for a three-credit class in Sociology or Abnormal Psychology at a White liberal-arts college."

Theoretically, the book is about "cool poses" young Black men adopt so the aforementioned "dilemmas" of racism will not find them behind this camouflage and will bypass them for other prey, like a shark sensing movement. Cool, says the book, is the chameleon change by which young Black men avoid a world that has vowed to devour them. I don't know. I always thought cool was simpler and lots more enviable than that. Even eight-year-old White boys know what it is. They pronounce it "coo-ul." Most broadly, I think cool applies to a person, place, action, or thing that is acceptable, proper, right in the eyes of the beholder. Being specific, cool could be anything from Miles holding a sibilant note, to Denzel Washington telling a woman thanks but no, to a basic black baseball cap emblazoned with white script. CoCo Chanel would probably call all of that cool—as would Public Enemy.

However, the professors would have us believe the majority of "cool poses" are designed to "combat feelings of oppression." This, to me, is too broad a generality, and they ought to say so somewhere. Indeed, cool is a zone one can enter to freeze out the people, but there is a limitation to this isolation. I'm sure the authors have done the research. Damned sure. They constantly cite other scholars, using last names only, as if we know these people the way we know Tiffany and Yusef from across the street. The authors also utilize disembodied one-line quotes from the likes of "Sonny, 17." Sonny nails it by saying, "Sometimes [cool] means he's a calm person, or a person who is naturally himself."

They should give Sonny his three credits.

I'm sure there are "knuckleheads" (a cool word for kids who are not "down," another word for cool; I learned none of this in the book) who act out behaviors they believe are cool in order to form a buffer against oppression. I venture an uneducated guess: To your average sixteen-year-old, peer pressure is more motivational than any perceived oppression. How many of us who were poor and oppressed knew it as kids? Television can tell you how oppressed and poor you are, and often does these days, but there are some hard, applicable facts about our complex society that sixteen-year-olds haven't had time to experience, let alone fathom. Another segment of sixteen-year-olds aren't trying to act cool to combat feelings of oppression, unless the inviting glances of sixteen-year-old females are considered oppressive these days. I'll hazard another guess: Many young Black males, like their White and Brown counterparts, act cool to try and impress girls. Translation: hormones. If a man carries a "cool pose" into his forties, he's trying to tell you something. In his teens, he's trying to tell Annette something. Annette who? Never mind. Wouldn't want you to blow your cool.

Cool is what you make it. The party of Ronald Reagan made being a greedy, race-baiting, irresponsible politician cool, at least to many people, with predictably disastrous results for the subjects of this thought-provoking book on "cool pose." Some of the behaviors listed in the book are uncool, such as the dreaded "acting White," e.g., trying to do one's best in school. There are said to be states of "cool pose" where trying to do one's best in school is considered bad, as in not good. If you're dumb enough to believe this fool's cool—a.k.a. "misery loves company"—that is in part fostered by high school and college athletic departments and educators who believe White men are the only ones who ever wrote anything, and therefore are the only ones who can decipher writing. If you go for all that crazy hype (cool words) you end up unskilled, unemployed, sixty years old, down at the local Safeway giving grandmothers a ride home in your jitney for gas money, if you make it that far in life against those "dilemmas," which is not at all likely.

If you need proof that sincerity and good intentions are never enough, here it is in *Cool Pose*. It's amazing what college professors can do to obfuscate a fascinating subject once they knuckle down to the task of explaining it. Tenure, anyone?

Cool is not dead. Long live cool—if you can find it. Age has something to do with the location. My son said to me yesterday, "Don't get cysed over it, Dad. You can still be cool. We'll let you in." I then chastized him for not pronouncing "psyched" properly. He said, "No, *cysed*. It means overexcited, overanxious. This whole conversation about cool has you *cysed*, man."

I don't know. I don't know when I lost it.

What Black People Haven't Done Yet

Black people have already done everything that can be done on earth within the reach of the human spirit. Black people have done everything except recognize each other for it. Black people wait for the White person whose recognition we cherish to tell us when we've done something meritorious, worthy of note and study. Black people might call a thing great, but they wait and see if White people will agree with them before starting to believe it themselves.

Black people watch how they're depicted by White people to know how to depict themselves. Black people rarely offer each other heartfelt congratulations unless they've gained permission from White people. Otherwise, the congratulations are dry, insincere, given in hopes the Black person being congratulated will come back down to earth, into the dirt, where most Black people belong, or so we're led to believe.

Black people think their own standards and values mean less than the standards and values set by White men. If a Black award in journalism were to come about, call it the Wells Award, Black people would rather get a Pulitzer Prize. Black people create everything but self-respect—they'd rather pout and wait the interminable wait for White people to see them within the same value system and give them awards that White people thought up for themselves, really, no matter how they cry, "Fair play! We are judged the same! We judge ourselves to be the best! It's just a coincidence!" How convenient. Black people don't give each other credit.

But perhaps in time . . .

I could tell Arthur Ashe did not care too much for me at first glance. I came into the quiet of the University of California at Berkeley Faculty Club, sidling against the wood paneling, asking to interview him for a column, back in 1980. Arthur was retiring from tennis. He was then engaged in animated conversation with people his tennis background had introduced him to—the atmosphere at faculty clubs can be heady. "Brother Ashe," I said. Arthur couldn't hide his distaste. I was congenitally scruffy, with my uniform of ragged hair, an uneven and scraggly beard, a wrinkled suit. The way he hoisted the corners of his mouth up into little curls, like delicate china cup handles, let me know he was not pleased. But I understood. He was meticulous about his appearance. I was not meticulous about mine—only about the work. He was a great Black tennis player who was retiring. That was what I came to record. He was thirty-six at the time.

I would meet Arthur a few more times over the years, and I must say that oftentimes we were in disagreement. We simply saw some things differently. He still hitched the corners

of his mouth into those china cup handles, but after a while
he grew to expect to see me and I grew to expect to see him,
and slowly his greetings became warmer. If nothing else, he
could appreciate my stick-to-it-iveness. I hadn't agreed with
him when he went to South Africa to play exhibitions, but I
admired him because he went anyway, no matter what I
thought; he stuck with his principles, not mine or anybody
else's. Philosophically we are apart, but then, so what?

I began to see him more often. He seemed to become even
more active, if that was possible. Helping this person form
that organization. Serving us here. Serving us there. Now,
instead of heading Davis Cup teams, he was advocating human rights for Haitians, protesting apartheid in South Africa.
He had a wife and daughter and was good to them. Once I
met him at Columbia University in upper Manhattan, where
he'd given a seminar. We retired to a restaurant. He invited
me to a retreat that he and other Black people participated
in. I said I would come if I could, but the work. . . . He
smiled wanly, as though resigned to something. He said, "Are
you going to step up?" It was one of his favorite sayings.
Are you going to step up? He seemed weak, and as a tennis
player made of heart, eyes that shone like diamonds, and a
rawhide and deceiving musculature, he'd never seemed weak
before.

"The struggle is hard," I thought. I thought his open-heart
surgery had taken more from him than his public would ever
know. He seemed to have a perpetual and disconcerting sheen
of perspiration on his face, above his upper lip. I wondered
what was wrong, but I never asked him, because I never
doubted that he would overcome it, whatever it was. You
see, Arthur Ashe was synonymous with a quiet triumph of
the soul, the spirit, the mind, and the body. He was grace. It
never occurred to me that he might need my—our—help.

Not long after this, he saw me again in New York. He'd
brought along a copy of a small book I'd written entitled *Why*

Black People Tend to Shout. "Would you autograph this for me, Ralph?" he asked. I was taken aback. I knew Arthur Ashe was a great man, a facile diplomat, a good negotiator, almost the opposite of my persona. I'm not great, and I can be confrontational. I had no idea he would ever read any of my material. If he did read it, I thought, he would likely hurl that material directly into the fireplace, not bring it to me to autograph. We had often served on opposite sides of the same panels on education and the future of Black people.

I was pleased to do anything for him. He had done so much for me and people like me—not by winning any tennis tournaments, though winning the United States Open in 1968 and Wimbledon in 1975 were not small feats. What I looked forward to was Arthur Ashe, who was not even fifty, coming into his next, best prime, his years of power and influence and maturity and wisdom, where the contacts he had made in the White world of power, through tennis, could synthesize with the contacts he had made in the Black world of great love, horrible problems, and vast potential. There is no limit to what a man like Arthur Ashe might be able to do for all humanity, I thought. Oh yes, I admired him, if distantly.

When *USA Today* tennis writer Doug Smith, a Black man and lifelong friend of Ashe's, broke the story in 1992 that Ashe was HIV positive and had AIDS, an uproar swelled. Only the uproar was not over how we could save Arthur Ashe. The uproar was over whether this was an example of ethics or the lack thereof in journalism. Ethics has nothing to do with journalism. And what does it matter? I understood so many things now. I understood that what Black people haven't done yet, most of all, is save themselves from this biological disaster brought on by—dare we even ask? Magic Johnson and Arthur Ashe had both been diagnosed HIV positive, yet it was supposed to be a virus threatening homosexuals and intravenous drug users, a virus/disease of the blood. Yet, neither Magic nor Arthur were homosexual or I.V. drug addicts. Neither received the virus as a result of such activities. They *were* Black men—and not just run-of-the-mill Black men, but men of greatness. I had not yet seen a White heterosexual male come forward with the AIDS virus.

People say that this sounds paranoid. The graves are being filled up as you read this, yet I am paranoid. Yes, I suppose I am paranoid. I am a Black man in the world today. I wish the Jews in Germany had been paranoid in the 1930s. I wish the Black people in Tulsa, along the Black Wall Street, circa 1920, had been paranoid. I wish the Cherokee, when told it wasn't that long a walk to Oklahoma, had been just a little bit paranoid. Maybe they all might have lived.

After all, who does being paranoid hurt? AIDS hurts people—kills them. And since necessity is the mother of invention, who is most likely to find a vaccine or a cure? It certainly does not appear that White heterosexual males have anything to lose by not finding a vaccine or cure for AIDS. Yet Black people run to them and say, "Doctor, what can I do?" When the White male heterosexual doctor shrugs and says, "Nothing (stay Black and die)," my people shamble away and prepare their shrouds and say nothing, for fear they will be called dumb and paranoid if they ask questions.

"Where did it come from, this virus, tell me that?" I said to an acquaintance of mine, a television interviewer who often spoke to Arthur, and less often to me. I mentioned I kept hearing about a low-dose alpha interferon treatment out of Kenya. My friend scoffed at any possible treatment, especially one out of Kenya. "I haven't heard of anybody who has survived it yet," he said, almost proudly. He is White. "Yes, exactly. That's too efficient," I said. "I know of no other so-called disease with a kill ratio of 100 percent. That is like man-made." My acquaintance turned quiet then.

This is what I've heard: Two Black American doctors, a

man, Abdul Alim Muhammad, and a woman, Barbara Justice, have claimed real progress against AIDS, with treatments based on the original out of Kenya. The Kenyans claimed to have a 97 percent success rate of treating HIV-positive patients, with a scant amount of the key substance. Dr. Muhammad claims to have achieved an 82 percent success rate treating HIV-positive patients here. White people will scoff at this. I already know that. But ask yourself, why? If a man named Salk comes up with a vaccine against polio, who cares if he's Jewish? If Justice comes up with a vaccine against HIV infection, who cares if she's African-American? Why allow her to be scoffed at merely because she is Black and claims to know something that might help us? Explain that to me.

Dr. Muhammad was interviewed by the ABC network in 1992. The interviewer appeared to be debunking him, saying this new treatment would cost upwards of $2,500—doubting whether $2,500 might be worth a life. I cannot understand why Black people would not back Drs. Muhammad and Justice and their research with all the resources at our disposal. Suppose they are not charlatans? Why do we assume they are? All their papers and degrees are in order, even White people would admit this. Why do we ignore what they have to say? I'll tell you why—because they are Black, and what Black people haven't done yet is come to respect each other to do the best we can.

The AIDS virus is the acid test. We either beat it or we die. Since I know how Black people work under pressure, I say when the breakthrough is made, we should name it the Ashe vaccine, and not allow giant pharmaceutical companies to steal it, and share it with the world. That will be fitting.

Do All Black People
Know Each Other?

Wind in the desert. We stood together at an Eastern outpost in the Sahara, looking west. Wondering. The wise spoke in whispers so as not to disturb the softly omnipotent directives of the zephyr, which had for thousands of years carried dust from the Sahara across the Atlantic Ocean to the Amazon River basin. This zephyr carried the spores of life, taking and giving. Some of us spoke brassily over it, as if mindless of the challenge stretched out beyond the horizon—the endless challenge of journeying. There were any number of us out here now, and a few of us did know some of the others. But those of us who did know some of the others did not believe we knew the ones we knew all that well.

"Do all Black people know each other?" It's a question a

friend of mine named Grace told me she'd been asked by a White friend of hers. At least Grace said he was a friend of hers. Grace had laughed and asked me to consider it for my next review, and this desert setting seemed appropriate. There were many "Black" people at this tiny spot in the vast Sahara. We were all in a group, yet it appeared even those of us who were most alike had our differences.

We began talking, my two Black American friends, Joe and John, and I, recounting stories of growing up on the other side of the world. Our commonality in this arena at first seemed to be that we were all raised in the New World as New World men. After talking and revealing just enough about each other to remain safe, I suspected we were more nearly the same than different, and the big difference came from our rivers. The African in me pointed a sure finger up out of my soul and said, "You can tell a lot about a man from his river." I had come up near a big fishhook in the muddy Mississippi, around ten years before Joe came up near the Hudson, Harlem, and East rivers, while John was raised near where the Allegheny and Monongahela form the Ohio, around ten years before me. The other differences between us were circumstantial, differences mostly of time.

Time. I was amused by Henry Quarles, at least for a time, which turned out to be too long of one. Other African, Arabian, and Mediterranean Black, Brown, Bronze, Red, and Ivory men from Nigeria, Kuwait, Saudi Arabia, Algeria, Egypt, Ethiopia, Somalia, and the Sudan had passed by us in the cool of the early morning, offering "Good morning" or "As-Salaam-Alaikum" or saying nothing at all, merely smiling, or saying nothing and not smiling, but eyeing us with interest, or disinterest. Or ignoring us totally. You could never tell, could you? You could only wait and see.

Then Henry Quarles came by, a slight bob hitched to his gait, with what some of the old brothers back home used to call a "glide in his stride and a dip in his hip," and said, "Yo, what it is, what it look like? Think I'm gonna run down there and lay, and chill out for a few, but I'll come back up in a minute and we'll kick it. Cool?"

As a group we were so stunned that at first we gave Henry no quick reply. He became adamant. "Yo, is it cool? What it be like?" He sounded precisely like one Lenny Henry, a British comic. We nodded, sure, it was cool, even though the scene had become so surreal I almost looked around for a clock to see if it was melting. Then I laughed. I always laugh when there is some question about appropriate conduct. My theory is, how much can one be faulted for laughing?

"You know popular American colloquialisms even better than we do, friend," I said heartily.

"Colloquialisms?" Henry said, perplexed and not appreciating the feeling. "What are they?"

I explained what I thought colloquialisms were. Henry tilted his head to the side and said, "I can dig that, G." What made this so interesting was that we were in Egypt, and good old Henry, our new cut, was from Ghana, and, what's more, had never even set foot in America. He protested to the contrary and said he'd passed through America. I could tell by the way he talked that what he knew he'd gotten through rumor, recycled television programming, and the movies, or perhaps from Black American servicemen or others who never revealed their true selves to him, only gave him what they wished him to know or, indeed, all they knew.

Soon the crowd's business in the desert was finished for the morning. Joe, John, and I had not had the good sense to disperse. We were soon surrounded by small groups of Black and Brown people from the African continent and the Middle East and the Mediterranean who were curious about us. They wanted to see if we were as advertised. So smoothly had we been cordoned off, each Black American found himself in a group. Likewise each group seemed to hold one Egyptian, one person from east Africa, one from southern Africa, west

Africa, and so on—or so it seemed in my group. I attempted to look at Joe and John and see how they had done with their own personnel, but my attention was brought back by the animation and enthusiasm of my group, beginning with Henry Quarles, who seemed ecstatic that he'd gotten a live one.

We began to talk. I talked a very little bit about America, for there was only so much I knew about America that would make sense in a short conversation. The story of Black people in America takes some time to relate, if you are trying to tell it right, anyway. I figure if you're not going to tell it right, better to not tell it at all. I did mention to the brothers—we were all men in my group—that the Caribbean was a place where Black people should pay more attention. "First of all, it's very, very beautiful," I said. "Secondly, there are plenty of Black people already there, and they've been there for years and years and years, doing wonderful and horrible things. It's worth thinking about, the Caribbean, especially if you can take a business or creative enterprise there. I believe it has a lot of potential. We should all be interested in it. Also Brazil and several other places in South America, and of course America, but America can be kind of tricky and you need to know that up front. The New World is still new."

The others chimed in with stories of home countries. They told me of places they'd been where they had seen Black people in spots one might least have expected them—that is to say, on the good and productive side of things, either potentially or in fact, striving and achieving. They told me how heartened they were by this, but how saddened by other places and bad occurrences. It was a good discussion.

I noticed one young man staring at me intently as I continued to kick in my end of the stuff of conversation. He was from Nigeria, and his name, he said later, was Monsuru-O-Femi Oyehburi. He was one of the most handsome young men I had ever seen in my life, which threw me off briefly because he also was Black as velvet at midnight. Since I'm

American as well as Black, such a combination—wonderful handsomeness and midnight, velvety blackness—is rare to me in that sorry way I've been taught to see things. Monsuru-O-Femi brought a multiple to his own handsomeness as well, and without trying to do so. It was the way he held his head and the corners of his mouth and his gaze. His bearing made him handsome, as much as his keen-flat features, which were beautiful—there is no other word for it—in graceful combination of bas-relief. He was handsome in part because he didn't think he was ugly. The pattern of exquisite scarification at the edges of his oval face accentuated his copper eyes and bone-white teeth. He modestly offered little except his name and home country. Those he said proudly and matter-of-factly at the same time. Then he watched the rest of us and listened.

Meanwhile, Henry was putting on the African equivalent of a New World minstrel show. At least from him I found out how to pronounce Accra (ah-KRAH) in the manner of one who is native to its land. Henry bemoaned his fate since leaving his beautiful Ghana for some other parts of the world he had been curious about. He was not particularly pleased with how he came to be in Egypt, although I'd have to say he looked none the worse for wear and didn't seem to have missed any recent meals. He was first in line for the mass lunch, which was served inside the cool yellow shade of a vast tent (though, as I think back on it, he may have been more hungry than he appeared). Everything might be all right, Henry said, except for, first of all, his parents. He dismissed them with a wave of his hand, and I thought I saw the hint of a first reaction of any kind from Monsuru-O-Femi. It was not a pleasant reaction, I don't think, but I couldn't really tell because it was only a hint and either well disguised by the Nigerian or quickly passing. Perhaps it was my imagination.

I was looking at everyone generally and at nobody specifically. I could see Henry cutting his eyes at me whenever he thought he had made a point I might appreciate about the state of the world. Why he would be trying to impress me, of all in the group, was quite understandable. I was the Black American in the group, and to Henry, even by dint of the history of his own given name, I was the one to be studied until a proper use could be found for me. I was to be looked to for means, like an animal carcass, or a harvested crop, or a mine with a vein of precious mineral.

Henry began ranting a bit about the rigors White men have put Black men through for lo these many years, how they had raped us of everything and denied us, starting right there in Egypt and then around the belt of the world. And what were we going to do about it (eyes cutting to me), since it was up to us now, and up to those of us with the most resources (eyes cutting to me) to lead us out of the wilderness and into the new way, the New World (eyes resting on me).

Really. I sighed, which put Henry off but made Monsuru-O-Femi seem more interested in what I had to say next. I can't remember it all exactly, but it was something like this: "Look, friend Henry, and all of you (including you, Hassan— I can't tell you how much you look like a fellow I went to high school with named Tony, Hassan, but that's neither here nor there, except this gathering reminds me of my old high school). We've a problem, true enough, but it may not be insurmountable, nor has it been fatal in our cases up to this point. In fact, none of us even look sick."

"How can you say that," Henry interjected heatedly, "when we've been written out of history!"

"Written out of one outdated version of history," I said to Henry. "Why are you here today, Henry?"

He was there, as were the others, to play extras in the filming of *Malcolm X*. The point I was trying to make to him was in triplicate: The image of a Black man was being created by other Black men, and Black men were getting paid even for being the scenery around it. And the sun would come up tomorrow, whether we were there to meet it or not.

"So, may I continue?" I asked. "The point is, Black people are everywhere on earth, now and ever have been, and for all I know have already done everything twice and are working on new items now. You know or can know Black people everywhere. You're from everywhere. I'm from everywhere. And what we have to do is whatever we have to do whenever we have to do it. There is no mass bulletin board telling us the schedule of events. Only we know what is for us to do.

"I would not be so bold as to come here and offer you up some kind of universal plan for what to do about what has happened to us in the past. That would make me as patronizing and condescending as any White man has ever been. I don't know your circumstances the way you know them. I'm sure of this: I represent more aid to you than distress. I'm not looking to trip you up. I'm here to back you up, not vaccinate you with a sedative. Or worse. All of our circumstances are different, but there is one common rule. One must become fit for self in order to do for self, and one must do for self before one can seek to accept help or to help others.

"It is not just the Christian God who helps those who help themselves. It is any wise God. Without belief in action, help would not aid you; help would not aid me. Without a strong and determined sense of self, it would be like helping water into a sieve. This may sound harsh to you, I don't know. You see me as American, strong and smart and powerful. I see myself as smart, yes—but power is another thing. Power is what I would seek for others like me, but not necessarily for myself. Power is not to be taken lightly by anyone. Nothing comes without a price. I don't have much power. I'm not so sure I wish I did. Better to bequeath it, like undeveloped property. All I say is, be wary of men."

"What kind of brother are you?" Henry asked.

"I'm only one, and that's my point," I said. "I won't be here long, not in comparison to how long we'll be here, and have been here. I am only one man. All I can do is take one step forward—or one step back. I am determined to take that one step forward. For the most part, I try to live my life that way. If I take one step forward, then I have done all that I can do with the life given to me."

"But," protested Henry. "But . . ."

"I am serious about this. A man has to be careful not to bite off more than he can chew," I said. "Why, I'd be out of my mind to believe it to be any other way. I believe we were out here to take our appointed step and to help others to take theirs along with us. Some of us will take a step backward and try to convince others to come along with us by our actions, thoughts, words, and presence. Some of us will take that step forward and drag others along, or glide along with their help. So I'm sure that if we are going in the same direction, we'll run into each other, and not just once, but time and time again—and we should do what we can for each other at each meeting. If that amounts to nothing more than offering encouragement, then that's what it is. If it is more, then it is more when that happens. Each one of us knows his own circumstances and makes his own plan. Each of us is joined in action by like-minded people."

"I'd like to join you," said Henry. And it wasn't that he was insincere. It was that he was desperately insincere.

"Hmm," I said. Monsuru-O-Femi said nothing.

We broke up at that point, as they had to go to lunch. It was only then that Monsuru-O-Femi spoke to me. "You are a good lecturer," he said, shaking my hand. I told him I didn't know lecturing was what I'd been doing, but I appreciated him giving me credit for having any skill, and took down his name and age. He was twenty-three years old, a student; something impressive was his field of study. He was not very forthcoming about it. He said he would talk to me later and went off to eat lunch with Tony, er, Hassan, who in this country would have been called Yellow Tony by his own folks.

Later, I heard that Monsuru-O-Femi did come back looking for yours truly, but I had gone to see the Pyramids with John and Joe and had missed him.

We had passed the Pyramids in the blue mist of that morning while riding through Giza in a small van. John had looked over and said casually, "Oh, there are the Pyramids," as a river boatman might point out a familiar landmark that gives a feeling of comfort and direction to a long journey. "Oh, there are the Pyramids." I looked over and they were there, all right, in the blue mist. The sight of them caught my breath in a mitt and threw it back hard. Breath lodged in my chest and wouldn't budge. Later that same day, when we returned to investigate the grounds around these antiquities more thoroughly, the wind of the desert reached between my lips, down my throat, and took my voice completely. "Is it laryngitis?" asked Joe. If I could have answered him, I probably would have said, "No, Joe, I believe it's awe."

So I missed the return of Monsuru-O-Femi Oyehburi to our temporary stomping grounds. I missed the twenty-three-year-old student from Nigeria, who had been looking for me, but only to speak with for a while and get to know a little and smile at and feel right and proper about, to exchange numbers, to reach agreements in principles—not to join. I was a bit sad about missing him. But I figured I'd see him later anyway. I believed he would live trying to take the step forward.

Henry was waiting for us, even though it was long past dark when we returned. Henry was a little too available. "Henry," I rasped, barely making a sound. My voice was lost to the desert air. My mouth opened. ". . . . . ."

I wanted to ask him what he was doing there, but I didn't have to say a word. He began talking about coming to America with a sponsor, or just hanging out for a few days, or doing something else that would be an imposition if I had asked it of him. He gave me a photograph of himself. I didn't know what else to do, so I took it. I stared ahead of myself inside the large tent and reached down and picked up a handful of the Old World and felt the sand slip between my fingers and blow away West. Darkness falls very heavily over the desert, like a sodden blanket over a bed of embers. The chill smothered any sound in me. The desert had taken it all away, and I could feel my life slipping away into it.

Henry was oblivious to any feelings I had. He thought I was trying to avoid him, and wasn't giving me enough credit. If he had any gut instinct, he would have known that if I were trying to avoid talking to him, I would have simply said so, and not very nicely at that. Henry stared rudely, and for a second the glimmer of his contempt shone through. "Are you in a cult?" he asked.

That was the end of Henry Quarles, at least in my mind. Unless he changed directions completely, he was a backstepper, or so I had read him. I do not remember anything else about him or that evening, other than it took a very long time to get back to the hotel room on the banks of the Nile, and that there were several large, sweet oranges and tangerines in a silver bowl in my room, which helped soothe my throat. I threw the peelings on the pillows, and I slept and dreamed of barges floating on rivers, of riverbanks, of fruit, women, singing, and rain . . .

Much later, after I had been back in the New World for so long I'd stopped showing the photos I'd taken of my brief time in the Old World, I received a collect telephone call from H. Quarles Who Was Once of Ghana But Now Searches for Better. "You remember me, of course," he said. "I've a job offer in Jerusalem. It will pay me $500 a month. I need some money to get there. I was wondering when you could send it. You could send it directly to the express office here."

"And what about your parents?"

"My parents, them, what do they know?" he said.

I told Henry I could not help him in the manner he wished in the time he proscribed. Perhaps I could aid him later if he changed directions and didn't ask for much. When he rang back a few weeks later, I didn't accept his collect call. I often wonder how Monsuru-O-Femi Oyehburi is faring with his studies. I wonder how and where the wind takes him. I shall try to tell him a good story if we meet again.

Portrait of the Politician as a Man Reborn

Former mayor and newly sworn City Councilman Marion Barry made his customary late entrance into the swearing-in ceremonies for Advisory Neighborhood Commissioners, held in Room 33 of the Washington, D.C., Convention Center on January 2, 1993. Stout men and women resplendent in kente swirled contentedly about the room. A former public relations liaison in Barry's old mayoral administration said such late entrances are well planned. And indeed, I have witnessed him even coming into the Metropolitan Baptist Church late, taking the play away from the ministers. "Yes," said the ex-liaison, "coming late is planned for effect. Takes control of the room. That's the same old Marion."

There's a chilling thought: *The same old Marion.*

Barry certainly didn't look the same, in navy-blue semiformal Nehru-effect kente-bordered suit with a hatchet *kufi* hat. The broad mahogany face beneath that hat seemed beatific. The Convention Center room was full of players—from the nine city council members and council president, a wisecracking John Wilson, to Mayor Sharon Pratt Kelly, to Rev. Jesse Jackson.

The audience was sprinkled with Barry supporters bused en masse from Ward 8, along with the friends and relatives of thirty-three Advisory Neighborhood Commissioners from Ward 8. Barry proceeded to swear them in with studied aplomb. Kelly was careful to have her picture taken smiling with him. People shook his hand, admired and feared him. Some chanted, "The righteous Black man's back on the scene!" Children from the Duke Ellington School for the Arts sang. Fruit of Islam marched. A voice rang out: "You the man!"

"Marion has strong ties with the unions and many grassroots neighborhood political organizers—a strong parlay," said a newly elected ANCer from Ward 2, Al Coles. "The kente brings him back to activist level, where he made his political bones, although he had become part of the power structure. He also has to thank the selective amnesia of the voters of Ward 8, who blame Sharon Pratt Kelly for things Marion Barry never did for them. It will be interesting to see who aligns with him on the council in the belief that they are shifting with the political winds."

I moved in quietly. Barry asked, "Who are you with?" In the way of a seasoned politico, he was finding out what organization an inquisitor represented, the better to know how to handle him or her. I said, "I'm with no one." He didn't appear thrown. I asked if he had made a religious conversion after his stay in prison in the manner of Brother Minister Malcolm X. He said, "I'm still a Christian. Labels don't mean anything. We are working for each other, I'm inspiring my constituents in Ward 8, and I'm being inspired by them, those who have been neglected for so long."

He is known as Anwar Amal in some circles now, Arabic for "Bright Hope." But then, in some circles I'm known as Malik al Din, "Warrior of the Faith," and I am about as much Muslim as Chuck Berry. But I know I'm in a war, and it's a question of identity, stripes, and rank.

Later, Barry had an inaugural party up in the Panorama Room at Our Lady of Perpetual Help, on a hill in Southeast. The party waxed large, attended by Mr. Wilson, Ms. Kelly, and other Black politicians in Washington with a sense of survival, among others. Marion Barry stood with his arms behind his back, taking in the great view. One of his large, soft hands grabbed the other wrist as he overlooked the Anacostia River, auto-pouting his lips out at the Gulag Potomac. Washington, G.P., the home of taxation without representation. I remembered what I had asked him earlier at the Convention Center: "What do you say, Mr. Barry, to those who'd question your sincerity and motives?"

"Nothing," he told me. "To them I say nothing. That is their problem, not mine."

There is no such thing as objectivity in media. It is a question of controlling one's subjectivity as much as one can. I know I have as much faith in the altruism of Marion Barry as I have in the sobriety of, say, Todd Bridges. But let us be frank. We are not talking about altruism. We are talking about politics. I know why I feel disappointment—doubt. It is because Mr. Barry hurt me badly, worse than he hurt his most frenzied supporters among the lifetime residents of Ward 8. And this is why.

Thirty years ago, my mother moved from a position teaching at Owen Junior College in Memphis, Tennessee, into the heart of Ward 8, on 14 Halley Place, at the fork of what was then Nichols Avenue and South Capitol Street. I came with her, more or less. A few years earlier, Marion Barry had come up out of the Delta himself, from Mississippi, to study at LeMoyne College in Memphis.

Marion Barry too would eventually come to Washington, D.C., as we had. But my mother, Marion, and I always had another home in common. There are indelible lessons that the Delta teaches you. You have to be twice as good to go half as far. But of course. We all know that, don't we? But more than most, Black people from the Delta know what many White people are capable of and are not surprised by anything they might do in the way of holding up the progress of Black people. So when Barry was videotaped hitting the pipe, he hurt me, not because he was the Black mayor of Washington, D.C., but because he was mayor of Washington, D.C., and a Black man who had come up out of the Delta and had made his way and been twice as good and was now gutted in public because he'd forgotten who he was, what he represented, how he'd gotten there, where he'd come from. He'd been foolish and inexcusably naive about the lengths to which some White folks will go to discredit you if you are Black and independent and good at what you do.

Marion then sat up and said, among other things, "It's racism!" Of course, to a great extent it was racism. Racism is something we deal with every day. Even small children in the Delta know this. No sensible Black person ever forgets it. So it hurt me that Marion Barry would forget. I'd thought Black people who came up out of the Delta, having been historically victimized so terrifyingly by power themselves, would have a much deeper understanding of its effect on them when and if they were hard-working and fortunate enough to attain some semblance of power.

To rub salt in the wound, while in prison Barry was said to have received an unscheduled conjugal visit from a woman of renown in the craft of oral copulation, which she allegedly proceeded to demonstrate in a semipublic area. This allegation was publicized. Later, Marion said *that* was racism—that he could not be suspected of allegedly getting these same kinds of visits big-shot White prisoners got without arousing uproar and outrage.

I could not believe he had not learned his lesson—that he can't act in the way of the corrupted powerful and have people accept it because he'd been a big shot and big-shot rules should apply over racism. His actions seemed to say, "It's racism if you don't look the other way when a Black man does what he should be ashamed of, when you do look the other way when White men do them." We don't look the other way when White men do them. The White media looks the other way. They're just waiting for Barry to drop his guard. If sex and drugs are your *raison d'être*, better to be an artist, living alone, dying young, out of public sight.

At the same time, I'm sympathetic to any story of sin and redemption involving a Black man in America. I feel I have to give Barry every chance to redeem himself—not because I fear what he might be able to do to my political career. I don't have one. And not that I fear what he might be able to do to my access as a political writer—I rarely write about politics. I have to give him a chance because I never know when I may need redemption myself, as a fallible human being and a Black man in America.

The way he went down was so sad, with all those FBI agents waiting in the next hotel room, as though he were Machine Gun Kelly (no relation to Sharon) or Public Enemy No. 1, as Hazel Rasheeda Moore literally begged him to hit the pipe—moving out of camera range to tease him with her body, and then replacing her body in his hands with the pipe. I'm sure sex is what Marion wanted all along, in this case, although he did seem to have developed a taste for certain controlled substances at the time.

What happened to Marion was pitiful. It was similar to what could happen to any Black man—if he was naive enough to let it happen. A Black man out of the Delta should have seen something like that coming a mile away, had he not been blinded by the drug of power. Marion should remember this: *You never had any power. The people of the Gulag Potomac had invested their power in you. And what the people give, the people can—and will—take away.*

Two days after the swearing-in ceremony, Councilman Barry's black-cherry Chrysler was stolen from in front of the District Building, the keys having been mysteriously lifted from his coat pocket in his own office. The car was later found in Southeast. Barry hesitated to take possession of the car; no telling what might have been planted in it or under it. "No, not me," he said. The very next night, one of the worst fires in memory swept across Halley Place, next door to number 14, which was once home to me, my mother, and my stepfather. Five people were burned alive. The reason I bring up the last fact is to point out that any intrigue about stolen cars, and planted "evidence," and politics, and the use of power, pales next to the loss of human life. We are all lucky to be alive. Nothing is promised to us except a battle.

As for Marion Barry, I wish him Godspeed. And if he should hurt Ward 8, I shall write about him again.

Identity and Purpose

(Text of a presentation given on Youth Day, January 29, 1989, at the Mount Pisgah C.M.E. Church, Memphis)

I am laughing. I'm laughing because I'm standing on the wellspring of my soul, right here, and when you do that you'd better laugh. If you laugh, something good might happen.

Youth Day. Someone once said, "Youth is wasted on the young." I disagree. I think young people are the only ones who deserve youth. They are the only ones who can handle it.

And if you've been paying attention to the service today, as I have, listening to the eloquence of the young men and women to my left and right, you know what I mean.

I'm not going to take up a lot of time. I know how Methodists are about the length of their services. I'm going to talk for a little while about Identity and Purpose.

Another reason I laugh is because—Identity and Purpose— my grandmother, who used to sit right over there in that pew, a member of something called Stewardess Board Number One, predicted this on me when I was a boy. She said, "Son, have you been called?" And I knew what she meant. She meant had I been called to preach the gospel. I was a shy boy, so I just said, "No'm, I haven't been called and I don't expect to be. I do like to write though, Grandma."

She said, "Take my advice. Write sermons."

So that's why I'm thrilled to be here. I mean that literally. First of all, I know I didn't have to be here. Many I grew up with are here, and I'm glad to see them, they are part of my strength, they're in me, I'm in them. But many I grew up with are dead. I was reminded of death, that Old Clockmaker, two nights ago when I arrived. I'd been running around doing my job, my two or three jobs, not getting much rest, not eating very well, eating when I was hungry, running through airports. I'd been running around so much I was susceptible to illness. When I got here, my neck became stiff. A big knot of pain welled up in my neck. So I asked around about this and a so-called expert told me it was probably the flu. And I bought into that. I wanted to believe something that made sense. So I said, my goodness, I have the flu. So I was dosed with teas and concoctions. I couldn't afford to have the flu. I had to be here, do this. About four-thirty that morning I sat bolt upright in bed and said, "I have the flu." That pain was in my neck so heavy . . . so I knew I had one option left. I had to dial God's number. You know when it gets to that point where you just have to dial.

Now, as you go along in life, if you're smart you'll try to learn things. Eventually, people will "learn" you that God is a vague concept at best, a medium used to hold down oppressed people, an inferior concept to science, because science is pure. And you might even buy into all that for a little while, right up until some hurt and pain you know you aren't strong enough to handle come down on you. Then you put in that emergency call. To God. I woke up the next morning—no flu. I never had it all along, that's what a scientist would say. "Well, Mr. Wiley, you never had it in the first place." But I don't know.

I was thinking about this when the bellman brought breakfast up. I was staying in a hotel. He was quiet, efficient, did his job well. But I was thinking about scientists and not paying any attention when he said,

"Raaaalph!"

Now this was brother Aubrey Pruitt. Aubrey grew up with me, right here, going to this church, when we both were young. It's amazing. I had written a book, and in the first chapter of the book Mount Pisgah is in there, and Aubrey and I are outside. It's a book about boxing, about life, and you have to learn how to box, and you have to learn how to live life. And here was my old friend Aubrey, with me again. A scientist would call it coincidence. But I don't know.

By the way, Aubrey was doing very well. And do you know why? Because he knows his identity. You see, the one skill all people do have is the ability to be mean. It takes no talent to be mean. Hurting somebody is the easiest thing in the world to do. So as you go out in life, young people, you are going to have to realize that it is not always going to be this right, this close, this sure, this certain, as it is in this sanctuary. It's not like that in the life you must learn to lead. There are tests to it. Hurt, pain, and disappointment. Fear, envy, and resentment. Murder, robbery, and the Old Clockmaker. The Old Clockmaker is out there. Waiting. And all you have to fight with against all that is your identity. In the end, that's all you have.

Now, mean people, people who want to hurt people, would say, "He's got nerve, coming in from out of town with his good job, staying in hotels and not with his own people, talking about Aubrey Pruitt bringing his breakfast like that." Mean people. That's how people without an identity talk. They ramble. They try to hurt you. All you have to fight with is your identity. Aubrey didn't think like that. We laughed and talked about the old days. Do you know why? Because he knows his identity. It's rooted deeply, here, in his spirit.

He knows he's not a job, a title, a temporary condition. He's Aubrey. The good jobs, the long titles, the expensive cars, the pretty girlfriends and fine boyfriends and athletic ability and high intellect and good looks and all that—just snap your finger. All those things can be stripped from you like that. Snap. Like you're snapping your finger. Like that. And your identity is the only thing you have that keeps you from falling into the abyss when you have been stripped of those worldly things. That is when your character is truly tested. What kind of person are you?

Your identity is who you are. People—White people—say, "Why is it, Ralph, that Black people have no culture?" I say, "Well, that's because most of it is out on loan to White people. Interest-free." We are a good-hearted, big-hearted people, and we will let them borrow it anytime.

One part of our culture is this institution. Some of our institutions are gone, like the high school you knew was there, and you knew you were going to go there. Institutions. My mother taught at Owen Junior College. I thought it was a good place. Tall trees, wonderfully idiosyncratic buildings, educated, learned people. You think I'm some kind of accident? You think I just learned how to write without a proper way? This was all there. All those institutions were there. I was there. But now they're gone. Many of those institutions are gone. I want to talk of this institution because we still have this institution left. All the institutions that have been boarded up and folded up that used to be here and thriving before pseudo-integration debilitating re-segregation, this is one that's left. This is the strong thing. One of them.

All I know is once there was a man with hair like lamb's wool, and he was the only man or woman who was close to being perfect. So I would say to the youth, and the youth in all of us, I would not ask you for perfection, but I would ask that you try for it. See how close you can come.

You'll make mistakes, I know, because I made my share. I

did not have a perfect road, as many of the people who know me out here understand. But so what? If you have an identity, when you get knocked down, anytime you get knocked down, you can get up, wipe it off, and keep going because you know who you are. You know you weren't made to stay in the dirt. And if you don't, heaven help you in this world and this life. Heaven help Michael Jackson. I love the young brother, but heaven help him. And I know you understand me.

Now, this man with the lamb's-wool hair—I'm sure you know who I'm talking of—lived not far away geographically from the Nile River Valley. Now we're going to talk about identity. White people will tell you that you have none. That's because your identity would frighten them if they admitted how deeply your identity ran within them, within everyone. The Nile River Valley is part of your identity just as surely as Mount Pisgah Church is. The Nile River Valley stretches from down in upper Egypt, down near Ethiopia, to lower Egypt, up by the Mediterranean Sea. It is the only river running south to north in Africa—and the Nile is the mightiest river in Africa. It runs up from Sudan and Ethiopia. It was traveled by all the scholars who came east from the empires of Mali, Songhai, and the great center of Timbuktu. The northern half of the Nile Delta in Egypt is called Lower Egypt, and the southern half of the Nile is called Upper Egypt. Because the river runs south to north. One great city in the Nile River Valley was named Memphis. Yes, it was. Great peoples lived there. The Nile River Valley is the cradle of civilization, where the Greeks and later the Romans went to find out things. They might have even had brochures and weekend specials, for all we know. They might have had travel agents. "Travel to the Nile River Valley. Special this month—four days and three nights. Cheap."

Mathematics, agriculture—name it—architecture, art, medicine, astronomy. It was all there, in the Nile River Valley, the most beautiful place on earth, and one of the oldest civilizations in recorded history, some four thousand years before the man with the hair like lamb's wool, some two thousand years before the Greeks, way back. Who really knows for sure? If we're counting the years by the thousands, then we can only say they were awfully old.

Some people say the Pyramids were built by alien beings from outer space. Have you heard that one? No, the Pyramids were built by Black contractors from Ethiopia. Maybe they used slave labor. Maybe they didn't. We don't know, do we? We're ignorant, aren't we? If they did use slave labor, then we know why something bad eventually happened to them, don't we? The pharaohs said, "We need a place to hang out." Contractors said, "We can build it. This is the fee." The most perfect buildings on earth are still the Pyramids.

Did you see or hear of the King Tutankhamen exhibition as it toured America? King Tut? All the people went to see it at the museum? You must remember. Fabulous inlaid gold and precious metals, the mummy case, and the beautiful decorative ornaments. Do you remember the golden face of King Tut on the case? I do. He looked like Aubrey Pruitt.

Identity. After you establish who you are and you're safe with that, then you have to ask, "What can I do with what I am?" And you have to be honest with yourself. You have to find what your purpose is. Once you find it, purpose and identity will give you direction. Whatever you do and in whichever direction you go, try to do well, and go well.

Because when you go out in this cold, merciless world I'm telling you about today, and you find your friends saying, "Yo man, got that crack, man," or when your rivals say, "You know, you're really not that good at this job. I don't even know why you're trying to do it," I want you to be able to laugh and say, "No thank you on that crack, no thank you, man," and be comfortable saying it because you know who you are. Or to those rivals, I want you to be able to say, "Well, it's nice to know you have an opinion, opinions are good to have, everybody's got one, like something else. But I can roll. I know it." That will make people sit up straight and realize they have to deal with you, and can't just run some conversation on you and have your character, your identity be so weak you buy into it. "Oh, I guess I'm not very good, just like you say." I learned better within a two-mile radius of right here.

I want all you young people to know that you are descended from a great people. I look around here right now, why, it's like being in the Nile River Valley. I see the faces of Sheba, and Tutankhamen, and Nefertiti. I see faces that came before them that left me no names to call.

I grew up two blocks from here—this way. Six liquor stores were within a block of the house I grew up in. Yet we all know this was a nice neighborhood, wasn't it? It was nice because people cared. It certainly was nice once. The nearest library was—well, outside of those libraries in the institutions, outside of my mother's library; the nearest library was twenty blocks that way. And I would not have been welcome there had I tried to go at that time. Turned away at the door, "What do you want?" they would've asked. What do I want? I want to *know*. That's what I want. What do you want?

You can forget what you don't want to remember. When you think you have no identity, you want to forget that. Any fool can get high, and I should know. It's easy. It's like turning on television. Automatically there. Quick fix. Want it now. Let me have it. Miracle diet. A purpose is not so easy to come by. A purpose takes you through years, drives you to survive. A purpose supersedes a quick fix, a quick hit.

It pays to enjoy your purpose. Sometimes I think people enjoy my purpose more than I do. "He gets paid to sit around and watch," they say. But what I'm really doing is studying, analyzing, seeing what makes things tick, because I have very little margin for error in my work.

Invariably a purpose involves work. If you fear work, you may as well go talk to the Old Clockmaker now. "Old Clockmaker, I don't want to work." "Well, you might as well come with me Junior, because it's not going to be any fun for you here." Without work, people wither in the soul. There is no greater pleasure than a job well done.

By my reconnoiter, which can be curious I admit, the greatest purpose in life is teaching. I look around today and see Miss Dean, Mr. Powell, Mrs. Echols, Mr. Wilburn, Mr. Lee, thought about Mr. Goodlow. In my time with them, they made me shake my head more than once. "Whoa," I'd say, "What do they want?" They wanted me to know. So they showed me, whether I liked it or not. And usually I didn't like it. Or I went against the grain because I just wanted to see, could I. Now these days, if I were in a rural suburban academy and acted the way I acted at Melrose High, why my goodness, I would've been called a troublemaking hyperactive idiot, with no I.Q. at all. "We just can't teach him." Ha.

But these teachers of mine put up with me because they knew something, they saw something in me, they said, "Let him run, let him go, let him see what he can do, don't bust him down until the last moment possible." And it worked.

Because if you can teach a person one useful thing, then you have achieved the fruition of purpose. You have passed it along. So I feel the same way here today. If there is one young person who remembers and acts on what I have attempted to pass along, then I have achieved some degree of purpose—what people once called your good deed for the day.

Now Brian here, who introduced me, asked me something last night. He seemed to be really curious. He doesn't know because he's in the bosom of this sanctuary and all of you, but he's heard about this racism. He's heard about it, but he doesn't have to see it and deal with it—just in a general sense, but not quite specifically. Brian asked, "Mr. Wiley, is being Black a handicap, trying to do the job?"

Brian. Being Black is a gift from God. It may handicap others, your Blackness. It may handicap their ability to perceive you correctly or their ability to treat you fairly. But it is that very Blackness, that Nile River Valley, that very identity, which allows you to stride right through it. It means nothing, this racism. If racists want to call out the Old Clockmaker, and very often they do, well, they will have to account for that someday. But no, Brian, no amount of racism can stop you because *talent . . . will . . . out.*

Purpose and Identity. I'm going to leave you now by saying I can't wait to shake hands with all you Tutankhamens and Nefertitis, Askias, Hatshepsuts and Shebas, and all the well-spring of my soul, from the Nile River Valley to the Mississippi River Valley, from the Memphis of Egypt to the Memphis of Tennessee, from the mighty river that runs south to north to the mighty river that runs north to south—and there is no God? It seems there is a God. And God is in each and every one of you. And you are among the great people of this earth. I thank you.

Index

baseball and baseball games
(*continued*)
and Blacks in minor leagues,
39–41, 43, 45
and Cincinnati Reds, 40–45
and Clark, 48, 52–56
Creamer's writing on, 140
and Davis, 40–43, 45–46, 60, 62
fans at, 42
and Henderson, 42, 48–52,
55–56, 60, 62–63
integration of, 46
racism of, 43–45
why Blacks don't go to, 38–63
and writing, 129
basketball, 239–54
constants and variables in,
244–45
at Memphis State, 285–93
see also specific players
Bass, Vernell, 154
Bassett, Angela, 191, 215
Bedford, William, 291
Beiderbecke, Bix, 277
Bell, Derrick, 317
Bellow, Saul, 26, 29
Bernal, Martin, 34
Bernhard, Sandra, 102
Berry, Chuck, 347
Berry, Halle, 311–12
Billson, Janet Mancini, 324–27
Bingham, Howard, 166, 168, 170
Bird, Larry, 244–52
Johnson and, 244–51
Jordan and, 249–52
Black Entertainment Television
(BET), 93–94, 238
Black Issues in Higher Education,
315
Blacks:
and acting White, 305
business acumen of, 10–11, 69,
73, 79
consumerism of, 11
in controlling own images,
219–20

creativity of, 9
as crime victims, 153
decision making of, 244
demonizing of, 150, 160
exploitation of, 145
generosity of, 354
handsomeness of, 337–38
heritage of, 334–35, 337, 339–
41, 354–56, 359
in holding selves back, 7
identity of, 355–57, 359
internal problems of, 111
killing of, 9–10
lynching of, 5, 88–89, 119–20,
124, 156, 171
myths about sexuality of, 119–
20, 157, 159
neoconservatives among, 305
new songs for, 6
oppression of, 78
in overaccessorizing, 305–6
paranoia of, 332
poverty of, 264
recognition from Whites for,
328–29, 332–33
reparations for, 9–10
salvation of, 339–41
self-confidence of, 219–20
self-hatred of, 34, 122
self-respect of, 110, 333
sense of self for, 340
slogans representing, 302
spokespeople of, 4–6, 8
standards and values of, 329
stereotyping of, 20
temerity of, 171
temperance, social graces, and
redeeming values of, 4
torture of, 145
unemployment among, 153
unification of, 6, 8, 10–11
waiting strategy of, 8
Blanchard, Terence, 188, 202
Bland, Bobby, 266
Bloch, Paul, 228
Bloom, Allan, 23–29

362

Index

About the Author

RALPH WILEY is the author of *Why Black People Tend to Shout* and *Serenity: A Boxing Memoir*, and co-author, with Spike Lee, of *By Any Means Necessary: The Trials and Tribulations of the Making of* Malcolm X. His work has appeared in *Sports Illustrated*, *Emerge*, and *Premiere* magazines. He lives outside Washington, D.C., where he is currently working on his first novel, *Flier*.

BROTHERMAN
The Odyssey of Black Men in America—An Anthology

Edited by Herb Boyd and Robert L. Allen

A groundbreaking collection of essays, memoirs, social histories, novels, poems, slave narratives, short stories, biographies, autobiographies, and position papers, and spanning the complete life cycle of African-American men. Including one hundred of the strongest and finest black male voices in the literary canon, this superb anthology features the work of such notables as:

Ayi Kwei Armah, Ralph Ellison, W.E.B. Du Bois, Frederick Douglass, Henry Dumas, Alex Haley, James Alan McPherson, Walter Mosley, Richard Wright, Charles Chesnutt, Haki Madhubuti, Charles Johnson, Paul Robeson, Clarence Major, Julius Lester, Ishmael Reed, Derrick Bell, John Killens, Arthur Flowers, Martin Luther King, Jr., Ernest Gaines, John Edgar Wideman, Chester Himes, Brent Wade, Shelby Steele, Stephen L. Carter, Jake Lamar, John Henrik Clarke, Claude Brown, Maulana Karenga, Dudley Randall, Gordon Parks, Albert Race Sample, Jawanza Kunjufu, Malcolm X, Amiri Baraka, Ralph Wiley, Jess Mowry, and Claude Brown.

One World Books
Published by Ballantine

Coming to bookstores in February